MW00352556

Breakdown and Reconstitution

Breakdown and Reconstitution

Democracy, the Nation-State, and Ethnicity in Nigeria

Abu Bakarr Bah

LEXINGTON BOOKS
Lanham • Boulder • New York • Toronto • Oxford

LEXINGTON BOOKS

A division of Rowman & Littlefield Publishers, Inc.
A wholly owned subsidiary of The Rowman & Littlefield Publishing Group, Inc.
4501 Forbes Boulevard, Suite 200
Lanham, MD 20706

Estover Road
Plymouth PL6 7PY
United Kingdom

Copyright © 2005 by Lexington Books
First paperback edition 2008

All rights reserved. No part of this publication may be reproduced,
stored in a retrieval system, or transmitted in any form or by any
means, electronic, mechanical, photocopying, recording, or otherwise,
without the prior permission of the publisher.

British Library Cataloguing in Publication Information Available

Library of Congress Cataloging-in-Publication Data

Bah, Abu Bakarr, 1969–
  Breakdown and reconstitution : democracy, the nation-state, and ethnicity in Nigeria /
Abu Bakarr Bah.
     p. cm.
  Includes bibliographical references and index.
  1. Nigeria—Politics and government—1960- 2. Democratization—Nigeria. 3.
Nigeria—Ethnic relations—Political aspects. I. Title.
JQ3090.B34 2005
320.9669—dc22   2005002157

  ISBN-13: 978-0-7391-0954-0 (cloth : alk. paper)
  ISBN-10: 0-7391-0954-5 (cloth : alk. paper)
  ISBN-13: 978-0-7391-2793-3 (pbk. : alk. paper)
  ISBN-10: 0-7391-2793-4 (pbk. : alk. paper)

Printed in the United States of America

Contents

Figures

Tables

Preface

My interest in Nigerian politics dates back to many years before I even started my graduate studies. I was first exposed to the complexities of Nigerian politics and society during my secondary school history classes. As I read about colonial rule and the nationalist movement in West Africa, I realized a huge difference between Nigeria and other countries, such as my native Sierra Leone. During the early 1990s, I had the chance to mingle with many Nigerian students in Sofia, Bulgaria. During those years, I became aware of the politics of ethnicity and the struggle against military rule in Nigeria. In retrospect, I benefited a lot from my Nigerian roommate who transformed our tiny apartment into a popular political-talk-shop for Nigerians, especially those from Eastern Nigeria.

My research interest in Nigeria began at the New School University in New York. As I studied issues of political transformation in Europe, Latin America, and Africa, I began to appreciate the complexities of Nigerian politics. Eventually, I saw the Nigerian experience as a lens through which I could further study the problems of democratization and nation building in divided societies.

Many scholars have written very insightful and groundbreaking works on issues of political transformation and ethnic conflicts. This book is intended to be a modest contribution to those works. The book deals with the synergy of democratization, nation-state building, and ethnicity in Nigeria. It pays special attention to the role of ethnicity in the breakdown and reconstitution of democracy and the nation-state, the problems of leadership, and the challenges of institutional design in a postcolonial multiethnic country. The study points to a cycle of breakdown and reconstitution of democracy and the nation-state in Nigeria. Notwithstanding the formidable political problems in Nigeria, the study emphasizes the creativity and experimental nature of democratization and nation-state building in Nigeria.

This book is a revised version of my doctoral dissertation which I defended at the New School University in 2003. While I take responsibility for any shortcomings in this work, I want to express my deep gratitude to the numerous individuals and institutions that have supported me throughout my education. First of all, I want to thank my dissertation advisors: Professors Andrew Arato and Jose Casanova. Both of them gave me tremendous support throughout my years at the New School. I am deeply indebted to them for their intellectual guidance and institutional support. I would also like to thank professors Courtney Jung, Dianne Davis, and Orville Lee for supporting my dissertation work.

I am also grateful to the numerous individuals in Nigeria who gave me tremendous support while I was conducting field research in 2002. First of all, I owe a special word of thanks to Dr. Wale Adebanwi of the University of Ibadan for his extraordinary support. He hosted me, drove me around, showed me the resources, and above all helped me make sense of the many things that I had been reading about Nigeria. I should also express my deep gratitude to Professor Adigun Agbage and his family for their hospitality and intellectual support. I also want to thank Dr. Emmanuel Remi Aiyede and Oladapo Omi of the Development Policy Center in Ibadan. Remi gave me tremendous research support and insightful comments. Remi and his family also showed me great hospitality. Oladapo was my energetic research assistant who helped me dig the national archives at the University of Ibadan. I am also indebted to the following scholars and community leaders who volunteered for in-depth interviews: Dr. Olutayo Adesina, Professor Adigun Agbaje, Professor J. F. Ade Ajayi, Professor J. A. A. Ayoade, Professor I. B. Bello-Imam, Moshood Erubami, Professor Eghosa E. Osaghae, Professor Oyeleye Oyediran, Dr. Rotimi Suberu, and Dr. John Ademola Yakubu. Each of these individuals gave me invaluable insights into Nigerian politics.

I also want to recognize the various institutions that supported my research. I thank the Gradate Faculty and the Transregional Center for Democratic Studies (TCDS) at the New School University for their generous financial support. In addition, the TCDS helped me establish networks in Nigeria. It was through the TCDS that I met Dr. Adebanwi, Dr. Aiyede, and Professor Agbage. At the TCDS, I am particularly indebted to Dr. Elzbieta Matynia for her intellectual guidance and institutional support. I am also very grateful to the Todda Institute for its generous financial support during my graduate studies. At Northern Illinois University, I would like to thank my colleagues at the sociology department for their support and encouraging words. I also extend my gratitude to Leonard Walther of the geography department for helping me with the graphics. I would also like to thank Cambridge University Press and Lynne Rienner Publishers for giving me permission to use some of their materials.

In Nigeria, I am indebted to the Development Policy Center, the Programme on Ethnic and Federal Studies (PEFS) at the University of Ibadan, and the Political Science Department at the University of Ibadan. All of these institutions gave me access to their libraries and supported my work. At PEFS, I want to express special words of thanks to Professor Eghosa Osaghae and Lwazi Lushaba. I would also like to thank Dr. Rotimi Suberu and Professor Alex Gboyega of the Political Science Department and the members of the Joint Action Committee of Nigeria (JACON) for their support.

Finally, I want to thank my parents, wife, siblings, and friends for their tremendous emotional, moral, and material support, without which I would not have had the chance to acquire a western education. In particular, my parents have had to make difficult choices. I thank them for their wisdom, sacrifices, and commitment to education. I also want to pay my respect to all those who have been victims of ethnic/racial violence and discrimination.

Chapter 1

Introduction: Democracy, the Nation-State, and Ethnicity

Since gaining independence from Britain on October 1, 1960, Nigeria has witnessed no less than ten changes of government—either through coups or through elections. Looking closely at the pattern through which the military dictatorships replaced elected civilian governments and vice-versa, one can identify a cycle of breakdown and revival in the Nigerian political order. In either case, the problems are democracy and national integration. Democracy was ushered in to Nigeria toward the dawn of the First Republic (1960 to 1966). In 1966, the military overthrew the democratic regime, and shortly thereafter the Nigerian Civil War began (1967 to 1970).[1] Democracy was restored in 1979, marking the birth of the Second Republic. From 1984 to 1999, Nigeria was ruled by successive military governments.[2] Democracy was once again restored in 1999 at the birth of the Fourth Republic.[3] So far, we can identify three periods of democracy and two periods of military rule in postcolonial Nigeria.

One of the most intriguing questions in Nigerian political development is the relation between democratization, nation-state building, and ethnicity. The declared goals of the pioneers of the First, Second, and Fourth Republics have been to make the government more representative and accountable to the citizens and to promote an integrated nation-state. The Nigerian Civil War, the Ogoni uprising, the annulled 12 June 1993 presidential election, and the numerous incidents of ethnic violence demonstrate the difficulties in realizing these goals. However, it is interesting to note that these incidents of ethnic violence have also inspired campaigns and reforms geared toward a more inclusive democracy and nation-state. Thus, one can argue that democratization and nation-state building are lively, albeit troublesome, projects in Nigeria. Furthermore, a cycle of breakdown and reconstitution characterizes Nigeria's path to democracy and nation-state building. Taking the birth of the First, Second, and Fourth Republics as the high moments for democracy and nation-state building in Nigeria, one can also identify the two low moments. The first low moment is from the January 1966 coup to the Nigerian Civil War and the second is the period around the annulled 12 June 1993 presidential election, the Ogoni uprising, and the growth of ethnic militias. In order to make sense of the cycle of breakdown and reconstitution, one will need to look at the ascending phases that lead to the high moments and the descending phases that lead to the breaking points. Each wave in the cycle consists of the phase of ascendance, the climax of reconstituting democracy and the nation-state, and the descending phase. In between the waves are the breaking points, which link one descending phase to the next ascending phase.

The aim of this work is to systematically analyze the synergy and potential conflicts between democratization, nation-state building, and ethnicity in Nigeria as well as the challenges of transforming a postcolonial multiethnic country into a stable democratic nation-state. I argue that the recurring breakdown of democracy and crisis of the nation-state in Nigeria are not isolated problems. Given the globalization of democracy and the importance of national integration for the consolidation of democracy, it is vital to pay attention to the linkages between democratization and nation-state building. Furthermore, I want to analyze the impact of ethnicity on the breakdown as well as the reconstitution of democracy and the nation-state in Nigeria. My modest desire is to identify some of the pitfalls in the institutional designs that contribute to the breakdown of democracy and threaten the survival of the nation-state, and to suggest alternative approaches to the problems. Thus, the project seeks to address the following questions. First, what is the link between democratization and nation-state building in Nigeria? Second, what forces led to the reconstitution of democracy and the nation-state during the First, Second, and Fourth Republics? Third, what are the forces that contributed to the decline of the First and Second Republics—the descending forces? I am aware that in both cases, the forces can be numerous and interrelated—ranging from external forces to elite manipulation, religion, and ethnicity. Without minimizing the complex interplay of forces, I want to pay special attention to the problems of ethnicity. I focus on ethnicity because it has been at the center of the "stateness" problem in Nigeria and it is a potential barrier for the consolidation of multiparty democracy. This leads me to the next question: What mechanisms have been used to address ethnicity and thereby foster democracy and national integration in Nigeria? In speaking of a cycle of breakdown and reconstitution, one might think of democratization and nation-state building in Nigeria as alternating virtuous and vicious cycles. This leads to the final questions: What progress has been made? What challenges remain? Unless one thinks that Nigeria is a total failure, these should be crucial questions for understanding Nigeria's tortuous path to democracy and nation-statehood.

The fact that Nigerians have been actively looking for creative ways to overcome the formidable problems of ethnicity in their country makes the Nigerian experience a paradigmatic case. It magnifies both the problems and the potentials for forging stable and democratic postcolonial multiethnic nation-states in sub-Saharan Africa. Nigeria is not only the most populous and ethnically heterogeneous country on the continent, but also the one that has most consistently campaigned for democracy, and the one that has tried a variety of institutional arrangements to address the problem of ethnicity. The Nigerian dilemma started before independence, when the three ethnically dominated regions—North, East, and West—could hardly agree on what the new Nigeria should be. The problem was addressed in the 1951, 1954, and 1960 constitutions. This is also true of the postcolonial Nigerian constitutions of 1963, 1979, 1989, and 1999.[4] Each new constitution has been an innovative step toward addressing the ethnic politics that plagued the previous institutional arrangement. Though Nigeria is not yet a success story, the country is remarkable for its learning experience. In particular, the Nigerian experiment has consistently employed consociationalism to restore democracy and avert the breakup of the nation-state. It must also not be forgotten that Nigeria has been transformed from a federation of three regions to a federation that now consists of thirty-six states.

Theoretical Perspectives and Contributions

Democracy, nation-state, and ethnicity are concepts that are employed in a wide variety of historical, cultural, and social contexts. While these concepts tend to convey a universal meaning, grounded in scholarly debates and historical realities, it is important to concretely relate them to the Nigerian context. Given the scope and interconnectedness of the issues addressed in this study, I believe that such a clarification is urgently needed.

Attempts to define democracy often face the problem of reconciling the ideals envisioned by the enlightenment philosophers and the practical problems of realizing such ideals in contemporary developing countries. To go the ideal way, in which case democracy implies not only one person one vote but also economic and social justice, will amount to making democracy only a dream. Yet, a democracy that does not take into account social and economic injustice runs the risk of being unattractive.[5] This dilemma is well illustrated by Scott Mainwaring when he identified two approaches in the attempt to define democracy—the outcome oriented and the procedure oriented. Contemporary students of democracy have taken a pragmatic position and settled for the procedure-oriented approach, with the hope that social and economic injustice can be addressed later.[6] The basic elements of this procedure-oriented minimalist democracy are freedom of association, freedom of expression and a free media, right to vote and seek public office through competitive, free and fair elections, and the existence of an independent electoral commission and judiciary.[7] This minimalist democracy can be traced back to Joseph Schumpeter's critique of the classical doctrine of democracy. He saw democracy as a system of government in which the leaders of government acquire the power to make decisions through a competitive struggle to win the votes of the majority of the people.[8] Following Schumpeter's minimalist definition and Max Weber's focus on the political institutions of democracy, Seymour Lipset sees democracy as a function of conflict and cohesion.[9] The puzzle for a democratic society is how to face continuous conflict among its members and groups and still maintain social cohesion and the legitimacy of state authority. Essentially, the electoral process has now become the key means of expressing both conflict and cohesion.[10]

The underlying assumption of minimalist democracy is that if citizens have an input in decision-making through the electoral process, their concerns for social and economic justice will eventually be addressed. However, the problem in divided countries, such as Nigeria, is not just about individual participation, but also group representation.[11] In multiethnic countries like Nigeria, where political institutions are still in their infancy, it is imperative that we emphasize that institutions should not only be designed for conflict and consensus among individuals or voluntary groups, but also among involuntary groups in which membership is ascribed, such as ethnic groups. Thus, democracy in Nigeria is not just about conflict and cohesion among individuals, but also about conflict among the ethnic groups to which they belong. As J. A. A. Ayoade argued, "In Nigeria, ethnic groups are real and to the extent they are real, they must be accorded rights."[12] A close look at the three moments of democratic revival in Nigeria will show that democracy has been understood to mean free and fair multiparty elections that would not only represent citizens, but also fairly represent the diverse groups of people in the country. While it is individuals (not groups) that cast the vote it is clear from the institutional arrangements and the political discourse that, in Nigeria, participation is measured more by the degree to which groups are represented in the institutions of power than by individual participation in the electoral process. Indeed, democracy is one person, one vote; but it should also produce an arrangement that gives each of the constituent groups a voice and makes the group visible in the institutions of power.

While the discourse on democratization makes a clear distinction between democratic and non-democratic (i.e., totalitarian, Sultanist, and authoritarian) regimes, very little attention is paid to situations in which the regime meets most, if not all, of the criteria for a minimalist democracy, but fails to mature into a consolidated democracy.[13] However, such regimes are not uncommon in Nigeria and Africa in general. I will refer to such regimes as quasi-democracies.[14] Essentially, these are regimes in which the government is elected, usually during transitional multiparty elections, but through institutional designs or extra-legal means, they foreclose any real possibility for change of government through the ballot box. Such regimes tend to promote institutions that are, either by design or management, discriminatory toward certain ethno-cultural groups in the country. Furthermore, the leaders tend to have a limited sense of responsibility toward the electorates. Instead, they rely heavily on clientelism, force, and manipulation of ethno-cultural differences in the country to maintain their grip on power. In general, such regimes are characterized by conditions of democratic decay. In particular, electoral rules are often arbitrarily changed to the advantage of the governing party, elections are generally violent and rigged to the disadvantage of opposition parties, and vital institutions, such as the courts and the electoral commission, are often subjected to undue government interference. Because such regimes violate democratic values, they create conditions that invite the use of civil disobedience or arms to remove them from power.[15]

Students of democracy do not only face the problem of defining the concept of democracy, but also the difficulties of identifying the most appropriate institutional arrangements to make democracy work. As Donald Horowitz points out, "Democracy is a popular destination, for which it is difficult to give directions."[16] Very often, political actors are forced to choose between: liberal and consociational arrangements, parliamentary and presidential systems, federal and unitary structures, proportional representation and simple majority systems.[17] While such choices may be necessary, they often tend to be a narrow approach to institutional design. In Nigeria, such institutional choices cannot be disassociated from the configuration of the nation-state. Thus, institutional design should be seeing as a dual endeavor to establish institutions that can promote democracy and the nation-state at large.

To understand the nature of the nation-state in Nigeria, it is important to analytically separate the concepts of state and nation. Though historically interconnected, the processes of state-building and nation-building are not necessarily the same, especially in the case of African countries where the colonial powers created states and at the same time tried to undermine the formation of a common national identity.[18] The state can be viewed as a complex set of institutional arrangements as well as a structured relation among the various groups of people that inhabit a defined territory. In this sense, the Nigerian state can be seen as a defined territory, with institutions that have persisted for nearly a century. Furthermore, there is an authority which, to a large degree, has received the loyalty of Nigerians and monopolized the use of violence.[19] The Nigerian state can also be seen as a field of contestation where the various ethnic and regional groups are struggling for power.[20] Most notably, this is manifested in the rivalry among the three dominant ethnic groups (Hausa-Fulani, Igbo, and Yoruba), the minority-minority issue, the North-South regional divide, and the Muslim-Christian conflict over *sharia* (Islamic law).

While the state is viewed as a sovereign political entity within a specific territorial boundary, the nation is more fluid and directly linked to culture and sense of identity.[21] Very often, the nation is either viewed as a product of primordial and perennial forces or a socially constructed unit.[22] Johann Herder, for example, saw the nation as a natural unit that is characterized by objective and subjective features, such as climate, ancestry, and mythology.[23] In his study of nationalism, Florian Znaniecki viewed the nation as a product of secular culture invented through written language and the growth of literature.[24] The emphasis on written language is of great significance because it tells us about the creation, standardization, preservation, and transmission of cultures, as well as the formation of national identities. In a similar way, Benedict Anderson sees the nation as an imagined political community that is limited in its membership and sovereign in its claims. It is the product of cultural artifacts and the conjunction of discrete historical forces. Though these artifacts are for the most part accidental, Anderson argued, "once created, they became 'modular,' capable of being transplanted, with varying degrees of self-consciousness, to a great variety of social terrains, to merge, and be merged with a correspondingly wide variety of political and ideological constellations."[25] In Nigeria, the seed of this imagined political community was sowed during the period of colonial rule. Even though the policy of the colonial government was to divide and rule, it unwittingly created the conditions for the emergence of a common national identity. As colonial rule became more oppressive, the colonized people started to see themselves as one people fighting a common enemy. Since the attainment of independence, the challenge in Nigeria has been to strengthen that fragile identity and hold the country together.

Though for analytical purposes I have addressed the state and the nation separately, I acknowledge that they are closely intertwined concepts.[26] Thus, what is actually under investigation in this study is what I call the postcolonial multiethnic nation-state—the multiethnic Nigerian state that is being transformed into a nation. Given the colonial legacy of Nigeria, it is important to emphasize the transplantation of the European models of the nation and state to Africa. As Sheldon Gellar has argued, nation-states in Africa are shaped by their neo-patrimonial features as well as by their colonial inheritance.[27] In particular, he emphasized the continuity of colonial structures in the postcolonial state, the dependency on former colonial powers, and the promotion of a postcolonial identity around the state that was created by the colonial powers. By state, I refer to a territorial entity that is internationally recognized as a sovereign political entity and the institutions through which its inhabitants are governed. Thus, I see the state as the institutional machinery through which a country with a defined territory is governed and linked to the international political and economic order. By nation, I refer to a society whose members see themselves as a people with some common cultural characteristics (such as language, religion, political values, or a common history) and a political destiny tied to a sovereign state that they call home. Their common attributes may or may not have been forced upon some or all of the members. The key to this definition is self-identification based on objective and subjective features. In short, the nation-state is an internationally recognized sovereign territorial entity with institutions designed to govern a group or groups of people who share some common cultural attributes and a political destiny. In this sense, nation-state building refers to the process of maintaining the nation-state and promoting integration and harmony among the various groups of people who constitute the nation-state.

To understand the problems associated with democratization and nation-state building in Nigeria, it is important to also deal with the issue of ethnicity. As we shall see, ethnicity is a crucial factor in both the breakdown and reconstitution of democracy and the nation-state in Nigeria. Until recently, it was common to refer to the various linguistic and cultural groups of people in African countries as tribes and the problem of cohabitation among them as tribalism.

However, as Gellar points out, "what is called tribalism in Africa is part of the universal and timeless problem of how culturally pluralistic societies hold together and function within the framework of a single political system."[28] Recently, social scientists have tried to replace the term "tribe" with "ethnic group." Thus, what used to be a uniquely African phenomenon becomes comparable to the problem of cohabitation in other parts of the world. While tribe was a colonial fabrication, ethnic group is a postcolonial politically correct term for the same social formation.[29]

An ethnic group is a relatively homogeneous body of people who claim a common ancestry and share a common language and culture. Such a group may be internally differentiated by dialects, religious practices, and customs.[30] Usually, an ethnic group is concentrated in specific areas of one or more countries; and countries with more than one ethnic group are referred to as multiethnic states. Multiethnic states exist in all parts of the world, especially in sub-Saharan Africa. In some multiethnic states, the groups are few in number and there is an overwhelmingly dominant majority group. In such cases, ethnic relations tend to be hegemonic. However, most of the multiethnic states in sub-Saharan Africa are composed of many ethnic groups with no clear majority group. Rather, there is a proliferation of relatively equal groups competing for control of the state. I will refer to ethnic relations in these kinds of cases as contested.[31]

The problem of cohabitation among ethnic groups can be broken down into ethnocentrism and ethnicity. Ethnocentrism is the attitudinal dimension of ethnic relations. It is usually inward looking and promotes a sense of pride and positive image of the group's beliefs, customs, and identity in relation to others. Ethnicity emerges during the process of interaction among ethnic groups inhabiting the same state. This interaction is frequently characterized by fierce competition for resources and power at the national, state, or local level.[32] Conflict arises out of the attempt to include one's members and at the same time exclude people from other ethnic groups in the distribution of resources. The urge to include and exclude fosters a collective consciousness among group members, making them not only a "group in itself," but also a "group for itself."[33] Ethnicity has either been viewed as the result of innate tendencies to be loyal and support one's group or the result of elite manipulation and corporate interest.[34] While the former emphasizes the strength of primordial identities, the latter stresses social construction. Whether it is a natural tendency or socially constructed, ethnicity does exist in Nigeria. As Okwudiba Nnoli points out:

> The media of socialization such as the family, press, and private as well as public conversation had become infected by the ubiquitous malaise of ethnicity . . . . This development intensified the polarization of the society into subnational ethnic cultures further separated in terms of identity and loyalty. . . . Consequently the ethnic factor assumed a self-fulfilling and self-sustaining dynamic of its own which daily reinforced the individual's internalized ethnic

sentiments. The persistence and growth of ethnicity in Nigeria had become inevitable.[35]

I will not dwell on the origin of ethnicity. Rather, I will take it as an empirical phenomenon and focus on its implications and the things Nigerians are doing about it.

This study will contribute to three interrelated theoretical debates that are central to the ongoing political transformation in Nigeria and other divided societies. These are: the synergy between democratization and nation-state building, the relevance of ethnicity in the democratization and nation-state building process in postcolonial sub-Saharan Africa, and the nature of democratic transitions and institutional design.

The first question, concerning the relation between democratization and nation-state building, is inspired by the experiences of the failed African democracies that emerged during the independence period, the failure of the authoritarian regimes that then followed, and the recent wave of democratic revival in the continent.[36] It is no secret that the advocates of one-party rule and military regimes consistently argued that nation-state building could not be effectively combined with multiparty democracy, and that the former should be the first priority. Though this argument has been challenged by pro-democracy activists as merely an attempt to monopolize power, it cannot be denied that the multiparty democracies of the 1960s failed in most African countries largely due to lack of national integration. Though the democratic breakdowns of the 1960s and 1970s may have boosted the authoritarian argument, their failure to build the nation has equally discredited the advocates of one-party and military regimes and strengthened the position of the pro-democracy activists of the 1990s. The cycle of democratic breakdown and crises of the nation-state in Nigeria can be very illuminating for understanding the synergy and potential conflict between democratization and nation-state building. The Nigerian experience indicates that democratization and nation-state building are tightly intertwined processes.

Over the past decades, there has been a growing interest in political transformations within the field of sociology and political science. However, most of the studies take the existence of the state, and sometimes the nation too, for granted. Despite the huge body of works in historical comparative and political sociology that have addressed the problems of nation-state building and democratic transitions, especially in Europe and Latin America, rarely do my fellow sociologists (and political scientists) pay attention to the fact that in most of the postcolonial countries that are democratizing, the nation-state is still in the making. Most importantly, few have tried to rigorously look for the links between these two intertwined processes. Claus Offe's analysis of the multiple transitions in Eastern Europe is helpful, but it falls short of the kind of systematic analysis of the interface of democratization and nation-state building envisioned in this project.[37] As Juan Linz and Alfred Stepan rightly note, "modern democratic governance is inevitably linked to stateness. Without a state, there can be no citizenship; without citizenship, there can be no democracy."[38] Despite their brilliant work, their question, "under what empirical conditions are the logics of state policies aimed at nation-building and the logics of state policies aimed at crafting democracy congruent?" still deserves further investigation.[39] In order to understand the empirical conditions they are referring to, we need to simultaneously deal with the processes of democratization and nation-state building. This study will take Linz and Stepan's work further by systematically analyzing a case where democratization has been undermined by problems of stateness and at the same time, democratization is being used to address the stateness problem.

I should make it clear that this work is intended to be a criticism of neither the existing studies on democratization nor those on nation-state building. On the contrary, I want to make a positive contribution to these bodies of work. My first contribution is to bridge them by showing that in essence they are all addressing the same question of peace and stability, albeit from different angles. While the literature on states and nations looks at the historical developments that generate institutions, structures, actors, common identities, and shared political values that help to maintain an orderly nation-state, the literature on democratization looks at the different political systems that have emerged and the struggles of the vast majority of people for political freedom and a voice in the running of the state. What is missing in both sets of literature is a rigorous and systematic analysis that links these two dimensions of the problem of peace and stability in most of the postcolonial multiethnic countries.

Second, the study will contribute to a deeper and balanced understanding of the impact of ethnicity on democratization and nation-state building in Nigeria and other postcolonial multiethnic countries. Ethnic violence is a common occurrence in Nigeria and many other parts of the world. In Nigeria, ethnic violence led to the virtual collapse of the federation during the Nigerian Civil War, and in recent times the Ogoni uprising and the activities of ethnic militias have raised concerns about the survival of the federation. Ethnicity has been demonized and identified as one of those evil forces that stand in the way of progress. Nnoli argued: "Ethnicity is not a critical variable. It lacks explanatory potency. Its role in African politics, although sometimes considerable, is more apparent than real. Its potential as a force for changing the objective realities of African life is very minimal."[40] Yet, he agrees that ethnicity is worth studying. In fact, he did study it in detail. He saw ethnicity as that evil force that "helps to perpetuate imperialism, and militates against the imperative of revolutionary struggle by hampering the development of a high level of political consciousness by its victims."[41] Thus, real change cannot come until we understand ethnicity and counteract its negative effects on the revolutionary process. Though for different reasons, I agree with Nnoli that we must study ethnicity in order to effect significant political and social changes in Nigeria, and Africa at large.

The project at hand seeks to go beyond this simplistic denial or demonization of ethnicity. Whether it is an epiphenomenon or not, it cannot be denied that ethnicity is a part of the Nigerian reality that is associated with tremendous troubles. To begin with, ethnicity is a major source of grudges and violence that destabilize democracy as well as the nation-state. However, while ethnicity contributes to the breakdown of democracy and creates a crisis of the nation-state, ethnicity can also serve as a driving force for democratization and nation-state building. When disadvantaged groups, such as the Ogoni, raise their voices for equality and adequate representation, in essence they are also calling for more democracy and national integration. As we shall see, the cycle of breakdown and reconstitution of democracy and the nation-state in Nigeria points to this dual character of ethnicity. On this note, one can draw from the works of Mahmood Mamdani and those of Basil Davidson that saw ethnicity as both an oppressive and a liberating force in the struggle against colonial rule. Indeed, while the colonial powers used ethnicity to oppress Africans, the victims managed to use ethnic sentiments as a vehicle to galvanize the revolt against colonial rule.[42] Though Mamdani's work dealt with a specific mode of oppression in Africa, decentralized despotism, his analysis leaves room for ethnicity to be seen as a constructive force in the struggle against oppressive rule. This dual character of ethnicity is most evident in postcolonial Nigeria, where the violent manifestation of ethnic grievances has led to conscious attempts to factor ethnicity into the design of democracy and the nation-state.

Finally, this work contributes to the discourse on democratic transitions and institutional designs by underscoring the intrinsic relation between the breakdown of democracy and its reconstitution. Contrary to the traditional notions of democratic transition, the Nigerian experience suggests that the breakdown of democracies, quasi-democracies in particular, can actually create opportunities for the reconstitution of a more representative democracy and inclusive multiethnic nation-state. Thus, the democratization process is neither unilinear nor necessarily a vicious cycle. In fact, democratization and nation-state building in Nigeria can best be described as a series of experimentations with institutional arrangements aimed at promoting a stable democracy and an inclusive nation-state. Furthermore, instead of seeing the designing of institutions as an attempt to come up with a one-time, fix-all solution, I emphasize the historical nature of the institutional design process and the collective learning experience it generates for the citizens of the multiethnic nation-state.

Organization and Scope

In order to demonstrate the dynamics between democratization, nation-state building, and ethnicity in Nigeria, I have traced the genesis of the multiethnic nation-state, looked at the manifestation of ethnicity, and analyzed the various institutional designs that Nigerians have employed in their effort to build a democratic multiethnic nation-state. To answer the questions raised in this study, I have relied on various official and unofficial documents on the manifestation of ethnicity, the numerous constitutions that have been promulgated in Nigeria, the decrees passed by various military governments, and the reports of government commissions that have dealt with issues such as revenue allocation, boundary adjustment, and minority problems. Most of these documents are available in the rich National Archive at the University of Ibadan in Nigeria. Furthermore, I have benefited from the expert opinions of a variety of Nigerian scholars, activists, politicians, and community leaders. I also had the opportunity to participate in numerous seminars dealing with a wide range of Nigerian political issues held in Ibadan and the New York metropolitan area.

This work is organized into several chapters that address the relevant theoretical and historical questions at hand, describe the Nigerian ethno-political landscape, and examine the various approaches and institutional arrangements that have been employed to promote a stable democracy and an integrated nation-state. Chapter 2 deals with the historical genesis of Nigeria and the legacies of colonial rule. It highlights the role of the colonial power in the making of Nigeria as well as the challenges of maintaining unity among the various ethnic groups after the withdrawal of the colonial power, which was the common enemy that held the country together. The chapter also points to the potential difficulties of reconciling multiparty politics with ethnic politics. In the third chapter, I demonstrate the magnitude of the problem of ethnicity in Nigeria. In particular, I discuss various incidents of violent ethnic conflicts that are rooted in the struggle for power and resources, and analyze their impact on multiparty democracy and the stability of the nation-state. The fourth chapter outlines the main objectives of nation-state building in Nigeria and examines the various forms of leadership and policies pursued by successive military and civilian governments in their attempt to build the nation-state. In the fifth chapter, I explore the varieties of institutional arrangements that have been devised in Nigeria as well as the conditions under which they were constructed and eventually crumbled. In particular, I explore the synergy between democratization and the nation-state building, the complexities associated with the process of designing institutions, and the role of ethnicity in both the breakdown and the reconstitution of the various institutional arrangements that have been devised to promote a democratic and inclusive nation-state in Nigeria. The final chapter sums up the main lessons that can be drawn from the Nigerian experience. In an attempt to stimulate further debate about the kinds of institutional arrangements that can promote a democratic and inclusive multiethnic nation-state in Nigeria, I suggest some specific changes that can be made to balance the federation and create a more equitable and fair system of revenue generation and distribution. Overall, I call for an institutional arrangement that is decentralized and builds capacity. Above all, I emphasize the need to complement institutional designs with good leadership and the development of a political culture that inculcates the values of tolerance, equity, fairness, liberty, and patriotism. In keeping the spirit of the work, I should emphasize that institutional design is a process. As such, my suggestions should not be seen as a one-time, fix-all solution. To the contrary, the suggestions should provoke more debates about the process.

Notes

1. The Nigerian Civil War is also referred to as the Biafra War.

2. With the exception of the interim civilian government led by Chief Ernest Shonekan that replaced the Babangida government in August 1993. However, this government was overshadowed by the military. In November 1993, General Abacha, who was the defense minister, forced Chief Shonekan to resign and quickly transformed the government to a military dictatorship.

3. The Third Republic was aborted.

4. As well as the 1995 draft constitution.

5. Claude Ake, *Democracy and Development in Africa* (Washington: The Brookings Institute, 1996), and Claude Ake, *The Feasibility of Democracy in Africa* (Dakar, Senegal: CODESRIA, 2000).

6. Scott Mainwaring, "Transitions to Democracy and Consolidated Democracy: Theoretical and Comparative Issues," in *Issues in Democratic Consolidation*, ed. Scott Mainwaring et al. (Notre Dame: University of Notre Press, 1992), 294-341.

7. Robert Dahl, *Polyarchy: Participation and Opposition* (New Haven: Yale University Press, 1971).

8. Joseph Schumpeter, *Capitalism, Socialism, and Democracy* (New York: Harper Colophon Books, 1942).

9. Seymour Martin Lipset, *Political Man: The Social Bases of Politics* (New York: Doubleday & Company, 1960).

10. Juan Linz and Alfred Stepan, *Problems of Democratic Transition and Consolidation: Southern Europe, South America, and Post-Communist Europe* (Baltimore: Johns Hopkins University Press, 1996), and Adam Przeworski, *Democracy and the Market: Political and Economic Reforms in Eastern Europe and Latin America* (New York: Cambridge University Press, 1991).

11. Donald Horowitz, *Ethnic Groups in Conflict* (Berkeley: University of California Press, 1985); Donald Horowitz, *A Democratic South Africa? Constitutional Engineering in a Divided Society* (Berkeley: University of California Press, 1991); and Arend Ljphart, *Democracy in Plural Societies: A Comparative Exploration* (New Haven: Yale University Press, 1977).

12. Interview with Professor J. A. A. Ayoade in Ibadan, August 2002.

13. Linz and Stepan, *Problems of Democratic Transition*; Scott Mainwaring et al., *Issues in Democratic Consolidation*; Guillermo O'Donnell and Philippe Schmitter, *Transitions from Authoritarian Rule: Tentative Conclusions about Uncertain Democracies* (Baltimore: Johns Hopkins University Press, 1986); and Juan Linz, *The Breakdown of Democratic Regimes: Crisis, Breakdown and Reequilibration* (Baltimore: The Johns Hopkins University Press, 1978).

14. Abu Bah, "Changing World Order and the Future of Democracy in sub-Saharan Africa," *Proteus: A Journal of Ideas* 21, no. 1 (Spring 2004): 3-12.

15. This is not to endorse military coups or rebellions. Rather, my aim is to emphasize the way in which the anti-democratic features of quasi-democracies contribute to the manner of replacing the government.

16. Horowitz, *Democratic South Africa*, xi.

17. Giovanni Sartori, *Comparative Constitutional Engineering: An Inquiry into Structures, Incentives, and Outcomes* (New York: New York University Press, 1997); Linz and Stepan, *Problems of Democratic Transition*; Horowitz, *Democratic South Africa*; and Arend Lijphart, *Democracy in Plural Societies*.

18. Mahmood Mamdani, *Citizen and Subject: Contemporary Africa and the Legacy of Late Colonialism* (Princeton, N.J.: Princeton University Press, 1996); David Welsh, "Ethnicity in sub-Saharan Africa," *International Affairs* 72, no. 3 (July 1996): 477-91; James Coleman (edited by Richard Sklar), *Nationalism and Development in Africa: Selected Essays* (Berkeley: University of California, 1994); and Basil Davidson, *The Black Man's Burden: Africa and the Curse of the Nation-State* (New York: Times Books, 1992).

19. Gianfranco Poggi, *The State: Its Nature, Development, and Prospects* (Stanford: Stanford University Press, 1990); Charles Tilly, *Coercion, Capital, and European States, A.D. 990-1990* (Cambridge, Mass.: B. Blackwell, 1990); Charles Tilly, "Reflections on the History of European State-Making," in *The Formation of National States in Western Europe*, ed. Charles Tilly (Princeton, N.J.: Princeton University Press, 1975), 3-83; Joseph Strayer, *On the Medieval Origins of the Modern State* (Princeton, N.J.: Princeton University Press, 1970); and Max Weber (translated, edited, and with an introd., by H. H. Gerth and C. Wright Mills) *From Max Weber: Essays in Sociology* (New York: Oxford University Press, 1946).

20. Theda Skocpol, "Bringing the State Back In: Strategies of Analysis in Current Research," in *Bringing the State Back In*, eds. Peter Evans et al. (New York: Cambridge University Press, 1985), 3-37.

21. Ernest Gellner, *Nations and Nationalism* (Ithaca: Cornell University Press, 1983).

22. Anthony Smith, *Nationalism and Modernism: A Critical Survey of Recent Theories of Nations and Nationalism* (London: Routledge, 1998); Anthony Smith, *The Nation in History: Historiographical Debates about Ethnicity and Nationalism* (Hanover, N.H.: University Press of New England, 2000); and Eric Hobsbawm, *On History* (London: Weidenfeld & Nicolson, 1997).

23. Johann G. von Herder (edited by F. M. Barnard), *J. G. Herder on Social and Political Culture* (London: Cambridge University Press, 1969), and Johann G. von Herder, *Reflections on the Philosophy of the History of Man* (Chicago: University of Chicago Press, 1968).

24. Florian Znaniecki, *Modern Nationalities: A Sociological Study* (Westport, Conn.: Greenwood Press, 1973).

25. Benedict Anderson, *Imagined Communities: Reflections on the Origin and Spread of Nationalism* (New York: Verso, 1991), 4.

26. Coleman, *Nationalism and Development*.

27. Sheldon Gellar, "State-Building and Nation-Building in West Africa," in *Building States and Nations*, Volume 2, ed. Shmuel Eisenstadt and Stein Rokkan (Beverly Hills: Sage Publications, 1973), 384-426.

28. Gellar, "State-Building and Nation-Building," 409.

29. Mamdani, *Citizen and Subject*.

30. Onigu Otite, *Ethnic Pluralism, Ethnicity, and Ethnic Conflicts in Nigeria* (Ibadan, Nigeria: Shaneson C. I. Ltd., 2000), and Horowitz, *Ethnic Groups*.

31. Taking into account the coincidence or non-coincidence of social class with ethnic origin, Horowitz identified two kinds of ethnic group relation. As he argued, "where the two coincide, it is possible to speak of ranked ethnic groups; where groups are cross class, it is possible to speak of unranked ethnic groups . . . if ethnic groups are ordered in hierarchy, with one super-ordinate and other subordinate, ethnic conflict moves in one direction, but if groups are parallel, neither subordinate to the other, conflict takes a different course." See Horowitz, *Ethnic Groups*, 22.

32. Aidan Campbell, *Western Primitivism: African Ethnicity; A Study in Cultural Relations* (London: Cassell, 1997); Okwudiba Nnoli, *Ethnic Politics in Nigeria* (Enugu, Nigeria: Fourth Dimension Publishers, 1980); and Horowitz, *Ethnic Groups*.

33. Nnoli, *Ethnic Politics*.

34. Horowitz, *Ethnic Groups*.

35. Nnoli, *Ethnic Politics*, 175.

36. Stephen Riley, *The Democratic Transition in Africa: An End to One Party State?* (London: Research Institute for the Study of Terrorism, 1991); Michael Bratton and Nicholas van de Walle, *Democratic Experiments in Africa: Regime Transitions in Comparative Perspectives* (New York: Cambridge University Press, 1997); John Wiseman, *The New Struggle for Democracy in Africa* (Aldershot, England: Ashgate, 1996); and Bah, "Changing World Order."

37. Claus Offe, *Varieties of Transition: The East European and East German Experience* (Cambridge, Mass.: MIT Press, 1997).

38. Linz and Stepan, *Problems of Democratic Transition*, 28.

39. Linz and Stepan, *Problems of Democratic Transition*, 25.

40. Nnoli, *Ethnic Politics*, 12.

41. Nnoli, *Ethnic Politics*, 13.

42. Mamdani, *Citizen and Subject*, and Davidson, *Black Man's Burden*.

Chapter 2

The Genesis of Nigeria and the Elimination of the Common Enemy

What is now known as Nigeria—as a defined territory, a political entity, and a set of people—is a fairly new phenomenon that dates back to the British conquest of the territories of the Niger delta. As James Coleman notes, "the artificiality of Nigeria's boundaries and the sharp cultural differences among its peoples point up the fact that Nigeria is a British creation and the concept of a Nigerian nation is the result of British presence."[1] The Berlin Conference of 1885 gave official recognition—in the West—to the conquest. It is well known that the region was inhabited by different groups of people, such as Hausa-Fulani, Yoruba, Ibibio, Igbo, Urhobo, Ijaw, Itsekiri, Ogoni, Atyap, Birom, Tiv, and Jukun, who were later given the unenviable task of forming a Nigerian nation-state. Onigu Otite (2000) has identified as many as 387 ethnic groups in Nigeria (see table A.1). Of these ethnic groups, the Hausa-Fulani, Yoruba, and Igbo are the dominant groups, accounting for around two-thirds of the Nigerian population.[2]

Nigeria is currently divided into thirty-six states and a Federal Capital Territory (see figures A.1-A.7). Each of these is further divided into Local Government Areas (LGAs). Furthermore, Nigeria is informally divided into geopolitical zones and regions.[3] Currently, there are six geopolitical zones: Northwest, Northeast, Middle Belt, Southwest, Southeast, and South-South.[4] The most prominent division, however, is the historic North-South regional divide, followed by the North-East-West regional divide.[5] The North-East-West regional divide reflects the dominance of the three major ethnic groups: Hausa-Fulani, Igbo, and Yoruba, respectively. Of course, none of the geographical divides does justice to the full range of the ethnic diversity in Nigeria. In fact, they just marginalize the millions of Nigerians who belong to the relatively smaller groups, which are nevertheless quite large.[6] Yet, such a categorization is necessary to get a better picture of the political struggles in Nigeria. In fact, the increase from two regions to six geopolitical zones, like the growing number of states and LGAs, is a reflection of the ethnic struggles for power and resources in Nigeria.

The North is an open savannah that stretches all the way down to the Middle Belt of Nigeria. The major ethnic groups in the core North are the Hausa-Fulani and the Kanuri. The Kanuri are mainly in the northeastern corner around Lake Chad. The Hausa-Fulani, who form the majority group, are spread all over the North, but are concentrated especially in the western and central part of the North. The Hausa-Fulani actually consist of the Hausa and the Fulani people. Though historically the Hausa and Fulani were separate groups of people, they have come to be seen as a single ethnic group in Nigerian politics. The unification of the Hausa and the Fulani people began with the conquest of the Hausa states by the Fulani under the leadership of Uthman Dan Fodio in 1804 and the establishment of the Sokoto theocracy in most of what is now northern Nigeria. The less numerous Fulani overlords made vassals of the majority Hausa, settled among them, intermarried, and took up the Hausa language. In turn, the Fulani successfully converted the Hausa people to Islam. This integrated Hausa-Fulani community has now emerged as a single ethnic identity within the Nigerian political landscape.[7] Though many of the Hausa-Fulani people may be fully aware of the distinctions between the two groups, to many Nigerians not of the Hausa-Fulani, the Hausa and Fulani are the same people.[8] This view has been further strengthened by the united political front demonstrated by the Hausa-Fulani people. Thus, for all practical political purposes in contemporary Nigeria, the Hausa-Fulani have come to be accepted as a single body of people. The Middle Belt area is inhabited by clusters of smaller ethnic groups such as the Jukun, Nupe, Borgu, Igala, Ebira, Tiv, Birom, Atyap, and Idoma. In many ways, the Middle Belt serves as a geographic and cultural transition zone between the core northern and southern parts of Nigeria.

The South is mainly a forest zone and predominantly Christian. It is dominated by the Igbo in the East and the Yoruba in the West. Indeed, one can argue that these are distinct regions, especially in light of the fact that the two sides fought one another during the Nigerian Civil War and had been rivals even before independence. Most of the minority groups in the South, such as the Ebu, Urhobo, Itsekiri, Ijaw, Ibeno, Isoko, and the highly publicized Ogoni, are clustered around the Niger Delta area in the South-South zone.

The capture of Lagos in 1861 marked the birth of formal British rule in Nigeria. Since then, the history of Lagos, and that of Nigeria as a whole, has rarely been peaceful. In 1885, the British annexed the Niger Delta area and named it the Oil River Protectorate. In 1893, they expanded their rule to include the hinterland and renamed the area the Niger Coast Protectorate.[9] Having established a base in the coastal regions, the British followed the Niger River northward. In March 1903, Sokoto too fell to the British, marking the demise of the Fulani Empire. By 1900, the British had virtually conquered the colony of Lagos in the southwestern part of Nigeria and transformed the southeastern and northern territories into British protectorates. The regions were commonly referred to as Western Nigeria, Eastern Nigeria, and Northern Nigeria, respectively.[10] In 1914, these regions were amalgamated to form the colony and protectorate of Nigeria.

This marked the birth of Nigeria as a single political entity. The amalgamation began the establishment of the Nigerian state in that it created a single territory and a sovereign authority—albeit illegitimate—in the given territory. Since then, the process of nation building has largely involved establishing institutions to effectively control the territory and its people and link the country to the international system of states. Furthermore, the amalgamation initiated a common historical experience for the diverse groups of people inhabiting the territory of Nigeria, which has been the key unifying force among them. This common colonial experience, as indigenous Africans robbed of their land and oppressed by the British, became the seed of Nigerian identity and nationhood. The challenge for the various peoples that have been defined as Nigerians is to maintain that identity and promote national integration after the elimination of their common oppressor.

Colonial Rule

British rule in Nigeria was neither coherent nor uniform in the different parts of the country. It was customized to ensure a cost-effective administration advantageous to the colonial power. The administrative system of each region was customized according to the form of cultural and political organization among the various ethnic groups and the duration of their contact with the British. Though it is generally assumed that British rule was *indirect* while that of their colonial counterparts—the French—was *direct*, it is important to note that the British had their own version of direct rule, which they applied to their colonies. For example, the municipalities of Lagos, Port Harcourt, Enugu, Kaduna, Kano, and Zaria were under direct rule. Political power and the day-to-day administration of the municipalities were vested solely in the hands of expatriate officials of the imperial power. The rest of Nigeria was administered through indirect rule.[11] Indirect rule was first established in Northern Nigeria (between 1900 and 1913). It was introduced in Western Nigeria from 1916 to 1919. Around 1927, it was taken to Eastern Nigeria. By 1937, nearly the whole of Nigeria was governed through indirect rule.[12] Indirect rule relied upon subjugated indigenous rulers who continued to exercise authority over their people, subject to the supervision of the colonial agents. The relation between the traditional rulers and the British was based on an understanding that the former would deliver what the colonial power needed: taxes, forced labor, unhindered access to raw materials and agricultural products, and order. In turn, the British allowed them a free hand over their people as long as they did not go against British interests. Those rulers who did not cooperate, and many did not, were replaced with puppet chiefs who are commonly referred to as warrant chiefs.[13]

Indirect rule in the northern region relied upon the existence of a powerful and centralized aristocracy, which the British came to associate themselves with and defended. Ironically, the British pacified the people in the eastern and western regions by preaching against African cultures and working toward their destruction in the name of progress. At the same time, in the northern region, where the autocratic elements of the local culture worked well with the colonial agenda, the British wholeheartedly promoted traditionalism. They insulated feudal structures from change, manifested negative conservatism, and hindered local initiatives for progressive change. Not surprisingly, in 1937 British officials prevented the Emir of Hadejia from appointing to his council a man who was considered to be very able, simply because he was of slave origin.[14]

Inspired by the success of indirect rule in the northern region, the British also introduced indirect rule to the western and eastern regions. They engaged in mischievous social engineering to make room for indirect rule among the various people in the South. Already, they knew that a strongly hierarchical power structure was the key to the success of indirect rule. As such, they searched for kings and imposed them where they did not exist. The problem is that some of these societies did not have a rigid and hierarchical power structure. This is particularly true of the Igbo whose societies have been described as small-scale democracies built around secret societies, oracles, and group participation. Translated into modern political language, Igbo societies could be described as grass-roots democracies. So too was the case of the Kantana of the Benue Valley, whose elders describe their traditional governments as a hierarchy of masquerade.[15] It is not surprising that in their search for chiefs, the British often appointed people whose caliber was far from what one would expect of a chief. For example, the Mwahavul of Mangu tricked the British into appointing an idle man who had refused to farm and wandered from place to place as a chief. The people saw such a man as an appropriate person to follow the British around. These were the kinds of people that became warrant chiefs—corrupt and exploitative.[16]

The imposition of indirect rule in the western and eastern regions not only involved imposing chiefs where they had not existed, but also redefining borders, subjugating one people under the jurisdiction of another group (thereby furthering the divide-and-rule tactics of the British), and inventing customs and traditions.[17] In this way, the Algo Kingdom of Doma was forcibly integrated with the much more recent Lafia Kingdom. In the Alafinate of Oyo, the powers of the Alafin (King) were increased at the expense of the comprehensive traditional system of checks and balances. The Oyo Mesi (Queen Mother) was marginalized and the people's right to demand the Alafin's suicide in cases of gross abuse of power was eliminated.[18]

Colonial rule led to the breakdown of the social fabric of the various societies in Nigeria. Furthermore, it was exploitative. British officials who could barely make a living in their home country were paid big salaries and benefits in Nigeria. It is estimated that in 1936, when Nigeria's total income was £6,259,547, colonial officials sent home around £1,156,000, in addition to pension payments.[19] Worst of all, the British policy of promoting traditionalism in the North and westernization in the South had a huge repercussion on the relation between the Hausa-Fulani of the North on the one hand and the Yoruba and Igbo of the South on the other hand, who as compatriots would have to live together. This created a climate of negative rivalry and an unbalanced competition among the different groups.

Nationalist Movement

Nigerian nationalism, which was essentially the struggle to end British rule, can be divided into two phases: traditional and modern nationalism.[20] Traditional nationalism refers to the early resistance toward British conquest and pacification. It was characterized by localized and religious forms of resistance against British rule. Though traditional nationalism was suppressed, it did lay a foundation for modern nationalism. Modern nationalism refers to the coherent and systematic struggle to end British rule and lead the country into nation-statehood. It was strategically oriented toward independence and led by westernized Africans, commonly referred to as nationalist leaders. These nationalist leaders were Africans who were recruited and trained by the British and who later became alienated from their British mentors. In turn, the nationalists used British laws, institutions, and political tactics to oust them.

In addition to the groundwork laid by traditional nationalism, modern nationalism was bolstered by the negative impacts of a money economy, urbanization, racism, the contradictory role of Christianity, the influence of Africans in the Americas, western education, and the precarious situation of westernized Africans who were left in limbo, hated by the British and alienated from their own cultures.[21] The nationalist movements led to the emergence of regional and national political leaders and political parties, a systematic constitutional reform that eventually led to independence in 1960, and the birth of ethnic politics in anticipation of British withdrawal. In an attempt to pacify the nationalist movement, the colonial government tried to entrench ethnic difference. In his criticism of the National Congress of British West Africa (NCBWA), which among other things was advocating for the creation of democratically elected legislative councils and responsible governments in the British territories, Governor Hugh Clifford stated that the policy of the colonial government was to maintain and support the various tribal institutions and forms of government.[22]

It is worth noting that there are debates as to whether there was more than one nationalist struggle in Nigeria. One can ask whether the nationalist movement was a unified Nigerian struggle against the British or whether the Igbo of the East, the Yoruba of the West, and Hausa-Fulani of the North waged separate battles against British rule.[23] The debate is a good indicator of the historical origins of the very problems of forging a democratic multiethnic nation-state in Nigeria. A close look at the struggle against British rule will show elements of both a unified struggle and ethnically oriented struggles, as well as inter-ethnic struggles to succeed the British. This is not a contradiction, however, though at first glance it may appear so. Rather it shows that the difficulties of the independent Nigerian nation-state had emerged at the very beginning of the nationalist movement. Indeed, all Nigerian nationalists had one clear and common objective which was to gain freedom for their communities. However, the various leaders used different tactics and tried to customize their demands for political change to fit the relative needs and advantage of their constituencies. While Nigerians were united in their struggle against their common oppressor, among themselves they were disunited, especially so after the elimination of the common enemy.

Regional leaders, who tried to become national leaders as well, were the main symbols of the nationalist movement. The main figures were Nnamdi Azikiwe (commonly referred to as Zik) from the Igbo East, Obafemi Awolowo of the Yoruba West, and Ahmadu Bello, Abubakar Tafawa Balewa, and Aminu Kano of the Hausa-Fulani North.[24] Zik was one of the most prominent of the nationalist leaders. Among other things, Zik is remembered for his support of the 1945 general strike which brought together 17 unions representing 30,000 public workers. Notwithstanding his courageous efforts to promote an independent nation-state in Nigeria, he has also been blamed for intensifying personal rivalries and ethnic chauvinism, which destroyed the Nigerian Youth Movement (NYM) and ironically undermined his very efforts to promote national integration.[25] In particular, he angered many non-Igbo Nigerians by stating: "The God of Africa has specially created the Ibo nation to lead the children of Africa from the bondage of the ages. . . . The martial prowess of the Ibo nation at all stages of human history has enabled them not only to conquer others but also to adapt themselves to the role of preserver. . . . The Ibo nation cannot shrink its responsibility."[26]

Some of the most prominent political organizations that championed the Nigerian struggle for independence are: the National Council of Nigeria and the Cameroons (NCNC), which was led by Zik, the Action Group (AG) led by Awolowo, and the Northern Peoples' Congress (NPC), which was headed by Ahmadu Bello.[27] For the most part, these organizations represented the Igbo in the East, the Yoruba in the West, and the Hausa-Fulani in the North, respectively. However, the first organizations that championed the nationalist cause were inter-territorial, leading a common cause on behalf of the peoples of all the four British territories in West Africa—Nigeria, Sierra Leone, Ghana, and the Gambia. The main organizations were the National Congress of British West Africa (NCBWA) which was inaugurated in 1920, and the West African Students' Union (WASU) led by Chief Oladipo Solanke. Among other things, the NCBWA demanded that chiefs be elected and deposed only by their people. Furthermore, they demanded the creation of an independent judiciary, an increase in the number of elected members in the Legislative Council, a university in West Africa, an end to the discrimination against Africans in the civil service, and stricter immigration controls against Syrians. Unfortunately, by 1930 the NCBWA was dead.[28] As the colonial administrations of the four territories became autonomous from one another, so did the Pan-West African organizations fade away. They were replaced with territorially based organizations which championed national causes. Thus, people in Nigeria began to see themselves as the citizens of a nation-state-in-the-making.

The Nigerian National Democratic Party (NNDP) was one of the first national organizations to develop. It was founded in 1923 and led by Habert Macaulay, C. C. Adeniyi-Jones, J. Egerton-Shyngle, E. O. Moore, Ibikunle Olorun-Nimbe, and A. Adedoyin. The Nigerian Youth Movement (NYM) was founded in 1934 and led by E. Ikoli, S. Akinsanya, Obafemi Awolowo, H. O. Davies, Samuel Akintola, and F. R. A. Williams. Although these parties purported to be national, they were, however, based primarily in Lagos. After 1944, parties with a much wider base of support emerged, though all of them were primarily associated with the home region of their leaders. The main parties were the National Council of Nigeria and Cameroons (NCNC), the Action Group (AG), and the Northern People's Congress (NPC). In addition, there were other small parties, such as the Northern Elements Progressive Union (NEPU) and the United Middle Belt Congress (UMBC).

The NCNC emerged out of an attempt to find an umbrella organization that could promote the nationalist cause, primarily in southern Nigeria. Nigerian students founded the organization in 1944, immediately after the King's College strike during which seventy-five senior students were expelled and eight of them conscripted into military service. Angered by the punishment, the Nigerian Union of Students (NUS) thought it necessary to have an organization to coordinate the efforts of the existing political parties, trade unions, professional organizations, and ethnic unions. A mass meeting was organized by the NUS on June 10, 1944, in the Glover Memorial Hall, Lagos. The participants deliberated over the King's College strike and agreed to set up a "National Council or Committee" (NC) and a national school. Over forty organizations met on August 26, 1944, for the inaugural meeting of the National Council and mandated the council to work in unity with other groups for the realization of the ultimate goal of self-government within the British Empire. Herbert Macaulay was elected president and Namdi Azikiwe was elected secretary general. From the outset, some of the leaders of the NYM were suspicious and saw the NC as an attempt by Zik and Macaulay to bring the nationalist movement under their control. Despite the suspicions, the Nigerian Union of Young Democrats (NUYD) affiliated itself with the NC, and by 1945 the NC had 87 member unions, three of which were from Cameroon. The NC was renamed National Council of Nigeria and the Cameroons (NCNC) and became very active in the struggle for constitutional reforms.

Initially, the NCNC scored big successes. Most notably, it successfully organized an eight-month tour across Nigeria and won elections in Lagos. During the tour, the NCNC raised £13,500 and received written mandates from twenty-four communities in the North, forty-eight in the West, eighty-one in the East, and the blessings of the traditional ruler of Lagos. Under the banner of their affiliate—the NNDP—members of the NCNC also won three Lagos seats in the Legislative Council. However, between 1948 and 1951, the organization declined and the NCNC was virtually dead by 1951. In March 1951, NCNC supporters tried to revive the organization. The move was seen as an effort by the Igbo to preempt their Yoruba opponents, who were under Awolowo's leadership, from controlling the nationalist movement. On March 27, 1951, Mbonu Ojike and Kingsley Ozuomba Mbadiwe, well known Igbo nationalists from the eastern province of Owerri, formed the Committee for National Rebirth. Though leaders of the NYM and members of the AG attended the meeting, they failed to create a united front. Members of the AG withdrew from the committee, leaving the NCNC alone to recreate itself into a political party with individual membership.[29]

The AG emerged at a time when relations between the Yoruba elite and the Igbo elite, who dominated NCNC leadership, were deteriorating very fast. In particular, there was growing fear that the NCNC would win the 1951 elections in the Western Region. It is no secret that the AG was set up by the educated Yoruba elite to ensure Yoruba political control of the Western Region, starting with the 1951 elections. The formation of the AG was facilitated by the existing Yoruba cultural organization, the Egbe Omo Oduduwa, which brought together the educated Yoruba elite and the traditional chiefs. In addition, the Egbe already had a political committee on constitutional reform in place. From the outset, it was clear that the AG was to consist of Egbe members and could count on the pan-Yoruba sentiment fostered through the Egbe to pursue its political goals. As Awolowo argued, chieftaincy carries an "incalculable sentimental value for the masses in Western and Northern Nigeria. This being so, it is imperative, as a matter of practical politics, that we use the most effective means ready to hand for organizing masses for rapid political advancement."[30] The AG was inaugurated on March 26, 1950, at the Ibadan residence of Awolowo, the general secretary of the Egbe. Though there was some initial opposition within the Egbe to the creation of the AG, for fear of duplicating the activities of the Egbe and encouraging internal rivalry, Awolowo and Samuel L. Akintola successfully argued for the establishment of the AG as an autonomous political body operating within the Egbe. Later, the AG became the de facto political wing of the Egbe. In 1951, the AG was unveiled to the nation as a political organization of the Western Region. The inaugural conference was held at Owo on April 28 and 29, 1951.[31]

The emergence of the NPC can be traced back to two significant meetings held in Kaduna and Zaria under the leadership of Malam D. A. Rafih and Dr. A. R. B. Dikko, respectively. On October 3, 1948, the Kaduna group formed the Jam'iyyar Mutanen Arewa A Yau (The Association of the Northern People of Today), and on October 12, 1948, Dr. Dikko and Malam Abubakar Imam, founded the Jam'iyyar Jama'ar Arewa (Northern Nigerian Congress) in Zaria. At the Zaria meeting, during which Malam Rafih was present, an agreement was reached to combine the two organizations into one, Jam'iyyar Mutanen Arewa (the Northern Nigerian Congress [NNC], which was later renamed the Northern Peoples' Congress [NPC]). The inaugural meeting of the NNC was held on June 26, 1949, in Kaduna. Initially, the NNC was intended to be a social and cultural organization dedicated to the development of the North. Nevertheless, it was clear that the leaders also had political objectives. Among other things, they wanted to reform the Sole Native Authorities system and to ensure that Hausa-Fulani would lead the nationalist movement in the North, instead of leaving it to the Igbo and Yoruba, who were seen as radicals and potential oppressors.

Soon, it became evident that the NPC could not hold all the northern elite together—the emirs (traditional rulers), the moderate educated elite, and the radicals. In August 1950, radical youths formed the Northern Elements Progressive Union (NEPU), which was seen as a vanguard political party within a conservative NPC. One of its main objectives was to reform the aristocratic institutions and free the Talakawa (commoners). Given the reservations of the emirs, the moderates realized that in order to transform the NPC into an effective political party, they would have to do away with the radical members of the NEPU. The conservatives and moderates supported a resolution which effectively expelled NEPU members from the NPC. The NEPU broke away and left the way clear for the transformation of the NPC into a conservative political party on October 1, 1951.[32]

Political organizations were the vehicles of the nationalist movement. Indeed, they were the best organizational response to the challenge because they fit well into the British model of political engagement. Moreover, in comparison to secret societies and religious organizations, political parties provoked fewer suspicions in the minds of the British. Their operation was facilitated by the improved means of communication, urbanization, the growth of political and cultural associations, the emergence of a dynamic press, and the proliferation of the English language—ironically the language of the enemy.

Politically active pan-ethnic organizations also developed beside political parties. In 1928, the Ibibio created the first ethnic union. In the 1930s, the Igbo formed Igbo unions in Port Harcourt and Lagos, which became the backbone of the NCNC. Later on, the Ibo Federal Union (renamed Ibo State Union in 1948), which was headed by Zik, emerged as an umbrella Igbo organization. However, Zik's involvement with the Ibo Federal Union further convinced non-Igbo people that the NCNC was an Igbo party. In 1945, the Yuroba founded the Egbe Omo Oduduwa. Its guiding spirit was Awolowo, who wanted to halt the internal divisions among the Yoruba elite and counterbalance the Ibo State Union. The emergence of these ethnic organizations opened the way for a bitter press war between Zik and the Egbe leaders. Unlike the Igbo and Yoruba, who tried to keep their ethnic organizations as distinct bodies from their political parties, for the Hausa-Fulani the NPC was the single organization that assumed both roles.

The general feature of the Nigerian party system during the nationalist movement was that each of the three major parties had a strong regional base and was dominated by one of the three major ethnic groups. Ethnic domination was clearly manifested in the composition of the leadership of the parties. For instance, in 1958 the NPC's national executive council was 51 percent Hausa-Fulani, the AG's federal executive council was 68 percent Yoruba, and the NCNC's top executive bodies were 49 percent Igbo. Even though Zik contested a seat in Lagos during the 1951 elections, and the NCNC gained a majority in the West in 1954, the political parties were hardly national. Essentially, they were regional parties. During the first general election in 1952, they each gained a large majority of the seats in their home region.[33] The situation left ethnic minorities in each of the regions worried. In the West, minorities of the Mid-West agitated for a separate region. In the East too the people of Calabar, Ogoja, and Rivers (the COR areas) stood up against Igbo domination. In the North, ethnic minorities formed the United Middle Belt Congress (UMBC) to resist Hausa-Fulani domination. Perhaps the only tangible way in which the major parties tried to maintain a national image was by aligning themselves with minorities in other regions. However, this did not change the regional and ethnic character of the parties.

Sadly, these anomalies in the party system were not properly addressed before Nigeria achieved independence. In fact, the prospect of independence intensified the ethnic struggle, while the British cared little because they were looking to advance their own postcolonial careers. Overall, the impact of political organization on the progress toward Nigerian nation-statehood is mixed. Indeed, political parties were crucial for promoting Nigerian independence and the development of multiparty democracy. However, the close link between political parties and ethnic organizations hampered the formation of truly national political parties with clear ideologies that could accommodate Nigerian ethnic diversity. In contrast, ethnic organization hastened the transformation of political parties into ethnic parties, which further complicated the process of building a democratic multiethnic nation-state.

Ultimately, the nationalist movement was a struggle to end colonial rule. The struggle itself centered around the existing political, economic, and social grievances. These grievances formed the ideological and substantive issues that sustained and intensified the movement. Politically, the nationalists denounced discrimination and subjugation, and called for equality and freedom. On the economic front, they demanded equal access to large-scale import/export and banking enterprises. Socially, they demanded better welfare policies and more access to social services such as education, health, and sanitation.[34]

After World War II, the nationalist movement took a much more radical turn. African participation in the war undermined the sense of European superiority which the British had carefully instilled in the people.[35] During the war, they interacted with average Europeans, who were quite different from those that had been groomed to maintain an image of perfection in Africa. Returning servicemen who had seen the inside of the white world realized that Europeans were no cleverer, better, or kinder than the people in their home villages.[36] Furthermore, the nationalist leaders seized upon the liberal ideas expressed in

President Woodrow Wilson's Fourteen Points issued during World War I and the 1941 Atlantic Charter drawn by Franklin Roosevelt and Winston Churchill. The nationalists demanded the application of the principle of self-determination advocated by the western leaders to the people of Africa.[37]

In addition to sending petitions and delegations to the Colonial Office in Britain and engaging in debates in the Legislative Council, the movement pressed its demands through street protests and industrial action. This was facilitated by the growing numbers of wage earners, estimated at around 300,000 in 1950, out of whom 120,000 were employed by the government.[38] In 1897, for example, employees of the Public Works Department successfully prevented changes in their working hours. In 1904, skilled railway workers went on strike to press for insurance and a pension scheme. In the Enugu collieries there was a series of strikes for better wages in 1920 and 1921. One of the most significant industrial actions against the colonial regime was the general strike of 1945. Seventeen unions representing 30,000 workers, including railway, postal, and telegraph employees, went on strike for 37 days. The strike received strong support from Zik's newspapers. Overall, the strike was a great demonstration of unity against the colonial government.[39] Trade unions, which numbered up to 70 after World War II, were the main supporters of the strikes. Two of the leading unions during the inter-war period were the Nigerian Union of Civil Servants and the Nigerian Union of Teachers. Later on, the Nigerian Trade Union Congress was formed as an umbrella organization for most of the unions.

Equally important for the growth of the nationalist movement was the African press that was owned and managed by the nationalists—such as Zik's *Pilot*. The African press became the mouthpiece of the nationalists and a weapon against colonial rule. The early papers and pamphlets were also vital in raising racial and political consciousness as well as nationalist sentiments. In particular, John Payne Jackson's *Lagos Weekly Record* (1891 to the 1930s) constantly called for national unity and concerted effort from the different ethnic groups to free their land. Other papers that emerged were the *Lagos Standard* (1903), the *Nigerian Chronicle* (1903), and the *Nigerian Times* (1914). In 1910, the Tika-Tore Printing Works was established in Lagos, which was a great boost to the African papers.[40]

During the 1950s, the political climate significantly changed. Radical confrontations (strikes, riots, and political trials) gave way to more conciliatory relations. The colonial government tried to co-opt the nationalist leaders. In particular, the University of Ibadan was opened in 1948. The colonial government also started to appoint Nigerians to high positions in the civil service. In 1953, for example, the number of Africans who held senior positions in the civil service increased to 786, from a low of 23 in 1939.[41]

Constitutional Development

The first constitutional reform in Nigeria occurred in 1922. The 1922 Constitution created a single council for the whole of Nigeria to replace the separate councils for the colony of Lagos and the rest of the country.[42] The new council, called the Legislative Council, consisted of twenty-six officials, fifteen nominated unofficial members (these were later on increased to "not more than thirty" and "not more than seventeen," respectively), and four elected members—three from Lagos and one from Calabar.[43] The three elective seats for Lagos were occupied by the NNDP until 1938 when the NYM ousted them.[44] In terms of democratization and nation-state building the 1922 Constitution created the first national political organ and introduced electoral politics in Nigeria. Since then, Nigerians have understood democracy to mean winning the mandate to govern through competitive elections among the various political factions within the country.

Substantial constitutional changes did not really occur until after World War II. The post-war constitutional development can be broken into two phases: the period of troubles (1944-1951) and the period of dyarchy or cooperation (1951-1959). The first period was characterized by growing economic difficulties and strikes, such as the General Strike (1945), the Buruntu Strike (1947), and the Enugu Colliery Strike (1949). The period was also characterized by militant political activism as manifested through the activities of the NCNC and the Zikist movement.

The most significant constitutional development of the first period was the adoption of the Richards Constitution in 1946. Under the 1946 Constitution, Nigeria was divided into three regions: Northern Nigeria, Eastern Nigeria, and Western Nigeria (see figure A.1).[45] Each had a Regional Assembly with a majority of unofficial members (North: twenty-four unofficial and eighteen official members, West: nineteen unofficial and thirteen official, and East: eighteen unofficial and thirteen official). The North had a House of Chiefs in addition to the Assembly. The primary functions of the Regional Houses were to choose regional representatives for the Legislative Council (which was the Federal Assembly), advise the governor, and approve the budget (i.e., Regional Estimates). The Legislative Council consisted of sixteen official and twenty-eight unofficial members. Of the twenty-eight unofficial members, four were directly elected from Lagos and Calabar and twenty elected by the Regional Assemblies.[46] Though the council's legislative powers were limited and the governor could bypass it, the 1946 Constitution significantly boosted the morale of the nationalists by giving them a majority in the Legislative Council. Furthermore, the 1946 Constitution signaled the development of a federal state. The central dilemma was how to find a system that could work both in the North where the Hausa-Fulani dominated and in the South where the Yoruba and Igbo dominated. While in the North traditional rulers were firmly in control and there was no political party of mass following, the South had an active and politically organized western-educated elite. Thus, right from its inception, Nigerian federalism was complicated by an uneven development between the regions. Despite the significant gains, the Richards Constitution fell short of the aspirations of the nationalists. In essence, it merely provided a forum for Nigerians to engage in political debates (with the colonial government and among themselves), but failed to empower them to act. Overall, the nationalists were not satisfied with the 1946 Constitution, especially because it was passed without properly consulting Nigerians, and it only got twenty-nine minutes of discussion in a nearly empty British House of Commons.[47] Not surprisingly, the nationalists intensified their campaign. In 1947, the NCNC sent a delegation to London to push for an early review of the Richards Constitution.

The period of dyarchy was ushered in with the 1951 Macpherson Constitution which was a significant step toward establishing a government that was representative and responsible to the people of Nigeria. The Constitution established regional legislatures that were empowered to make laws on matters such as local government, health, agriculture, and education. The legislatures consisted of an indirectly elected House of Assembly with a majority of unofficial members, the lieutenant governor of the region, and the House of Chiefs in the North and the West. The Federal Legislative Council consisted of 130 unofficial members (selected from members of the Regional Legislature by the Regional Legislatures themselves), and six officials. Half of the unofficial members came from the North while the West and the East were evenly represented. This arrangement, which essentially favored the Hausa-Fulani was a compromise that was strongly criticized by Zik and Awolowo.[48] Under the 1951 Constitution, Nigeria combined elements of both federal and unitary state models. Indeed, the country was in the hands of a well-established colonial administration under the command of the governor, his lieutenants, the heads of departments in Lagos, and their regional deputies. Yet, it also had some of the trappings of a federation, which was plagued by regional imbalances. The struggle between the North and South to control the federal legislature was a good indicator of what was in store for postcolonial Nigeria. Later on, the intervention of the military and the emergence of an oil-dependent economy further complicated the centralized and unbalanced federal structure.

It is also important to take note of the composition and character of the executive organ under the 1951 Constitution. The Council of Ministers consisted of the governor, six officials, and twelve ministers (i.e., four unofficial members from each region). However, this was not a cabinet in that it was not chosen or led by a prime minister. Most significantly, ministers maintained their regional allegiances and were not in charge of government departments. The regions too had similar executive councils.[49]

The period of dyarchy was that phase of the struggle for independence during which the colonial government started to take the nationalists much more seriously. Unlike the past, they were more or less considered partners of the government. Of course, the intentions of the colonial government in its change of policy from suppression to cooperation were suspicious. At any rate, it was clear that the colonial government had felt the weight of the movement and realized that things could not go on as they used to. Whether the policy change was a genuine attempt to withdraw or simply a tactic to co-opt and oppress is an open question. But if one draws a lesson from the way indirect rule was used to co-opt traditional African rulers into the colonial regime, one would have few doubts that the phase of dyarchy was another attempt to disarm the nationalists.

Apart from it being a period of rapid constitutional development with less confrontation between the nationalists and the colonial government, the period of dyarchy was also characterized by high expectations for economic and social improvement as well as internal struggles among the leaders of the three dominant ethnic groups. Politics became a game of payoffs, competition for booty, and internal fighting. As the British became less of an enemy, the bond among Nigerians grew weaker. Even though the country remained intact, it was not a fully united Nigeria that attained independence. Perhaps the strong desire for independence led the nationalists to take unity for granted at the expense of critical self-examination.

Dyarchy was followed by partial self-rule and eventually independence in 1960. Under the 1954 Lyttelton Constitution, Nigeria formally became a federation, consisting of the three regions (North, East, and West) and two federal territories (Lagos and the Southern Cameroons). The tricky problem was defining the respective powers of the federal and regional governments. Under the 1954 Constitution, the federal government had power over functions listed in the Federal Legislative List, such as: aviation, banking, census, copyright, currency, customs, defense, external relations, certain higher educational institutions, immigration and emigration, mining, police, railways, inter-regional commerce, trunk roads, inter-regional water, weights and measures, radio, and television. Both the federal and regional governments were empowered to legislate on issues in the Concurrent Legislative List.

The federal legislature consisted of 184 elected members (ninety-two from the North, forty-two from the West, forty-two from the East, six from Southern Cameroons, and two from Lagos), three officials, and up to six special members, representing minorities and others special interests. The 1954 Constitution still maintained the fifty-fifty distribution between the North and South in the federal legislature. The regional Executive Councils were to be led by premiers who would command majority support in their respective Legislative Assemblies. Though a significant development, the Executive Councils were still not real cabinets in that the respective lieutenant governors presided over Executive Council meetings and maintained some discretionary powers. The federal executive consisted of three ministers from each region and one from the federal territories appointed by the governor on the advice of whoever had majority support in the House of Representatives or the leader of the regional representatives. Still this was not a cabinet, as there was no prime minister. Furthermore, the members of the council were in fact representing the interests of their respective regions.

After the implementation of the Lyttelton Constitution of 1954, it became evident that Nigeria was on the verge of independence. In 1956, the West and East attained internal self-government, followed by the North in 1959. While the attainment of independence looked like a foregone conclusion, there were serious differences between the North and the South as to how soon it should happen. While the NCNC and AG wanted Nigerian independence to proceed as quickly as possible, the NPC asked for a moderate pace. By 1959, however, they all agreed that Nigeria should become independent in 1960. The Nigeria Independence Act, passed in the British Parliament, terminated the dependence of Nigeria upon Britain. Prophetically, the wording of the act sounded more like abandonment and a proclamation of innocence for whatever had happened or might happen to Nigeria. As it stated: "Her Majesty's Government in the United Kingdom shall have no responsibility for the government of Nigeria or any part thereof."[50]

The Legacies of Colonial Rule

The legacies of colonial rule are evident in the troubled political climate of post-colonial Nigeria. The key question is to understand how colonialism has affected the process of democratization and nation-state building in Nigeria. Indeed, without colonial rule there would not have been a Nigeria as we know it today. But the fact that we have a Nigeria does not imply anything inherently good or bad. Possibly, it might seem to be more the latter if one agrees with Chinua Achebe that "Nigeria is not a great country. It is one the most disorderly nations in the world. It is one of the most corrupt, insensitive, inefficient places under the sun. It is one of the most expensive countries and one of those that give least value for money. It is dirty, callous, noisy, ostentatious, dishonest and vulgar. In short, it is among the most unpleasant places on earth!"[51] From the perspective of nation-state building and democratization, the legacies of colonialism are truly paradoxical. While on the one hand, colonialism defined the territory and established the key political and economic institutions of the country, colonial rule worked against the integration of the various peoples that constitute Nigeria and created unbalanced structural and institutional arrangements that promoted conflict among the various ethnic groups in the country. Among the institutional legacies of colonial rule that promote nation-state building and democratization are the establishment of a modern bureaucracy, a judiciary, a standing army, and political parties. One should also mention the physical and economic infrastructure that was developed, which enhanced contact among Nigerians and linked the country to the international community. While these institutions contributed to state building and multiparty democracy, the reality is that they also hindered national integration and left deep divisions in the country. Colonial rule left a big mark on the political culture of Nigeria. The abuse of power in Nigeria can be traced back to the exploitative and dictatorial nature of colonial rule. Indeed, Nigerians learned the practices of the colonial masters very well. During colonial rule, Nigerian collaborators saw that European colonial officials were living in luxury. They took frequent vacations, lived in big and beautiful houses, had as much food as they wanted, and numerous servants to keep them in comfort. Soon court clerks and warrant chiefs developed a taste for this kind of luxury, which could only be secured through political repression and abuse of power.[52] This exploitative approach to power has now been perfected in Nigeria. It is well evidenced in the high level embezzlement of public funds and lack of accountability on the part of people in power. Such practices can hardly be conducive to sustaining democracy and promoting national integration.

One of the most pathological legacies of colonial rule in Nigeria is the ethnic and regional divide it fostered. Colonial rule created a huge disparity in the economic infrastructure and access to western education among the various groups. As Horowitz rightly noted:

> The dichotomy between backward and advanced groups arose during the colonial period out of the differential distribution of and response to opportunities among ethnic groups. . . . The location of an ethnic group's home territory often provided a head start. Groups located near the colonial capital, near a rail line or port, or near some center of colonial commerce—the siting of which was usually determined by capricious factors, such as a harbor or a natural resource to be exploited—were well situated to take opportunities as they arose. Such groups were to be found in the schools, government offices, and commercial houses established there.[53]

The disparity has made control of political power a crucial variable for balancing a federation that was economically and socially unbalanced. By promoting traditionalism in the North and westernization in the South, the British created an uneven field for the various groups—who now must live as compatriots—that could only be evened by disproportionate allocation of resources and political offices. In turn, this fostered large-scale ethnic consciousness and conflict.[54] In essence, nation-state building under colonial rule simultaneously led to strong regional and ethnic consciousness as well as inter-regional and inter-ethnic conflicts. Colonialism further entrenched ethnic consciousness through the policy of divide and rule, which was both a short and medium term strategy to subjugate the natives. The problem is that once fomented, ethnic consciousness took on a life of its own and reproduced itself in various ways. Given the history of ethnic conflicts in Nigeria, the puzzle is what holds the country together after the withdrawal of the common enemy.[55]

Given the way Nigeria came into being, it should not be surprising that the decade preceding independence and the whole of postcolonial politics has been caught up in a fierce ethnic struggle to control the state. The South, dominated by the Yoruba and the Igbo, benefited from the booming precolonial foreign trade and were exposed to western education and religion during colonial rule. This placed them in an advantageous position in a Nigeria that was built along western economic and political models. The Hausa-Fulani in the North were less exposed to western influences, western education in particular, which eventually placed them in a less competitive position. Thus, for the Hausa-Fulani, political power was a way to counterbalance the economic and social advantages of the Yoruba and Igbo. As we shall see, this struggle for political power has rendered the country unstable. To get a better sense of the political instability, it will be helpful to briefly look at the country's postcolonial political history.

On October 1, 1960, Nigeria gained independence and adopted a parliamentary system of government for the federation, which consisted of the North, East, and West. This arrangement lasted until January 1966 when junior military officers overthrew the NPC-led government and killed many senior politicians and military officers from the North. The civilian government they overthrew was plagued by a series of crises along ethnic lines. The government of Major General Johnson T. U. Aguiyi Ironsi, which came to power following the January 1966 coup, was also plagued with a series of problems. The very fact that the Igbo coup leaders killed many of the northern political elite (most notably, Ahmadu Bello and Abubakar Tafawa Balewa) did not bode well for Ironsi's government. Coupled with this was Ironsi's attempt to impose a unitary state which further antagonized the Hausa-Fulani. Although he abandoned the idea, "Northern alarm and bitterness persisted, culminating in a bloody countercoup by Northern officers in July, which killed Ironsi and many other Igbo officers and soldiers."[56]

The new military government headed by Lieutenant Colonel Yokubu Gowon also had its own share of problems. Its biggest dilemma was how to reconcile the deep mistrust that developed between the Hausa-Fulani North and the Igbo East. The challenge was to retain the East, which was about to secede, and at the same time to refrain from antagonizing the North, which insisted on its regional homogeneity and majority status in the federation. Gowon's solution to the stalemate was to further divide the federation into twelve states—six in the North, and three each in the East and the West. This solution, which was announced on May 27, 1967, did not satisfy the East. Three days later, Lieutenant Colonel Chukwuemeka Odumegwu Ojukwu, the governor and commander of the East, announced the secession and declared the Republic of Biafra. In July 1967, Nigeria slipped into a civil war. The war, which was extremely devastating (especially to the East), ended in January 1970 with a short-lived spirit of reconciliation blowing in the air. In October 1970, Gowon unveiled his program for transition to civilian rule. Unfortunately, he suspended the program in

1974, which led to widespread disillusionment and decline in the legitimacy of the regime.

In July 1975, Brigadier Murtala Mohammed overthrew Gowon and embarked on an anti-corruption campaign. On October 1, 1975, he announced a timetable for the restoration of civilian rule. In February 1976, Murtala Mohammed was assassinated in a failed coup attempt. His deputy and successor, General Olusegun Obasanjo, implemented the transition program.[57] In July and August 1979, state and federal elections were held and civilian rule restored, marking the birth of the Second Republic. Though the National Party of Nigeria (NPN)—which was a de facto successor of the NPC—won the elections, its victory, especially in the presidential election, was marred with many controversies. This led to a series of conflicts. Most importantly, as Diamond notes, the real danger was not just the conflicts, "but the aura of desperation and intolerance that infused these conflicts and the violence that often attended them."[58]

The NPN government, led by Shehu Shagari, was not only plagued by political violence, but corruption and ethnic favoritism also became the order of the day. On December 31, 1983, General Muhammadu Buhari overthrew the Shagari government and embarked on a massive anti-corruption campaign by putting public officials on trial for past wrongdoing. However, ethnic bias, excessive repression, and arrogance on the part of the military plagued the process. Added to these were the severe economic austerity measures of the government. On August 27, 1985, Major General Ibrahim Babangida overthrew his boss. Among other things, the Babangida government is best known for annulling the 12 June 1993 presidential election, which was supposed to restore democracy. With growing domestic and international pressure, Babangida was forced to resign at the end of August 1993. He handed power to an interim civilian government led by Chief Ernest Shonekan.[59] However, this government was overshadowed by the military. In November 1993, General Sani Abacha, who was the defense minister, took over the government. The Abacha government is remembered for being the most repressive in independent Nigeria. In particular, it imprisoned Moshood Abiola, the winner of the annulled 12 June 1993 presidential election and executed Ken Saro-Wiwa and his fellow activists campaigning for the rights of the Ogoni people. On June 8, 1998, Abacha unexpectedly passed away.[60] General Abdulsalam Abubakar, who succeeded Abacha, understood that Nigerians were tired of military rule and Hausa-Fulani domination. He did not waste time with the transition to democracy. In the January 1999 presidential election, Nigerians elected retired General Olusegun Obasanjo. Despite the optimism that followed the end of military rule, the Obasanjo government has been increasingly plagued by ethnic conflicts. It is estimated that around 10,000 people have already died in communal fighting since 1999.[61]

Conclusion

Nigerian politics has been characterized by ethnic struggles among the major groups. Apart from Ironsi, Gowon, and Obasanjo, all the heads of government have been Hausa-Fulani. The struggle for power began well before independence. On numerous occasions, the survival of the federation has seemed doubtful. Some have tried to explain the problem by introducing class analysis.[62] Certainly, one cannot ignore the role of the elite in manipulating the political scene for their selfish ends. Nevertheless, it is also true that ethnicity has been the main vehicle through which they manipulate their people. Even in the case of religious conflicts, Christians against Muslims, one can also locate elements of ethnicity in the conflict. After all, rarely do Yoruba Christians and Yoruba Muslims fight. Usually it is Hausa-Fulani versus Igbo or Yoruba. We should not forget that the Yoruba and Igbo—purportedly Christian brothers—fought on different sides during the Nigerian Civil War. Thus, I will argue, ethnicity is the key legacy of colonial rule that has been plaguing the development of a democratic nation-state in Nigeria.

Notes

1. James Coleman, *Nigeria: Background to Nationalism* (Berkeley: University of California Press, 1958), 45.

2. Onigu Otite, *Ethnic Pluralism, Ethnicity, and Ethnic Conflicts in Nigeria* (Ibadan, Nigeria: Shaneson C. I. Ltd., 2000), and Coleman, *Nigeria*.

3. John Paden, "Nigerian Unity and the Tensions of Democracy: Geo-Cultural Zones and North-South Legacies," in *Dilemmas of Democracy in Nigeria*, eds. Paul Beckett and Crawford Young (Rochester, N.Y.: University of Rochester Press, 1997), 243-64, and Jibrin Ibrahim, "The Transformation of Ethno-Regional Identities in Nigeria," in *Identity Transformation and Identity Politics under Structural Adjustment in Nigeria*, ed. Attahiru Jega (Uppsala, Sweden: Nordiska Afrikainstitutet, 2000).

4. Southwest (Lagos, Oyo, Osun, Ogun, Ondo, Ekiti); Southeast (Abia, Anambra, Enugu, Imo, Ebonyi); South-South (Edo, Delta, Akwa Ibom, Cross River, Rivers, Bayelsa); Northeast (Kebbi, Sokoto, Katsina, Jigawa, Kano, Kaduna, Zamfara); Northwest (Yobe, Borno, Bauchi, Taraba, Adamawa); Middle Belt (Kwara, Kogi, Benue, Niger, Plateau, Abuja [Federal Capital Territory], Nassarawa).

5. Prior to 1967, the units of the federation were referred to as "Regions" (see figures A.1-A.7).

6. Colonial Office, "Nigeria: Report of the Commission Appointed to Enquire into the Fears of the Minorities and the Means of Allaying Them" (London: Her Majesty's Stationery Office for the Nigerian Government, 1958).

7. Oshomha Imoagene, *Know Your Country Series: Handbooks of Nigeria's Major Cultural Areas, the Hausa and Fulani of Northern Nigeria*, vol. 1 (Ibadan, Nigeria: New-Era Publishers 1990).

8. Yusuf Bala Usman and Alkasum Abba, *The Misrepresentation of Nigeria* (Zaria: Center for Democratic Development Research and Training, 2000).

9. Coleman, *Nigeria*.

10. These three regions are also referred to as West, East, and North. Furthermore, the West and East are jointly referred to as the South.

11. Mahmood Mamdani, *Citizen and Subject: Contemporary Africa and the Legacy of Late Colonialism* (Princeton, N.J.: Princeton University Press, 1996), and Ibrahim Gambari, "British Colonial Administration," in *Nigerian History and Culture*, ed. Richard Olaniyan (Harlow, Essex, England: Longman, 1985), 159-75.

12. Okwudiba Nnoli, *Ethnic Politics in Nigeria* (Enugu, Nigeria: Fourth Dimension Publishers, 1980).

13. Mamdani, *Citizen and Subject*.

14. Elizabeth Isichei, *A History of Nigeria* (New York: Longman, 1983).

15. Isichei, *History of Nigeria*.

16. Mamdani, *Citizen and Subject*, and Isichei, *History of Nigeria*.

17. Mamdani, *Citizen and Subject*.

18. Isichei, *History of Nigeria*.

19. Isichei, *History of Nigeria*.

20. Coleman, *Nigeria*.

21. Coleman, *Nigeria*.

22. Coleman, *Nigeria*.

23. Tekena Tamuno, "The Independence Movement," in *Nigerian History and Culture*, ed. Richard Olaniyan (Harlow, Essex, England: Longman, 1985), 176-88.

24. Richard Sklar, *Nigerian Political Parties; Power in an Emergent African Nation* (Princeton, N.J.: Princeton University Press, 1963).

25. Isichei, *History of Nigeria*.

26. Quoted in Coleman, *Nigeria*, 347. Also note that Igbo is spelled as Ibo.

27. In 1961, the National Council of Nigeria and the Cameroons was renamed the National Convention of Nigerian Citizens.

28. Isichei, *History of Nigeria*.

29. Sklar, *Nigerian Political Parties*.

30. Quoted in Sklar, *Nigerian Political Parties*, 102.

31. Sklar, *Nigerian Political Parties*.

32. Sklar, *Nigerian Political Parties*.

33. John Mackintosh, *Nigerian Government and Politics: Prelude to the Revolution* (Evanston, Ill.: Northwestern University Press, 1966), and Isichei, *History of Nigeria*.

34. Tamuno, "Independence Movement."

35. Mamdani, *Citizen and Subject*.

36. Ng~ugi wa Thiong'o, *Weep Not Child* (London: Heinemann Educational, 1964).

37. Tamuno, "Independence Movement."

38. Isichei, *History of Nigeria*.

39. Isichei, *History of Nigeria*.

40. Coleman, *Nigeria*.

41. Isichei, *History of Nigeria*.

42. These were the Legislative Council (i.e., for Lagos) and the Nigerian Council (i.e., for the rest of the country).

43. Unofficial members usually referred to Africans. Also, see: W. E. F. Ward, *Government in West Africa* (London: George Allen & Unwin Ltd., 1975).

44. Tamuno, "Independence Movement."

45. These regions are commonly referred to as North, East, and West.

46. E. A. Keay and H. Thomas, *West African Government for Nigerian Students* (London: Hutchinson Educational, 1968).

47. Isichei, *History of Nigeria*.

48. Isichei, *History of Nigeria*.

49. Keay and Thomas, *West African Government*.

50. Quoted in Benjamin Nwabueze, *A Constitutional History of Nigeria* (New York: Longman, 1982), 60.

51. Chinua Achebe, *The Trouble with Nigeria* (Enugu, Nigeria: Fourth Dimension Publishing, 1983), 11.

52. Isichei, *History of Nigeria*.

53. Donald Horowitz, *Ethnic Groups in Conflict* (Berkeley: University of California Press, 1985), 151.

54. Larry Diamond, *Class, Ethnicity and Democracy in Nigeria: The Failure of the First Republic* (Syracuse, N.Y.: Syracuse University Press, 1988), and Nnoli, *Ethnic Politics*.

55. According to many Nigerians, oil is what really holds the country together. As Dr. Olutayo Adesina argued, "Nigeria is a peculiar country that you cannot actually understand like a textbook situation. It is a nation that exists in a state of flux. Nigerians speak to one another in the markets, they inter-marry. Apart from those things, the only thing we know to unify Nigerians is oil—that is the only thing. . . . Today we meet one another in the market, we buy from one another, and play. If tomorrow is daggers and arrows, then so be it" (Interview conducted in Ibadan, August 2002).

56. Larry Diamond, "Nigeria: Pluralism, Statism, and the Struggle for Democracy," in *Democracy in Developing Countries: Africa*, eds. Diamond et al. (Boulder, Colorado: Lynne Rienner Publishers, 1988), 43.

57. Olusegun Obasanjo is the current president of Nigeria.

58. Diamond, "Nigeria," 51.

59. The period around the annulled 12 June 1993 presidential election is generally referred to as the Aborted Third Republic.

60. A month later, Moshood Abiola suddenly died in prison.

61. Dan Isaacs, "Profile: Olusegun Obasanjo," *BBC News* April 23, 2003, http://news.bbc.co.uk/2/hi/africa/2645805.stm (April 25, 2003).

62. Diamond, *Class, Ethnicity and Democracy*; Nnoli, *Ethnic Politics*; and Otite, *Ethnic Pluralism*.

Chapter 3

Ethnicity and the Breakdown of Democracy and the Nation-State

Over the past five decades, Nigeria has witnessed no less than ten coups (successful or unsuccessful) and numerous threats of secession. Looking closely at the high levels of communal violence, the ongoing threats to the stability of the nation-state, and the pattern through which the military dictatorships replace civilian governments and vice versa, one can identify a cycle of breakdown and reconstitution in the Nigerian political order. In either case, the central question is how to promote a democratic and integrated nation-state in the context of ethnic diversity. Nigeria has undergone three periods of democratic restoration (i.e., the First, Second, and Fourth Republics).[1] However, both the first and the second democratic regimes collapsed amid threats to the survival of the nation-state. The current democracy is also plagued with ethnic violence and tensions that put in doubt the possibility of a peaceful change of government. This cycle of breakdown and reconstitution of democracy and the nation-state is illustrated in table 3.1.

As illustrated in table 3.1, Nigeria is characterized by a cycle of breakdown and reconstitution in repeated attempts to build a democratic and integrated nation-state. Each breakdown opens the way for the reconstitution of democracy and the nation-state. Unfortunately, the reconstituted democracy and nation-state often fell victim to the destabilizing force of ethnicity, which led to a new breakdown. The first wave of reconstitution began with the growth of the nationalist movement aimed at ousting the oppressive colonial regime. One of the watershed moments in the drive to end colonial rule was the adoption of the 1951 Macpherson Constitution and the introduction of dyarchy. The gains of the nationalist movement culminated in the attainment of independence in 1960. Independence ushered in a democratic regime and a sovereign state. Not too long after independence, however, Nigerian efforts to sustain democracy and promote national integration were shattered by outstanding ethnic conflicts. The breakdown was most evident in the census crisis, the Western Region crisis, the 1966 coups, and ultimately the Nigerian Civil War. A new phase of reconstitution began with the post-war peace and reconstruction program, the restructuring of the federation, and, under the Second Republic, the adoption of the Federal Character principle and a consociational presidential system. The new arrangement was again disrupted by the ethnic conflicts that flared during the 1979 and 1983 elections as well as the ethnic favoritism and corruption that plagued the Second Republic. This opened the way for the December 31, 1983 coups and a series of incidents (such as the Ogoni Uprising, the annulment of the 12 June 1993 presidential election, and numerous incidents of communal violence) that threatened the stability of the nation-state. The death of Nigeria's most notorious dictator, General Sani Abacha, brought a new window of opportunity for Nigeria. Democracy was once again restored in 1999 and some of the growing calls for political autonomy silenced. Unfortunately, the current democracy is shaky and its collapse may well prompt a renewed wave of secessionist claims.

Table 3.1: **Cycle of Breakdown and Reconstitution in Nigeria**

	1951 to 1970	1970 to 1998	1998 to 2003
Reconstitution: Democracy/or Nation-State	Nationalist Movement Independence (1960) Multiparty Democracy Parliamentary System Regionalism	Peace and Reconstruction Centralized Federalism Twelve-State Structure Second Republic (1979) Federal Character Consociational Presidentialism	Death of Abacha (1998) Informal Power Rotation Fourth Republic (1999)
Breakdown: Democracy/or Nation-State	Self-Rule Crisis Western Region Crisis Census Crisis 1966 Coups Civil War (1967-70)	Election Crisis (1979/1983) Corruption and Ethnic Bias December 31, 1983 Coup Annulled 12 June 1993 Election Communal Violence Ogoni Uprising Abacha Reign of Terror Ethnic Militia	?

Ethnicity and the Multiple Layers of Cleavages

The central question for us is to identify the forces that drive the breakdown as well as the reconstitution of democracy and the nation-state in Nigeria. Indeed, such forces include a variety of economic, social, cultural, political, and external factors. However, given the manner in which the Nigerian state was formed, the pattern of violent conflicts that continue to undermine democracy and the stability of the nation-state, and the form of corruption and discrimination that characterize Nigeria, I will argue that we need to focus more on the issue of ethnicity.

Democratic consolidation and national integration have been consistently undermined in Nigeria by conflicts among the various ethnic groups for control of resources and power. Some of the most notable incidents are the self-rule crisis of 1953, the 1962 census crisis, the Nigerian Civil War, the Ogoni Uprising, the 12 June 1993 presidential election, and the ongoing communal violence. To say that the problem of democracy and national integration in Nigeria is purely ethnic, I must acknowledge, would be a simplification of the numerous conflicts that have plagued the country. Nonetheless, ethnicity is a major problem in the Nigerian attempt to build a democratic and integrated nation-state. As Rotimi Suberu observed, "In Nigeria there are three major forms of sectional cleavages, ethnic, religious and regional, which significantly overlap. In relation to the others ethnicity is the most pervasive."[2] To see the relative significance of ethnicity, it is important to situate ethnicity within the multiple and overlapping forms of identities and cleavages that characterize Nigeria. Generally, these can be broken down into identities and cleavages that are based on territorial, religious, or ethnic affiliations.

In terms of the territorially based identities, the first major division is between the North and the South. The North encompasses the areas populated by the Hausa-Fulani in the far north and the Middle Belt region, which is mostly inhabited by a variety of smaller ethnic groups, such as the Tiv, Jukun, Igala, Nupe Atyap, and Beron. The most important features of northern identity are the administrative demarcations established under colonial rule, the extensive use of the Hausa language, the strong legacy of traditional rule (i.e., the emirate system), and the predominance of Islam. The South is made up of the Yoruba, Igbo, and numerous minority ethnic groups, such as Ibibio, Ijaw, Itsekiri, Urhobo, and Ogoni. Like the North, southern identity is a product of colonial administrative boundaries. Southern identity has also been fostered by the predominance of Christianity. Following the 1946 division of the South into East and West, a three-cornered regional identity emerged, namely: northern, eastern and western. The informal division of the country into six geopolitical zones during the mid-1990s has further promoted new forms of regional identity.[3] To a large degree, the emergence of the Middle Belt and South-South zones can be seen as a product of the struggle of minorities to carve out a separate political identity. One can also talk of the emergence of new forms of identities along the lines of state boundaries.[4] State identity tends to be stronger where the state overlaps with ethnic boundaries, especially in areas dominated by the minority ethnic groups.

Nigeria is also divided among Christians, Muslims, and people who practice a variety of indigenous religions. Though Christianity and Islam are world religions, they also tend to be domesticated and flavored with indigenous cultures. In Nigeria, this has given rise to different shades of Christianity and Islam to the extent that it is difficult to talk of a homogenous Christian brotherhood or Muslim *Uhnma* devoid of their ethno-cultural affiliations. This is most evident in the separation of the Yoruba and Hausa-Fulani Muslim communities. Nonetheless, the emergence of religious fundamentalism in Nigeria, possibly as a reactionary force to the failure of the nation-state, has sharpened the religious divide between Christians and Muslims.

Most significantly, Nigeria is fragmented along ethnic lines (see table A.1). Though there are debates as to the actual number of ethnic groups in the country, it is widely believed that there are anywhere between 250 to 400 ethnic groups in Nigeria. Onigu Otite has identified as many as 387 ethnic groups.[5] The Hausa-Fulani, Yoruba, and Igbo are estimated to account for around two-thirds of the Nigerian population. Though none of them is a majority, they are crucial power brokers in any national alliance. In 1963 for example, the three majority groups constituted 66.6 percent of the total population, which stood around of 56 million at the time.[6] In 1991, the population of Nigeria was estimated to be around 88 million (see tables A.2 and A.3). However, the figures are disputed and the distribution is often done by region and state, which does not neatly coincide with ethnic boundaries.

While each of the above-mentioned identities has a unique character, they strongly overlap. As J. A. A. Ayoade observed:

> Ethnicity is in a way not quite coterminous with regional cleavages. However, it is more or less the same ethnic thinking that reveals itself in the regional thing. What people actually call the North is the Hausa-Fulani, forgetting that there are non-Hausa-Fulani people living in the North. When you talk of the West, they say it is Yoruba. When you talk about the East, they think of the Igbo. What happens is that you have a core group and peripheral groups. . . . As far as we can relate ethnicity to regions, there is a way in which one can say they are conterminous; not necessarily in terms of area or size, but in terms of the insignificance of the peripheral groups. . . . To the extent that the peripheral groups are insignificant in decision-making, the majority groups represent the regions. So, North, East, and West more or less refer to the big ethnic groups.[7]

Equally, all Hausa-Fulani are regarded as Muslims. The Igbo are taken to be Christians, and the majority of Yoruba are sometimes considered Christians, despite the strong Yoruba Muslim community. This overlap between ethnic, regional, and religious identities reinforces the sharp divisions among the ethnic groups and blurs many of the internal divisions within the groups when it comes to national matters.

Because of the overlapping identities in Nigeria, it is difficult to classify some of the conflicts as purely ethnic, regional, or religious. Notwithstanding this difficulty, it is important to note the special place of ethnicity. According to a survey conducted by the Lagos-based Refuge Medical Service and the International Foundation for Election Systems between January and February 2000, nearly half of Nigerians considered their ethnic group as their primary social identity. When asked: "Beside being Nigerian, which specific group do you feel you belong to first and foremost?" 49 percent of the respondents selected their ethnic group. Another 21 percent selected their religious group, 18 percent identified with their occupational group, 10 percent with their class, and 2 percent maintained their individuality.[8] As Ayoade further argues, "the starting point is that people are born into ethnic units. That is the first and most important characteristic of every individual in Nigeria. . . . The ethnic group is also the symbolic owner of the land where they live."[9] To see the relative significance of ethnicity, it is important to note some of the features that characterize communal conflicts in Nigeria. To begin with, violent communal conflicts often involve people who identify themselves as members of different ethnic groups.[10] Indeed, there is a remarkable peace between Christians and Muslims within the Yoruba and the minority communities in the Middle Belt. Furthermore, communal violence along ethnic line dates back to the colonial period. In contrast, it was not until the early 1980s that religion became a violent issue in Nigeria.[11] As retired Major General Chris Alli, the son of a Muslim cleric and a born-again Christian mother, recalled, his dual theological heritage was generally accepted throughout his childhood. Muslims and Christians in his hometown of Onitsha lived in harmony, inter-married and joined one another during their respective festivals.[12] It should also be noted that though religious issues are a constant source of communal violence, such conflicts are not about doctrines, practices, or attempts to convert people who belong to other faiths. For the most part, they are about a people's right to freely practice their religion, the use of public space for religious purposes, and perceived acts of disrespect toward the religion associated with a particular ethnic group. As Nigeria's foreign minister, Sule Lamido, stated in his defense of *Sharia*: "Modern Nigeria cannot impede the right of Muslims to be Muslims. . . . Before I am a minister, I am first and foremost a Muslim. . . . I stand by Islam. If I have committed any fornication, I will also equally submit myself to that religion."[13] In this sense, religious conflicts themselves can be seen as an extension of the contestation for cultural rights among the various ethnic groups. To some degree, one can argue that in Nigeria "religious rivalry is a facade disguising the real competition, among ethnic groups."[14] As Otite rightly argued, ethnicity "overrides any of the other factors such as religion, which interact with and reinforce it."[15]

The shifting of regional blocs and state boundaries is also a strong indication of the fragility of territorially based identities. Today, neither the North nor the South can claim to be a unified body of people. For the most part, their homogeneity is an illusive image brought about by either "Hausanization" or Christianization.[16] In many ways, northern and southern identities have been undermined by subregional and state identities. In fact, the creation of more states and Local Government Areas (LGAs) has enabled a greater number of ethnic groups to assert their distinct political identities. In contrast, ethnic identity has always been pronounced and persistent in Nigeria. As Eghosa Osaghae puts it, "Historically, tribalism was the problem. Tribalism was a blanket term that referred to any one of these cleavages, with the exception of class. When you talk of region you are talking tribalism, when you talk of religion, in terms of the way it differentiates the Hausa-Fulani people and other ethnic groups in the country, you are talking tribalism. So tribalism—that is ethnicity—appears to be the most popular cleavage."[17]

While the growing disparity between the rich and the poor, elite and masses, can potentially make class differences visible, for now, Nigeria is not characterized by strong class boundaries.[18] For the most part, the rich and the poor are closely linked through extended family and ethnic networks. This is evident in the system of dependency, which links the elite with an extremely large body of family members, kinsmen, and townsmen.[19] As Ayoade confessed:

> If I go home I still have a family attachment which will make me run down the line to the lowest class—I must support them. As much as possible if someone in my family, who is less privileged has a son that is looking for a job, it will be my responsibility to get him employment because by getting him employed I will be reducing the dependence of his parents on me. Nigeria is not a country in which classes can be seen as antagonistic. They are not; there is a crosscutting social relationship that neutralizes the effects of class.[20]

Instead of class antagonism, what we actually have is an elite that manipulates ethnic sentiments among the masses and reinforces ethnicity. As Olutayo Adesina noted:

> It is easy for them to say that you Yoruba people are suffering because the Hausa-Fulani elite are actually destroying your future. So, when their minds are poisoned, they are ready to fight any Hausa-Fulani, not minding the fact that the Hausa-Fulani here (i.e., in Yorubaland) are not the ones responsible for their problems. The Hausa-Fulani are victims, like our people. . . . Of course, at times they back it up with little gestures: "Bring your brother, I will give him job." "Oh, take this fifty Naira to buy bread."[21]

Given the persistence and wider cultural significance of ethnic identities, the long history of ethnic tensions, and the tremendous violence that ethnic groups inflict on one another, more attention should be paid to the ethnic factor in order to understand the problems of democratization and nation-state building in Nigeria. Indeed, to many Nigerians, ethnicity is the unsolved national question around which a great deal of politics revolves. Yet, many African scholars and Africanists, especially those with a Marxist orientation, tend to downplay ethnicity.[22] For many, ethnicity conveys an inappropriate image for a civilized and modern state. In a sense, an ethnic war can hardly be justified as a fight for superior principles. Simply, it is seen as a savage act that further taints the image of black people. However, as much as we may want to be modern, the problem of ethnicity cannot disappear by simply denying it. Given the low level of economic development in Nigeria, the intense struggle for essential resources and the power to monopolize them cannot be dismissed as either savage or irrational acts. Ethnicity is a logical outcome of the political and economic conditions in Nigeria. As such, it is an integral part of the struggle to build a democratic and integrated nation-state. Instead of denying ethnicity, it seems to me that it is best to accept it as part of the contemporary Nigerian reality. As Lieutenant Colonel Ojukwu openly admits, "The very circumstances of Nigeria only permit an idiot to be 'detribalized.'"[23] By recognizing ethnicity, we can better address its problems and de-stigmatize the ethnic baggage of the modern African.

Manifestations of Ethnicity

In general, ethnic conflicts are the product of wider social, economic, and political forces that plague the nation-state. Besides the macro environment, however, ethnic conflicts are often linked to scarcity of resources, structural imbalances in the federation, internal colonialism, attempts to assert cultural rights and religious freedom, disputed territorial claims, and the imperatives of culture-bound occupations (such as cattle-rearing and farming). In Nigeria, ethnic conflicts take the form of social ostracism, ongoing favoritism in the struggle to access valuable resources (such as land, social services, education, jobs, and government contracts), and violent communal clashes. In Akoko-Edo (LGA) in Edo state, for example, the Etuno have discriminated against their Uneme neighbors. Historically, the Uneme were migrant goldsmiths who were outlawed for allegedly betraying their hosts (by making weapons for enemy forces) and engaging in adultery.[24] Even more disturbing is the widespread discrimination along ethnic lines. Very often, people in power favor their ethnic brothers over members of other ethnic groups in the distribution of resources. During the 1950s, for example, nearly all the contracts awarded by the AG-controlled Tender Boards in Western Nigeria were given to Yoruba people. Ethnic favoritism was also evident in the Nigerian Railway Corporation, which was headed by an Igbo. In 1964, for example, Igbo held 270 out of the 431 senior offices in the corporation.[25] As the political tide changed, Igbo themselves became the victims of discrimination in public service. As former Chief of Army Staff Chris Alli confessed: "Today, by August 1999, what has the Igbo nation to show after Sani Abacha? Out of seventy-two permanent secretaries in the Federal Civil Service, the Igbo have one. Out of fifty-seven police chiefs, that is thirty-six state commissioners, eighteen AIGs [assistant inspector generals], two DIGs [deputy inspector generals] and one IG [inspector general], the Igbo have only one."[26] Recently, the former president of the Southern Kaduna People's Union, Yaned Afuway, complained: "The government has been run by the Hausa. All the big contractors are Hausa. Nobody from one of our tribes has ever won a contract for even one million Naira. But the Hausa will get 100 million, 200 million Naira."[27] Social ostracism and discrimination in the allocation of resources provide a fertile ground for aggravated ethnic conflicts.

The most destabilizing ethnic conflicts are the ones that degenerate into communal violence. Often, such incidents are the culmination of long-standing ethnic grievances. Sadly, they have been increasing rapidly over the past years.

In fact, it is estimated that since 1999, around 10,000 people have been killed in communal violence.[28] Ethnically motivated communal violence in Nigeria can be categorized as follows: majority versus majority groups, majority versus minority groups, minority against minority groups, and intra-ethnic conflicts.

Majority versus Majority Groups

Conflicts among members of Nigeria's three majority ethnic groups date back to the colonial period. During the press war between the Igbo *West African Pilot* and the Yoruba *Daily Service*, for example, hostility between the two groups escalated so high that between July and September of 1948, "extremists on both sides bought up all available machetes in the Lagos markets in anticipation of ethnic violence."[29] While conflicts between Yoruba and Igbo are not rare, as evident in the Nigerian Civil War, more often the conflicts are between the Hausa-Fulani and the Igbo or the Yoruba. This may simply be due to the fact that the Hausa-Fulani have been in power for most of the time. One of the earliest incidents was the crisis surrounding self-rule, 1953 to 1956. It is ironic that the people of Nigeria, who had been resisting colonial rule since its inception, started to fight one another at a time when they should have been celebrating. March 31, 1953, the day when Chief Anthony Enahoro moved that the Federal House "accept as a primary political objective the attainment of self-government for Nigeria in 1956," should have been a day to rejoice. Alas, the session ended in an uproar. From the outset, the problem might look like a simple disagreement over timing. But one can ask why Alhaji Ahmadu Bello, the leader of the Hausa-Fulani dominated NPC, demanded that the words "in 1956" be replaced with "as soon as practicable." Bello pushed hard for the change even though he clearly understood what Chief Enahoro meant when he told the British "the bare idea of self-government is no longer attractive, is no longer enough. Whether it is expressed as 'self-government in our life time' or 'self-government in the shortest possible time' or 'self-government as soon as practicable,' it has ceased to be a progressive view, because Nigerian Nationalism has moved forward from that position."[30]

Yoruba and Igbo leaders, together with the people of Lagos, publicly rebuked the Hausa-Fulani for blocking the self-government motion. In response to the humiliation, the North threatened to withdraw from the federation. In the northern city of Kano, thirty-six people were killed and hundreds wounded during demonstrations against the visit of a combined NCNC and AG delegation. As Coleman points out, the crisis was "the surface manifestation of deep and unsolved tensions in two interrelated areas—northern fear of southern domination in a self-governing Nigeria, and southern dissatisfaction with the 1951 Constitution in particular and the frustration over the slow rate of advance toward self-government in general."[31] The stalemate over self-rule was temporarily resolved by a two-track approach. The Yoruba and Igbo demanded that self-government must be granted to their respective regions in 1956, but they also agreed not to coerce the North into self-rule. The North announced on May 30, 1956, that they would demand regional self-government in 1959.[32] Even though an agreement was reached, the solution underscored the deep mistrust between the Hausa-Fulani and their Igbo and Yoruba rivals. Back in March 1948, Mallam Abubakar Tafawa Balewa told his colleagues in the Legislative Council: "Many [Nigerians] deceive themselves by thinking that Nigeria is one. . . . This is wrong. I am sorry to say that this presence of unity is artificial and it ends outside this chamber."[33]

The Hausa-Fulani read the situation well and understood that self-government was the prelude to independence. Furthermore, they were aware that on the whole, the political arrangement was still centralized. Thus, one can understand why the Hausa-Fulani wanted to buy time to improve their competitive economic and social position. As stated in a February 18, 1950, editorial of the Hausa weekly (*Gaskiya ta Fi Kwabo*), northern fears were that "Southerners will take the places of the Europeans in the North. What is there to stop them? . . . There are Europeans, but undoubtedly, it is the Southerner who has power in the North. They have control of the railway stations; of the Post Offices; of Government Hospitals; of the canteens; the majority employed in the Kaduna Secretariat and in the Public Works Department are all Southerners; in all the different departments of Government it is the Southerner who has the power."[34]

Shortly after independence, the three major groups were again involved in a dispute over the 1962 census. What should have been a purely technical matter for demographers became a serious political crisis that threatened national stability. The census was held in the wake of a sweeping victory for the Hausa-Fulani dominated NPC in the Northern Region during the 1961 elections. Apparently, the political arrangement could hardly sustain a stable federation. As Dr. Michael Okpara, premier of the Eastern Region, argued, "Since the mere publication of census figures precludes a leader from a major political party from aspiring to the leadership of the nation, something must be wrong with the set-up in Nigeria when one can already know that he has won and his opponent lost a general election on the basis of census figures."[35] Since the allocation of seats in the federal assembly was based on population criteria and voting patterns were predetermined by ethnic affiliations, it was clear that the census was going to be a de facto political campaign, if not an indirect election. Not only was the census conducted immediately after the 1961 regional elections, but federal elections were also due in 1964. Thus, the political leaders in all regions took the census very seriously and worked very hard for a "good result"—meaning to show that the populations of their respective constituencies were larger than those of their opponents.

The contest was between the Hausa-Fulani dominated North and the South—represented by the Igbo in the East and the Yoruba in the West. The North wanted to maintain the majority position it had gained during the 1952-53 census: 16.8 million out of a total population of 30.4 million. The Igbo and

Yoruba, on the other hand, wanted to correct the 1952-53 census, which gave the south 13.6 million (see table A.2). They alleged that the census was British-engineered in favor of the Hausa-Fulani. In addition, they argued that many people in the South evaded the census because it was seen as part of British tax policy. Given the deep mistrust between the dominant ethnic groups and the delicate issues at stake, it was a foregone conclusion that the census would produce nothing like an accurate count. The 1962 census yielded the following result: North 22 million, East 12 million, West 8 million, Mid-West 2.4 million, and Lagos 0.45 million. In analyzing the figures, the chief census officer, J. J. Warren, noted that while the figures for the North were reasonable, those of the East had been inflated. According to the census organizers, "the biggest increase was in children under the age of five, and calculations show that the women of child-bearing age could not have produced this number of births had they all been pregnant for all the five previous years."[36]

Based on the census report, the minister of economic development, Alhaji Waziri Ibrahim, suggested that selected areas be verified for discrepancies. Initially, all four regions agreed to the plan. However, after realizing that the South would be in the majority, Dr. Okpara backed away from the recount. Nevertheless, the verification continued in the other regions. At the same time, accusations of rigging were bitterly exchanged, especially between the Hausa-Fulani and Igbo. After the verification, in January 1963 new figures emerged, which swelled the population of the North by more than 8.5 million.[37] This further inflamed an already volatile situation. In February 1963, Prime Minister Abubakar Tafawa Balewa annulled the 1962 census and called for a new census toward the end of the year.

New measures were taken to prevent rigging—"good results" as politicians called it. The new census was to be counting by sight and to last for only four days. More enumerators were brought in and officers from other regions were allowed to monitor and conduct a pilot census.[38] Amidst mistrust and escalating allegations of rigging, the figures from the new census, announced on February 24, 1964, were dubious and "too good" to be true. The new count gave the North 29.8 million, the East 12.4 million, the West 10.3 million, the Mid-West 2.5 million, and Lagos 0.7 million.[39] If anything was different this time around, it was the fact that all the regions openly engaged in rigging. From the point of strategic position within the federal power structure, the new census did not alter the 1952-1953 arrangement.[40] Not surprisingly, Dr. Okpara dismissed the results outright. In essence, the census was not about an accurate count of people, but scoring against other ethnic groups.

Eventually, politicians had to work out the arithmetic that demographers could not solve. The census stalemate was not officially laid to rest until the regional premiers and the prime minister gathered in Lagos for the Nigerian National Economic Development Council summit, May 11 to 14, 1964. By that time, it was clear that the Igbo had lost the census battle. The Hausa-Fulani dominated NPC federal government successfully co-opted the battered western premier, Samuel Akintola, as well as the leaders of the newly created Mid-Western Region. Dr. Okpara challenged the results in the Supreme Court, but the case was politely dismissed as "beyond the court's jurisdiction." Though northern "victory" was established, serious damage had already been done to interethnic relations. In the beginning of March 1964, the North and East started to prepare for a showdown.[41] The leaders of both regions traded disgusting insults in the press. In response to the insults from the eastern press Ahmadu Bello, the leader of the NPC, boasted: "my people, my government and my party are fully prepared at any hour of the day for any eventuality and would meet any challenge."[42] The North reacted to the insults by harassing its huge body of Igbo residents. On March 1964, the Native Authority gave Igbo traders at the Sabon Gari market forty-eight hours to leave. Dr. Okpara protested but obviously from a weak position.

In our exploration of "majority versus majority" ethnic conflict, we cannot forget the 1966 coups during which Igbo and Hausa-Fulani butchered one another in what seemed to be a rehearsal for the Nigerian Civil War. To a large degree, the civil war was between the Igbo and the rest of Nigeria, led by the Hausa-Fulani and Yoruba.[43] Indeed nobody wanted to let the Igbo secessionists go away with the oil. Despite the loss of hundreds of thousands of lives and the displacement of millions of people during the war, communal violence persists in Nigeria. The various ethnic groups have been regrouping and forming new quasi-cultural organizations to promote their political interests. In June 1976, for example, the Committee of Elders was formed in the North to monitor developments that could lead to disharmony in the ten northern states and suggest ways of defusing them.[44] Essentially, the committee was a strategic Hausa-Fulani forum for neutralizing the potential internal divisions that could follow the creation of new states. As ethnic tensions escalated during the 1990s, the various ethnic groups revived their old ethno-political organizations. The most notable of these are the Yoruba Afenifere, the Hausa-Fulani Arewa, and the Igbo Ohaneze Ndigbo. These organizations have already bred militant youth wings, such as the Oodua People's Congress, the Arewa People's Congress, and the Bakassi Boys, respectively.

Since the end of the Nigerian Civil War, sporadic fighting has continued among the three major ethnic groups. In December 1994, fighting erupted between the Hausa-Fulani and Igbo in Kaduna after Hausa-Fulani militants lynched the husband of an Igbo woman accused of using pages from the Holy Koran as toilet paper for her baby. Six months later, a fight between a Hausa-Fulani and an Igbo in Sabo Gari led to a violent clash between the two communities.[45] Toward the end of February 2000, hundreds of people were killed in fighting between Hausa-Fulani and Christians, the majority of whom were Igbo. The fighting was triggered by the decision to introduce Sharia in Kaduna. In Sokoto, a pro-Sharia student demonstration forced thousands of Igbo and minorities to seek refuge in police stations and army barracks.[46] A week after the massacre in Kaduna, more than 300 people were killed in the southeastern town of Aba when the Igbo attacked Hausa-Fulani people in retaliation for the kill-ings in Kaduna.[47]

Since the defeat of the Igbo during the war, most of the fighting has been between the Hausa-Fulani and Yoruba. The wartime alliance between the two groups crumbled during the Second Republic. During the 1979 and 1983 elec-tions, all three major ethnic groups clashed with one another. The tension was taken to an extremely dangerous height by General Ibrahim Babangida's an-nulment of the 12 June 1993 presidential election, won by a Yoruba, and the subsequent reign of terror unleashed by General Sani Abacha on Yoruba activ-ists campaigning for the restoration of the "12 June mandate." The mounting frustration of the Yoruba spilled over into a horrific clash with Hausa-Fulani in the middle of July 1999. The fighting, which took place in the town of Sagamu, left up to sixty people dead and dozens of homes, shops, and mosques burned. Sagamu, which is located thirty-six miles north of Lagos, is a traditional Yoruba town. However, Hausa-Fulani people have been living there for generations. The violence was sparked by the murder of a Hausa-Fulani woman who was allegedly caught watching a traditional Yoruba religious rite known as *Oro*. According to tradition, people who are not *Oro* members are expected to stay indoors during the festival. For the Yoruba, this violation was a sign of disre-spect toward them, while the Hausa-Fulani saw the whole episode as an indis-criminate attack on them. A few days after the Sagamu disaster, Hausa-Fulani in Kano retaliated against Yoruba. Up to seventy people lost their lives, many more were wounded, and hundreds of Yoruba were forced to flee their burned homes.[48]

Toward the end of November 1999, a dispute between Hausa-Fulani and Yoruba traders at the popular Ketu market led to two days of fighting in Lagos. Around one hundred people were killed, hundreds more were wounded, and many homes destroyed. The Oodua People's Congress (OPC) was blamed for most of the violence.[49] In Ibadan, the third millennium was greeted with a brawl between the Yoruba and Hausa-Fulani. Several people were killed during the early January clashes and many homes were burned. The fighting started after a fatal collision between a truck driven by a Hausa-Fulani and a taxi carrying Yoruba passengers.[50] Two months later, a similar incident in Ketu nearly led to renewed communal violence in Lagos. Luckily, the governor of Lagos quickly arrived at the scene and calmed the situation.[51] In mid-October 2000, the Yoruba and Hausa-Fulani again waged a battle in the streets of Lagos. Nearly one hundred Hausa-Fulani were killed, hundreds were wounded, and about 20,000 people were forced to abandon their destroyed homes and seek refuge in army barracks. The violence began after OPC members, who were pursuing suspected criminals, attacked a Hausa-Fulani settlement in Ijora, Lagos. A day before the attack, the OPC had clashed with the police in Ilorin, Kwara state, after they tried to replace the appointed Hausa-Fulani traditional ruler with a Yoruba chief.[52] The Lagos killing led to tensions in the North. Thousands of Yoruba were forced to seek refuge in army barracks and a curfew was imposed in Sokoto.[53] In February of 2002, Lagos was again in flames. Shortly after a fire at an army barracks that left more than a thousand people dead, fighting erupted between the Yoruba and Hausa-Fulani in Mushin district. At least 100 people were killed and many homes and shops were destroyed.[54]

Majority versus Minority Groups

Fighting between members of minority groups and the three dominant ethnic groups has been a common occurrence in all parts of Nigeria, especially in the Middle Belt where minorities are sandwiched between the majority ethnic groups. Most of the violence stems from attempts by the minorities to resist domination in places they consider their fatherland.[55] One of the bloodiest incidents took place from February to May 1992. It all began in the market town of Zango Kataf, inhabited mainly by the Hausa-Fulani but surrounded by Atyap communities. Even before the 1992 violence, there were long-standing grievances over Hausa-Fulani rule under the emirate system and ownership of the town. *Zango* itself means "market" in the Hausa language. The Hausa-Fulani claim to have established the town, while the Atyap argue that they are the indigene of the area and the Hausa-Fulani are strangers. The Atyap, whom the Hausa-Fulani refer to as Kataf, call the town *Zangon Kataf,* with the last *n* indicating that the market belongs to the Kataf. The February clash was instigated by the decision of the local government council, which for the first time had a Kataf as chairman, to transfer the market to a new location as of February 6, 1992. While the Kataf favored the relocation, the Hausa-Fulani saw the decision as an attempt to sabotage their trade. They sought a court injunction against the relocation. At the same time, Hausa-Fulani demonstrators harassed some Kataf women who went to the new market. The incident quickly flared into a fight between the two communities, resulting in the loss of lives and property. Fresh fighting broke out between the communities on May 15, 1992, after a Kataf farmer whose plants were vandalized was shot while investigating the incident. Kataf youths quickly spread word that they were at war with the Hausa-Fulani and later attacked them. As victims arrived in Kaduna, Hausa-Fulani promptly mobilized to retaliate against minorities and other Christians at large. The fighting left 471 people dead, 518 injured, and 229 houses and 218 vehicles destroyed in Kaduna.[56] A military tribunal sentenced retired Major General Zamani Letwot and other prominent members of the Atyap community to death for instigating the violence. As a clear sign of Hausa-Fulani power, no one from their community was arrested. So unfair was the conduct of the tribunal that the government had to hold back the sentences. On August 27, 1993, General Ibrahim Babangida commuted the sentences to five years. The inmates were eventually freed in 1995.[57]

On April 12, 1994, fighting in Jos, the capital of Plateau state, left at least four people dead and property worth over 329,278,659 Naira destroyed, including homes, shops, schools, and places of worship. The violence erupted during a demonstration by the Hausa-Fulani in support of Alhaji Aminu Mato, who was supposed to take over as chairman of the Caretaker Management Committee of Jos North (LGA). A week earlier, on April 5, 1994, the Birom, Anaguta, and Afizere people had organized a protest against the appointment of Alhaji Mato, who is a Hausa-Fulani. Despite the objection to the appointment of a Hausa-Fulani, on April 6, Alhaji Mato was sworn in as chairman. The indigenous minority groups vowed to do everything possible to prevent Mato from assuming office. To calm the minorities, the government halted the process. However, the government's decision angered the Hausa-Fulani community. On April 11, 1994, Hausa-Fulani butchers slaughtered cows on the highway to protest the government's decision. In the evening, the president of the Hasawa Development Association, Alhaji Yahaya Aga Abubakar, invited the Hausa-Fulani to the fatal demonstration on the following day.[58]

In May 1999, a similar incident left more than fifty people dead in Kafanchan, Kaduna. Minorities from neighboring villages, opposed to Hausa-Fulani traditional rule, erected barricades and set up bonfires to disrupt ceremonies marking the presentation of the staff of office to the eleventh emir of Jema, Alhaji Muhammadu Isa Muhammadu. The palace was burned and the emir forced to seek refuge with the security forces.[59] Two years later, at least 100 people were killed, mostly Tiv, hundreds wounded, and 17,000 forced to flee their homes during fighting between the Hausa-Fulani and Tiv in Lafia, the capital of Nasarawa state. The fighting erupted after unknown gunmen, whom the Hausa-Fulani suspected were Tiv, killed a prominent Hausa-Fulani chief.[60]

Once again in Jos, several hundred people were killed and many more wounded during a week of fighting between Birom (considered indigene) and Hausa-Fulani (considered settlers) in September 2001. The fighting erupted on a Friday after an argument between a pedestrian woman and Hausa-Fulani worshippers who had barricaded the street around the mosque at Congo-Russia to prevent traffic during prayer time. Local youths quickly responded to her call for help and spread a false rumor that a church had been burned. Just a week before the fighting, tension was already high between the two communities over the controversial appointment of a Hausa-Fulani, Alhaji Mukhtar Muhammed, as the poverty eradication coordinator in Jos North (LGA). His appointment was seen by the Birom and other minorities as a provocation, especially so because Muhammed was once forced to step down as chairman of Jos North (LGA) for falsifying his credentials. Minorities organized protests and made death threats to Muhammed. Just days before the fighting, organizations representing Birom and Hausa-Fulani had distributed provocative leaflets in the city.[61]

In early January of 2002, dozens of people were killed and hundreds displaced in Taraba state during fighting between native Mambilla farmers and nomadic Fulani. Long-standing tensions between the two communities further deteriorated after local government officials, who wanted to use the land issue as an electoral platform, threatened to redistribute land that was not effectively used.[62]

Going a bit southward to Kwara state, the Yoruba in Shaare clashed with their Nupe neighbors in Tsaragi at the beginning of July 2000. The fighting began as a dispute between a Yoruba and a Nupe farmer over a piece of land. On June 30, 2000, the two farmers, who had been uprooting each other's crops, eventually met on the plot and fought. Several people were killed and property destroyed during the clashes that ensued between the two communities.[63] Further down to the southwest, the Yoruba and Ijaw have been engaged in a series of disputes over ownership of oil-rich lands. In late September 1998, dozens of people died in fighting between the two communities near the disputed town of Apata. A year later, more people were killed in a series of fights between the two communities when the Yoruba tried to re-enter a town the Ijaw took in 1998.[64] In November 1999, the two groups fought pitched battles in Ajegunle, Lagos, leaving around forty people dead.[65]

One should not forget the bitter battles between minority ethnic groups and the Igbo during the Nigerian Civil War. Most of the minorities in the Eastern Regions refused to support the Igbo secessionists because they feared that they would then be under full Igbo domination. Apart from communal violence, minorities frequently clash with government forces, which are mostly under the control of the dominant ethnic groups. The most publicized case is the Ogoni Uprising during the 1990s. The Ogoni, led by the charismatic Ken Saro-Wiwa, stood against the Hausa-Fulani led federal government and Shell Petroleum Development Company in their struggle for political autonomy and adequate compensation for oil exploration and environmental damages to their land. The uprising left thousands of people in the Niger Delta dead, including Ken Saro-Wiwa and some of his fellow members of the Movement for the Survival of the Ogoni People (MOSOP). The impunity for crimes against minorities still continues under the Fourth Republic. In September 1999, the government of Olusegun Obasanjo massacred Ijaw people in Odi, Bayelsa. The government sent the military to avenge the killing of eight police officers by the *Asawana Boys*, a group of disgruntled minority youths turned bandits. After visiting the scene, Abdul Oroh, executive director of the Civil Liberties Organization, stated: "We saw no single livestock, poultry, or domestic animal except a stray cat. The community's 60,000 inhabitants had fled into the forest . . . [or] been arrested or killed."[66] Two years later, the army was engaged in a similar operation in Benue against the Tiv. During the Tiv-Jukun conflict, the Tiv brutally killed nineteen soldiers in Zaki Biam, whom they thought were Jukun enemies from Taraba. The victims, killed on October 11, 2001, were actually Nigerian soldiers from the 23rd Armored Brigade, stationed in the village of Vaase. On October 22, soldiers from the 23rd Armored Brigade returned to the area to avenge the killing of their comrades. They began by killing more than 200 people whom they had invited to attend a meeting at the Gbeji market. They then moved to the villages of Vaase, Ayiine, Ugba, Sankera, Kyado, and Zaki Biam where they engaged in widespread killing and destruction of property.[67]

Minority against Minority Groups

Apart from being victimized by the dominant ethnic groups, minority ethnic groups also fight one another. The conflicts among the minorities fit well into the overall pattern of struggle for resources in Nigeria. Minorities, from whose land Nigeria derives its oil wealth, are deprived. They have to fight for whatever little resources that filter down. In an attempt to get a bite of the Nigerian pie, minorities often fight for control of local governments and ownership of oil-rich lands.[68] In Warri, for example, the Itsekiri, Urhobo, and Ijaw have been engaged in a long battle for control of the local government and numerous strips of land. In 1951, a decision by the AG-led regional government to change the title of *Olu of Itsekiri* to *Olu of Warri* led to a series of violent confrontations that left several people dead and long-standing enmity between Itsekiri and Urhobo. The change of title allowed the traditional ruler of the Itsekiri to rule the whole of the Warri, even though Warri was traditionally owned by the Ijaw and Urhobo. It was not until 1999 that the government of Delta state accorded equal status to the traditional rulers of the various communities, the Olu of the Itsekiri, the Orosuen of the Urhobo kingdom of Okere, the Ovie of the Urhobo kingdom of Agbassa (Agbarha Ame), and the Amakusu of the Ijaw of Warri.[69]

Relations between the Itsekiri and Ijaw grew worse in 1997 because of attempts to relocate the headquarters of Warri South-West (LGA) from the Itsekiri town of Ogidigben to Ogbe-Ijo, an Ijaw town. The conflict led to violent clashes between the two communities that eventually claimed over 3,000 lives and displaced thousands of people.[70] In November 1999, people suspected of being Ijaw attacked a boat carrying Itsekiri passengers. The incident left eighteen Itsekiri dead and four wounded.[71] Five months earlier, hundreds of people were forced out of their homes during a land dispute between the two communities. Toward the end of May 2001, at least ten homes were burned and many people displaced by fighting between the Itsekiri and Urhobo. The fighting was ignited by an attempt to set up an Itsekiri-dominated local government council in Warri.[72] It is also important to note the dispute between the Ijaw and Urhobo over land ownership and water resources in Aladja.[73]

In the Southeast, fighting between Akwa Ibom and Cross River over the border between the two states left at least ninety people dead in May 2000. After the 1987 division of Cross River into two states (i.e., Cross River and Akwa Ibom) a border conflict developed between the two minorities-dominated states. At the forefront of the dispute were the Ibiobio of Itu (LGA) in Akawa Ibom and the Efik of Odukpani (LGA) in Cross River. The official border between the two local government areas is the Cross River. However, the Ibibio claimed that the real border between the two communities is the Okpokong River, which is five kilometers inside Cross River state.[74]

In the states of Taraba, Benue, and Nasarawa, the Tiv have been involved in a series of violent clashes with other minority groups, especially the Jukun. In the town of Wukari, for example, the Tiv and the Jukun have been involved in a long struggle for political dominance. During the 1991 boundary adjustment exercise (i.e., the creation of new states and LGAs), the two groups clashed over the location of the town. The Jukun wanted Wukari to be part of Taraba state, where they constitute a majority. In contrast, the Tiv wanted the town to be located in Benue state, where they form the largest group. At the end of 1991, the two groups again clashed during local elections. The Tiv contested the election of a Jukun candidate as head of the local government council on grounds that they were prevented from voting by the fighting between the two communities. In June 1992, Jukun burned two Tiv villages and killed twenty people in retaliation for the murder of a female Jukun member of the Taraba State Assembly. In November 2001, a land dispute in Taraba between the Tiv and Jukun left around fifty people dead.[75] Apart from the Jukun, the Tiv have also clashed with the Egon. At the end of June 2001, for example, Tiv warriors launched a surprise attack on the Egon in Tudun Adabu, killing around fifty people. The Tiv accused the Egon of supporting the Hausa-Fulani with whom the Tiv had a conflict.[76]

Intra-ethnic Conflicts

While ethnic groups tend to present a united front in the struggle against other ethnic groups, there are also cases of internal conflicts within ethnic groups themselves. Like inter-ethnic conflicts, intra-ethnic conflicts also center on the problem of access to resources and power among the various sub-units of a given ethnic group. One of the most troublesome cases is the Ife-Modakeke conflict among the Yoruba. The Modakeke people were refugees from the Oyo Empire who settled in Ile-Ife during the mid-1800s. The Modakeke maintained a separate identity and paid a token tax to their Ife overlords. During the colonial period, the two groups clashed over control of the Native Administrative Court and the distribution of proceeds from cocoa production.[77]

In recent times, the Ife and Modakeke have clashed on several occasions over local government and land matters. During the 1981 local government creation exercise in Oyo state, for example, the two communities clashed after the State Assembly refused to make Modakeke a separate local government area.[78] The Modakeke blamed the Ife political elite for blocking the creation of a Modakeke local government area as recommended by the Judicial Committee headed by Kayode Ibidapobe. In retaliation, the Modakeke switched allegiance from the Yoruba-dominated Unity Party of Nigeria (UPN) to the Hausa-Fulani dominated National Party of Nigeria (NPN). In order to punish the Modakeke, the incumbent *Ooni* (traditional ruler) renamed the streets in Modakeke and downgraded the status of the *Ogunsua*. This action caused violence to erupt between the two communities, which left many people dead and property destroyed. When the Modakeke LGA was created in 1996, the two groups clashed again over the location of headquarters. The Modakeke accused the Ife of manipulating the process, leading to the choice of Enuowa, an Ife area, as the headquarters. They forced the government to return the headquarters to Modakeke. However, this was unacceptable to the Ife people because the new LGA included places that were of high cultural significance to them. On August 14, 1997, an announcement that the headquarters was going to be moved to Oke-Igbi in Ife sparked a riot by the Modakeke. Several people were killed and property destroyed during days of fighting.[79] In December of 1997, six people were burned to death, several others kidnapped, and many houses destroyed during renewed fighting between the two communities.[80] Renewed violence erupted at the beginning of March 2000. At least thirty people were killed, 200 more wounded, and hundreds made homeless during three days of fighting over disputed land claims between the two communities. Hundreds of Modakeke victims failed to receive medical treatment because they were not allowed into Ife, where the two nearby public hospitals were located. A week later, another twenty-five people were killed. Eleven of the victims were from the Modakeke village of Olorombo.[81]

While most of the above-mentioned incidents may look like irrational acts, it should not take the critical observer too long to realize that they fit very well into the overall problem of resource distribution, democracy, and national integration in Nigeria. Given the system of patronage that is built around the extended family systems and ethnic affiliation, ethnic groups have vested interests in ensuring that their members gain immediate access to the resources of the state. As Adesina observed, "the nation-state has been seen as a honey pot from which everyone must taste. Each ethnic group is calculating how that honey pot or the larger part of it will come to its side. It becomes a problem in the sense of how many resources you can get depend on how close you get to the seat of government."[82]

Ethnicity and the Breakdown of Democracy and the Nation-State

Beyond the heartbreaking human and material costs, the real danger is that ethnicity contributes to the breakdown of democracy and threatens the survival of the nation-state in Nigeria. Even though ethnicity may be seen as involving normal conflicts over the distribution of scarce resources, it creates an environment that makes democracy, as well as national integration, very difficult to attain. This is most evident in the pattern of ethnic voting behavior and electoral violence that has undermined faith in the electoral process as an expression of the will of the people and a mechanism for ensuring political representation. By perpetuating a permanent majority, ethnicity undermines the very principles of majority rule, which "assume the possibility of shifting majorities, of oppositions becoming government, of an alterable public opinion."[83] Ethnicity breeds bad sentiments and diverts attention from the real social and economic issues that should be at the center of the political debate. As such, it perpetuates alienation and nurtures political grievances that can easily be translated into coups and secessionist movements.

Though political parties in Nigeria never openly confess that they are ethnic parties, it is widely understood that for a party to get hold of power in a particular area, it must establish itself as the party of the major ethnic group in the area.[84] As election results show, political parties (often dominated by the three major ethnic groups) have repeatedly won an overwhelming majority in their ethnic zones, notwithstanding the fact that there were hardly any substantial differences in their political manifestos or the quality of their leaders. During the First Republic, for example, all the parties dominated by the majority ethnic groups were able to gain a majority of votes in their home areas. Even among the internally divided Yoruba, the AG scored 61 percent of the votes cast in the Western Region (excluding the minority-dominated Mid-western constituencies) during the 1960 regional election. After the fall of the AG, another Yoruba party, the revived Nigerian National Democratic Party (NNDP), picked up 61 percent of the votes cast in the Western Region during the 1964 federal election. At the same time, support for the NCNC, which had initially tried to build a pan-Nigerian image, steadily declined in the Yoruba areas. As the NCNC became ethnicized, its support surged in the Igbo heartland. Its share of the votes in the Eastern Region increased from 63.2 percent of the votes cast during the 1957 regional elections to 64.6 percent during the 1959 federal election and 75.4 percent during the March 1965 federal by-election. In the Northern Region too, the Hausa-Fulani NPC took 60.8 percent of the vote cast during the 1959 federal election, 69.2 percent during the 1961 regional elections and a spectacular 82 percent during the December 1964 federal election.[85] So too the struggling Tiv minority United Middle Belt Congress (UMBC) took 85 percent of the votes cast in the seven Tiv constituencies in the Northern Region during the 1959 federal elections, leaving a mere 10 percent for the NPC.[86]

Despite the introduction of the Federal Character principle, ethnic voting continued during the Second Republic.[87] Each of the five political parties, the National Party of Nigeria (NPN), the Unity Party of Nigeria (UPN), the Nigerian People's Party (NPP), the People's Redemption Party (PRP), and the Great Nigeria People's Party (GNPP), monopolized the votes in the ethnic homeland of their leaders. The two Hausa-Fulani dominated parties (the conservative NPN and the radical PRP) and the Kanuri-dominated GNPP swept the vote cast in the North during the 1979 general elections, while the Yoruba-led UPN and the Igbo-dominated NPP did the same in their respective ethnic bases.[88] In the Federal House of Representatives, for example, the NPN won all ten seats for Niger and thirty-one seats in Sokoto, with the remaining two seats going to the

GNPP. In turn, the GNPP took twenty-two out of the twenty-four seats in the Kanuri state of Borno. In Kano, the PRP took thirty-nine seats with the remaining seven seats going to the NPN. Both the UPN and NPP failed to get even a single seat in the Federal House of Representatives from places such as Borno, Gongola, Kano, Niger, and Sokoto. The UPN won only one seat in Kaduna while the NPP managed to gain two seats in Kaduna and one in Bauchi (see table A.4).

In the Yoruba heartland of Lagos, Ogun, Ondo, and Oyo states, the UPN won all but four of the eighty-eight seats for these states in the Federal House of Representative during the 1979 elections. The NPN managed to take the remaining four seats, which were in Oyo. In the Igbo heartland of Anambra and Imo states, the NPP took all but five of the fifty-nine seats.[89] As for the minorities, they tended to vote against their immediate oppressors. Not surprisingly, the NPN won eighteen out of the nineteen seats in Benue state, twenty-two out of the twenty-eight seats in Cross River state, and ten out of the fourteen seats in Rivers state. In return, the NPP took thirteen of the sixteen seats in Plateau state. In Bendel state, all three major parties got a share of the minority votes. The UPN secured twelve seats, the NPN got six seats and the remaining two seats were taken by the NPP.

The pattern of ethnic voting was practically the same in the 1979 gubernatorial and presidential elections. The NPP secured the governorship in Anambra, Imo, and Plateau states, while the UPN won in all four Yoruba states and Bendel state. The NPN won in states such as Sokoto, Bauchi, Niger, Benue, Cross River, and Rivers. The PRP secured Kaduna and Kano states, while the GNPP took Borno and Gongola states (see table A.5). The presidential election was virtually a contest between the Igbo represented by Nnamdi Azikiwe (NPP), the Yoruba under the leadership of Obafemi Awolowo (UPN), and the Hausa-Fulani represented mainly by Shehu Shagari (NPN).[90] As expected, Awolowo scored no less than 82 percent of the votes cast in the Yoruba states, but less than 4 percent in states such as Bauchi, Borno, Kano, Niger, Sokoto, Imo, Anambra, and Benue. Equally, Azikiwe won 82.88 and 86.67 percent of the votes in Anambra and Imo states, but failed to even get 1 percent of the vote in Kano, Kwara, Ogun, Ondo, Oyo, and Sokoto states. Even with the brilliant ethnic balancing strategy adopted by the NPN, Shagari only managed to secure 4.1 percent of the votes in Ondo state, 6.23 in Ogun state, 7.18 in Lagos state, 12.75 in Oyo state, 8.80 in Imo state, and 13.50 in Anambra state. He took a comfortable 62.48 percent in Bauchi state, 66.61 in Sokoto state, and 74.88 in Niger state. Amino Kano had 75.89 percent in his native Kano state, and Waziri Ibrahim secured 54.04 percent of the votes in Borno state (see table A.6).

The pattern of ethnic voting was no different during the 1983 presidential election (see table A.7). The NPN took 91.83 percent of the votes in Sokoto state, 84.57 in Bauchi state, 67.88 in Rivers state, and 63.17 in Niger state. The UPN swept the Yoruba states, and the NPP won Anambra and Imo states. The only difference between the 1979 and the 1983 election was the level of rigging and violence, which dramatically increased to the advantage of the ruling NPN during the 1983 election.[91] To the disbelief of many Nigerians, the NPN secured a significant number of votes in all parts of the country, including the Yoruba and Igbo heartlands—37.65 percent of the votes in Oyo state, 20.03 in Ondo state, 33.26 in Anambra state, and 25.07 in Imo state.

The only serious exceptions to the pattern of ethnic voting are the 12 June 1993 presidential election and the 1999 presidential election. The difference is mainly due to the elaborate institutional arrangement and political bargaining processes that characterized these two elections (see tables A.8-A.10). As we shall see, the 12 June 1993 presidential election was conducted under a two-party system, which effectively forced Nigerians to vote for people that were not strongly affiliated with their ethnic group. As for the 1999 presidential election, the Nigerian political elite had a priori decided that the election was going to be a give-away to the Yoruba. Not surprisingly, the two candidates, retired General Olusegun Obasanjo and Chief Olu Falae, were Yoruba. Recently, it seems that the ethnic balancing and political bargaining processes have died. The 2003 presidential election was a virtual replay of the 1983 election. The Yoruba rallied behind the incumbent Olusegun Obasanjo, whom they shunned during the 1999 election. They supported Obasanjo even though they acknowledged that "his policies and administrative style in government has compounded the problem of poverty both in its absolute and relative terms."[92] Equally, the Hausa-Fulani dumped Olusegun Obasanjo and supported their own son, Major General Muhammadu Buhari. The Igbo too were not comfortable with Obasanjo. Alex Ekwueme, an Igbo presidential aspirant, described the PDP primaries as a "charade" after he failed to win the party ticket.[93] The Igbo argued that it was their turn to rule Nigeria. As the former attorney general of Oyo state, Ademola Yakubu, sums it up, "The issue of who becomes leader at any point in time is tied to the ethnic identity of the candidate. In the case of Shagari, what helped him to become a president was the fact that he is a Hausa-Fulani man. So too Obasanjo became president in 1999 because he is a Yoruba."[94]

The signs of ethnically rooted democratic breakdowns and threats to the survival of the nation-state are very clear in Nigeria. As ethnicity undermined trust in the electoral process, it also opened the way for the coups that ousted civilian as well as military regimes. The 1966 coup, for example, terminated Nigeria's parliamentary democracy. The coup itself was preceded by bitter ethnic politics among the three dominant groups. Not surprisingly, one of the coup leaders, Major Kaduna Chukwuma Nzeogwu, told Nigerians that the "enemies are the political profiteers . . . those that seek to keep the country divided permanently so that they can remain in office as ministers or VIPs, at least the tribalists, the nepotists."[95] Even though initially the coup seemed to be a nationalistic venture, it soon became apparent that it was aimed at uprooting the Hausa-Fulani. As former chief of army staff, Major General Chris Alli noted, "What is even more intriguing was that quota system was not applied to the distribution of casualties. Igbo leaders were spared and operations in the East were tempered. The coup planners were mostly Igbo idealists with a sprinkling of a couple of Yoruba and some minorities."[96] So too the Buhari coup of 1983 indefinitely suspended Nigeria's presidential democracy and peacefully retired Shehu Shagari. Even though the coup was more or less a Hausa-Fulani affair, it was not devoid of ethnicity. The Second Republic was plagued by ethnicity and corruption to the point that it hardly had any social legitimacy among Nigerians. Many people saw the Buhari coup as a strategic move to ensure the continuation of Hausa-Fulani rule. As Major General Alli observed: "It was perceived that the deposition of power to the North might be jeopardized unless northern officers took custody of it. . . . Its strategic objective was to deny the South access to the rotational presidency in due course, hitherto, a principle of the National Party of Nigeria, the ruling party."[97] One should not fail to note that both the Buhari and the Babangida coups, which replaced one Hausa-Fulani with another, were bloodless. These coups sharply differ from the bloody coups (successful or failed) that pit one ethnic group against another.

Ethnically motivated coups have also been plotted to oust military regimes in Nigeria. Certainly, the July 29, 1966 coup that ousted Johnson Ironsi was clearly driven by the desire of the Hausa-Fulani to revenge the January 1966 coup. On April 22, 1990, officers belonging to minority ethnic groups in the Middle Belt and in the South led by Major Gideon Orkar (a Tiv) and Major Mukoro (an Urhobo) made a bold attempt to overthrow Babangida. Though the coup was eventually subdued, the coup leaders were able to present their case to the Nigerian people. In his radio address to the nation, Major Orkar introduced himself as someone speaking on behalf of the oppressed minorities of the Middle Belt and the southern part of Nigeria. He emphasized that their coup was "not just another coup but a well conceived, planned, and executed revolution for the marginalized, oppressed, and enslaved peoples of the Middle Belt and the south with a view of freeing ourselves and children yet unborn from eternal slavery and colonization by a clique of this country."[98] As a clear sign of their anti-Hausa-Fulani agenda, the coup leaders temporarily excised the core northern states of Sokoto, Borno, Katsina, Kano, and Bauchi from the federation and gave people from these states living in other parts of Nigeria a week to return to their home states. To be readmitted, the above states were required to promise that they would never try to impose their "aristocratic domination" in any part of Nigeria. Three years later, Babangida more or less made an auto-coup by annulling the 12 June 1993 presidential election, which he had organized, after it became clear that a Yoruba had won.

Ethnicity has not only led to the breakdown of democracy, but it has threatened the survival of the nation-state, as is evident in the declaration of the Delta Peoples Republic in 1966 and most notably in the Nigerian Civil War. On numerous occasions, ethnic groups have threatened to secede from the federation. For instance, in 1953 an 1954, the Yoruba threatened to secede. Since the annulment of the 12 June 1993 presidential election, they have been making similar threats. The Hausa-Fulani also threatened to secede in 1953 as well as in

1966. Even before they declared the Republic of Biafa, the Igbo had made their intentions know in 1964.[99] Most recently, the Ogoni Uprising is a chilling reminder of the ongoing threats to the territorial integrity of Nigeria. The Ogoni Uprising was a struggle against the economic and political marginalization of minorities in Nigeria. As stated in the Ogoni Bill of Rights, "In over thirty years of oil mining, the Ogoni nationality have provided the Nigerian nation with a total revenue estimated at . . . over 30 billion dollars." In spite of their contributions, the Ogoni point out that they have received nothing in return. Among other things, the bill noted the Ogoni people are not properly represented in federal institutions. Furthermore, they lack pipe-borne water, electricity, and job opportunities. They see their plight as a direct result of the ethnic politics promoted by successive federal and state governments. Indeed, the poor economic, social, and environmental conditions in the Ogoni area are no exaggeration. To redress this injustice, the Ogoni Bill of Rights demanded:

POLITICAL AUTONOMY to participate in the affairs of the Republic as a distinct and separate unit by whatever name called, provided that this Autonomy guarantees the following: a) political control of Ogoni affairs by Ogoni people; b) the right to control and use a fair proportion of OGONI economic resources for Ogoni development; c) adequate and direct representation as of right in all Nigerian national institutions; d) the use and development of the Ogoni languages in Ogoni territory; e) the full development of Ogoni culture; f) the right to religious freedom; and g) the right to protect the OGONI environment and ecology from further degradation.[100]

The Ogoni are a minority ethnic group numbering around 500,000 people. They are mostly concentrated in the oil-rich Rivers state, especially in the Bori, Gokama, Eleme, and Nchia Khana areas. While the Ogoni have been resisting political marginalization since the days of colonial rule, their struggle became strong in 1990 when they issued the Ogoni Bill of Rights and formed the Movement for the Survival of the Ogoni People (MOSOP). MOSOP was initially led by Dr. Garrick Barilee Leton. However, it was Ken Saro-Wiwa who publicized the movement. Saro-Wiwa was elected president in absentia after the resignation of Leton, on June 1, 1993. Right from its inception, the movement confronted the Nigerian government by disrupting oil production, which is the lifeline of the country. It gave Shell Petroleum Development Company thirty days to leave Ogoni land. MOSOP organized a series of demonstrations to press for the Ogoni demands. Despite the energetic campaign, the Nigerian government turned a blind eye and a deaf ear to the Ogoni. In 1992, the Ogoni attracted international attention after Ken Saro-Wiwa presented their case before the United Nations. This changed the attitude of the military government. The government responded by engaging in propaganda, monitoring the movement, and harassing the activists. In October 1992, the Oil Mineral Producing Areas Development Commission (OMPADEC) was established. Its stated goal was to develop and rehabilitate the oil-producing areas, but it was merely cosmetic.

The government publicized the commission and made false claims about community development projects it had undertaken. In the end, "The commission could not point to one project it had completed in any state."[101]

At the same time, the government continued to persecute the activists. Saro-Wiwa's passport was confiscated. On Christmas Day, the State Security Service (SSS) detained Saro-Wiwa and Leton in order to preempt the January 4, 1993 protest. On January 10, 1993, four MOSOP officials were taken to Lagos for talks with the inspector general of police.[102] Soon after, they were invited to meet the secretary to the federal government, Alhaji Aliu Mohammed, the chief security adviser, Major General A. Mohammed, and chief of intelligence, Major General Halilu Akilu. The government made it clear to MOSOP that they would not grant the Ogoni political autonomy. Instead, they offered them the possibility of some local government areas. MOSOP was also asked to substantiate its claims of economic marginalization by providing a list of unemployed graduates and evidence of what minorities in other parts of the world were receiving from their governments. On May 4, 1993, the government passed the Treason and Treasonable Offences Decree, which was directly aimed at suppressing the Ogoni uprising. Among other things, the decree prohibited the display of anything that symbolized a new country, state, or local government area. The decree further stated, "a person who utters any word, displays anything or publishes any material which is capable of: a) breaking-up Nigeria or part thereof; or b) causing violence or causing a community or a section thereof to engage in violence against a section of that community or another community, is guilty of treason and liable on conviction to be sentenced to death."

The draconian reaction of the government outraged the Ogoni and led them to believe that the government was not sincerely listening to or addressing their complaints. Some of the MOSOP members called for a much more confrontational approach. The movement became divided over which strategy to pursue. Soon new factions emerged, such as the militant National Youth Council of Ogoni People (NYCOP), the Federation of Ogoni Women Associations (FOWA), the Council of Traditional Rulers Association (COTRA), the Ogoni Teachers Union (OUT), the League of Ogoni People (LOOP), and the Council of Ogoni Churches (COC). In the end, MOSOP became far more radical and confrontational in its struggle with the government. Building upon the January 4, 1993 protest, during which around 300,000 Ogoni marched to their headquarters in Bori, on April 30, 1993, Ogoni farmers resisted attempts by Shell to lay pipelines intended to send oil to the North. On the following day, around 100,000 Ogoni from Gokana, Tai-Eleme, and Khana joined the farmers.[103] Ogoni youths resorted to vandalizing oil installations and taking oil industry workers as hostages. On June 1, 1993, MOSOP voted to boycott the scheduled 12 June 1993 presidential election. The government arrested Saro-Wiwa and four others for sabotaging the election. Ogoni youths responded by attacking police stations at Kpor and Bori and destroying government vehicles. The Ogoni youths barricaded the highway leading to Port Harcourt and robbed travelers.

Incidentally, most of the victims belonged to the Andoni ethnic group. The Andoni accused the Ogoni of unnecessarily harassing them.[104]

The confrontation between the Ogoni and the Andoni opened a new front in the Ogoni uprising. As tensions mounted between the two communities, the government seized the opportunity to instigate communal violence, which later gave the military a pretext to suppress the Ogoni uprising. It is widely suspected that the government and Shell armed the Andoni and instigated more violence between the two communities. As Danu Mark of Kaa stated, "Before the attack, the policemen that were stationed here were withdrawn. A couple of days later we were attacked. Ogoni never had a quarrel with Andoni before. This was [a] planned attack organized by the Government, who used otherwise peaceful neighbors as proxies and fronts."[105] It was later revealed that government troops were actually involved in the fighting. The fighting ruined Kaa, a major Ogoni market town, and more than ten other villages. The main road from the Andoni and Ogoni areas to city of Port Harcourt was cut off and oil operations in Ogoniland suspended. The fighting left over 1,000 people dead and around 30,000 homeless.[106]

While the military government was clamping down on the movement, frictions were also developing between the Ogoni elders and youths, which eventually gave the government an opportunity to execute the MOSOP leaders. During the negotiations with OMPADEC, it was reported that Ogoni leaders had agreed to abandon the request for political autonomy. Believing that the elders had been bribed, the Ogoni youths accused the elders of betrayal and nicknamed them "vultures." On March 21, 1994, four prominent Ogoni leaders, believed to be traitors, were brutally killed by a crowd of around 2,000 Ogoni youths during a demonstration.[107] The victims were attacked while attending a meeting at the Gbenemene Palace Hall, following the Constitutional Conference Election. The government immediately alleged that the chiefs were murdered by NYCOP, which was led by Saro-Wiwa. He was accused of masterminding the attack and giving orders to the youths after government agents prevented him from campaigning for the Constitutional Conference Election. More than two hundred Ogoni were arrested and many more were declared wanted persons. Saro-Wiwa and fourteen other MOSOP leaders were tried for murder by a special military tribunal headed by Justice Ibrahim Auta.

The trial, which began on February 6, 1995, was neither open nor fair. The whole episode was a perfect opportunity for the government of General Sani Abacha to end the Ogoni uprising which was spearheaded by MOSOP. As Saro-Wiwa said in his final statement to the tribunal:

> My lord, we all stand before history. I am a man of peace, of ideas; appalled by the denigrating poverty of my people who live on a richly endowed land, distressed by their political marginalization and economic strangulation, angered by the devastation of their land, their ultimate heritage, anxious to preserve their right to life and to a descent living, and determined to usher this country as a whole a fair and just democratic system, which protects everyone and

every ethnic group and gives all of us a valid claim to human civilization. . . .
In my innocence of the false charges I face here, in my utter conviction, I call
upon the Ogoni people, the people of the Niger Delta, and the oppressed minorities of Nigeria to stand up now and fight fearlessly and peacefully for their
rights.[108]

Most of the evidence presented by the prosecution was circumstantial and wit-
nesses were either intimidated or bribed. In fact, Garrick Leton, the first
MOSOP president who fell out with Saro-Wiwa, was the key prosecution wit-
ness. In protest against the arbitrary nature of the tribunal, the defense team, led
by the renowned Chief Gani Fawehinmi, withdrew from the case.

On October 12, 1995, Saro-Wiwa and eight others were sentenced to death,
without the right to appeal. Despite numerous appeals for clemency from world
leaders, including Nelson Mandela, on November 8, 1995, the military government approved all the sentences. Saro-Wiwa and his eight comrades were executed on November 10, 1995. Nigeria was condemned from all corners of the
world, and was suspended from the British Commonwealth. Furthermore, most
western governments imposed some form of sanctions on Nigeria. For years to
come, Nigeria would become a pariah state. The executions sent a shock wave
to other ethnic groups and brought the country to the verge of collapse. Even
though the executions dealt a big blow to the Ogoni, the resistance continued
until the restoration of democracy in 1999. On January 5, 1996, MOSOP organized a rally, which was quickly dispersed by the police. Despite the introduction
of a new revenue allocation formula that guarantees mineral-producing states 13
percent of the proceeds from natural resources, the Ogoni demands are far from
satisfied.[109] In fact, this provision is being undermined by the separation of on-
shore and off-shore mining revenues and corruption. As such, the struggle for a
fair revenue allocation continues.

Conclusion: Demands for Ethnic
Inclusion and the Reconstitution Process

What is interesting about Nigerian democratization and nation-state building is
that each breakdown is followed by a renewed attempt to reconstitute democracy and the nation-state. In particular, ethnicity has been used to bring down
military regimes as well as quasi-democracies. As in the breakdowns, ethnicity
has also been a strong force that drives the reconstitution of democracy and the
nation-state. This is most evident in the kinds of demands put forward by disadvantaged ethnic groups. Whether they are coup-makers or prodemocracy activists, what they call for is greater representation in the institutions of power and
the right to a fair share of the resources of the state. These demands are essentially calls for more democracy and national integration. This raises questions
about the nature of ethnicity. The very ethnicity that contributes to the breakdown of quasi-democracy and the nation-state is also a rallying force for the

reconstitution of an inclusive democracy and the nation-state. Furthermore, the Nigerian experience leaves open the question whether the breakdowns are regressions or adjustment mechanisms in the process of democratization and nation-state building. The Nigerian case not only illustrates the formidable challenge for democratization and nation-state building in ethnically divided postcolonial countries, it is also characterized by a dynamic process of institutional design that takes ethnicity into account.

Notes

1. The would-be Third Republic was also an attempt but was aborted so quickly that it cannot be counted.

2. Interview with Dr. Rotimi Suberu in Ibadan, August 2002.

3. Southwest, Southeast, South-South, Northeast, Northwest, and Middle Belt.

4. Currently, the Federal Republic of Nigeria consists of thirty-six states and a Federal Capital territory (see figures A.1-A.7).

5. Onigu Otite, *Ethnic Pluralism, Ethnicity, and Ethnic Conflicts in Nigeria* (Ibadan, Nigeria: Shaneson C. I. Ltd., 2000), and James Coleman, *Nigeria: Background to Nationalism* (Berkeley: University of California Press, 1958).

6. Otite, *Ethnic Pluralism.*

7. Interview with Professor J. A. A. Ayoade in Ibadan, August 2002.

8. Survey reported in International IDEA, *Democracy in Nigeria: Continuing Dialogues for Nation-Building*, Capacity Building Series 10 (Stockholm, Sweden: International Institute for Democracy and Electoral Assistance, 2000), 92.

9. Interview with Professor J. A. A. Ayoade in Ibadan, August 2002.

10. Even in the case of intra-ethnic conflicts, there is often an "indigene-settler" dimension to the conflict, which puts into question the very homogeneity of the ethnic groups.

11. One of the earliest signs of religious tension was the Sharia crisis during the debates leading to the 1979 Constitution. As Oyeleye Oyediran recalled, Sharia was one of the hot issues that arose during the meetings of the 1975 Constitutional Drafting Committee in which he participated (Interview with Professor Oyediran in Ibadan, July 2002).

12. M. Chris Alli, *The Federal Republic of Nigerian Army: The Siege of a Nation* (Lagos: Malthouse Press Limited, 2000).

13. BBC News, "Minister Defends Nigeria's Sharia Law," November 4, 2002, http://news.bbc.co.uk/2/hi/programmes/hardtalk/2387627.stm (January 5, 2003).

14. Karl Maier, *This House Has Fallen: Nigeria in Crisis* (New York: Penguin Books, 2000), 217.

15. Otite, *Ethnic Pluralism*, 63.

16. Otite, *Ethnic Pluralism.*

17. Interview with Professor Eghosa Osaghae in Ibadan, August 2002.

18. Interview with Professor Ade Ajayi in Ibadan, July 2002.

19. Otite, *Ethnic Pluralism.*

20. Interview with Professor J. A. A. Ayoade in Ibadan, August 2002.

21. Interview with Dr. Olutayo Adesina in Ibadan, August 2002.

22. Okwudiba Nnoli, *Ethnic Politics in Nigeria* (Enugu, Nigeria: Fourth Dimension Publishers, 1980).

23. Quoted in Maier, *This House Has Fallen*, 286.

24. V. Adefemi Isumonah and Jaye Gaskia, *Ethnic Groups and Conflicts in Nigeria: The Southsouth Zone of Nigeria*, vol. 3 (Ibadan, Nigeria: The Lord's Creations for [the] Programme on Ethnic and Federal Studies, Department of Political Science, University of Ibadan, 2001).

25. Otite, *Ethnic Pluralism*, 101.

26. Alli, *Federal Republic of Nigerian Army*, 66.

27. Quoted in Maier, *This House Has Fallen*, 221.

28. Dan Isaacs, "Profile: Olusegun Obasanjo," BBC News, April 23, 2003, http://news.bbc.co.uk/2/hi/africa/2645805.stm (April 25, 2003).

29. Nnoli, *Ethnic Politics*, 229.

30. Quoted in Coleman, *Nigeria*, 399.

31. Coleman, *Nigeria*, 400.

32. See: Federation of Nigeria, "Report by the Resumed Nigerian Constitutional Conference" held in London, September and October 1958 (Lagos: Federal Government Printer), and Federation of Nigeria, "Report by the Nigeria Constitutional Conference" held in London, May and June 1957, (Lagos: Federal Government Printer).

33. Quoted in Coleman, *Nigeria*, 361.

34. Quoted in Coleman, *Nigeria*, 362.

35. Quoted in John Mackintosh, *Nigerian Government and Politics: Prelude to the Revolution* (Evanston, Ill.: Northwestern University Press, 1966), 556.

36. Mackintosh, *Nigerian Government*, 548.

37. Larry Diamond, *Class, Ethnicity and Democracy in Nigeria: The Failure of the First Republic* (Syracuse, N.Y.: Syracuse University Press, 1988).

38. Diamond, *Class, Ethnicity and Democracy*.

39. Mid-Western Nigeria was created in 1963 (see figure A.2).

40. Even though the populations of all the regions increased in terms of absolute numbers, their percentile shares did not alter significantly.

41. During this period, the West was weak and pacified by the North, partly due to internal divisions.

42. Quoted in Diamond, *Class, Ethnicity and Democracy*, 139.

43. Even though Yakubu Gowon actually belonged to a minority ethnic group in the North, he was installed and backed by the Hausa-Fulani.

44. Otite, *Ethnic Pluralism*.

45. Maier, *This House Has Fallen*.

46. BBC News, "Violence Erupts in Northern Nigeria," March 7, 2000, http://news.bbc.co.uk/2/hi/africa/669239.stm (March 15).

47. BBC News, "Nigerian Riots Kill Hundreds," March 1, 2000, http://news.bbc.co.uk/2/hi/africa/662246.stm (March 9, 2000).

48. Maier, *This House Has Fallen*, and BBC News, "Hundreds Flee Nigerian Ethnic Clashes," July 19, 1999, http://news.bbc.co.uk/2/hi/africa/398383.stm (July 20, 1999).

49. BBC News, "Nigeria Riots 'Killed 100,'" November 28, 1999, http://news.bbc.co.uk/2/hi/africa/540684.stm (January 10, 2000).

50. BBC News, "Fighting in Two Nigerian Cities," January 6, 2000, http://news.bbc.co.uk/2/hi/africa/593147.stm (January 8, 2000).

51. BBC News, "Twenty Die in Lagos Accident," March 8, 2000, http://news.bbc.co.uk/2/hi/africa/670746.stm (March 15, 2000).

52. Illorin is a historic Yoruba city that was invaded by the Hausa-Fulani shortly before the beginning of colonial rule. During the administrative division of Nigeria, the city was included in the North.

53. BBC News, "Ethnic Unrest Erupts in Northern Nigeria," October 20, 2000, http://news.bbc.co.uk/2/hi/africa/979428.stm (October 22, 2000).

54. BBC News, "Lagos Tense After Riots," February 5, 2002, http://news.bbc.co.uk/2/hi/africa/1802175.stm (February 6, 2002).

55. Colonial Office, "Nigeria: Report of the Commission Appointed to Enquire into the Fears of the Minorities and the Means of Allaying Them" (London: Her Majesty's Stationery Office for the Nigerian Government, 1958).

56. Maier, *This House Has Fallen*, and Rotimi Suberu, *Public Policy and National Unity in Nigeria* (Ibadan, Nigeria: Development Policy Center, 1999).

57. Maier, *This House Has Fallen*, and Otite, *Ethnic Pluralism*.

58. Mvendiga Jibo et al., *Ethnic Groups and Conflicts in Nigeria: The North-Central Zone of Nigeria* (Ibadan, Nigeria: The Lord's Creations for [the] Programme on Ethnic and Federal Studies, Department of Political Science, University of Ibadan, 2001).

59. BBC News, "Ceremony Sparks Violence in Nigeria," May 26, 1999, http://news.bbc.co.uk/2/hi/africa/353547.stm (July, 15 2000).

60. BBC News, "Thousands Flee Nigeria Clashes," June 23, 2001, http://news.bbc.co.uk/2/hi/africa/1404521.stm (June 27, 2001).

61. Organisation Mondiale Contre la Torture (OMCT) and Centre for Law Enforcement Education (CLEEN), *Hope Betrayed? A Report on Impunity and State-Sponsored Violence in Nigeria* (Geneva, Switzerland: Organisation Mondiale Contre la Torture, 2002), and BBC News, "Scores Die in Nigeria Clashes," September 10, 2001, http://news.bbc.co.uk/2/hi/africa/1535092.stm (September 18, 2001).

62. BBC News, "Nigeria Land Clashes Claim More Lives," January 8, 2002, http://news.bbc.co.uk/2/hi/africa/1748652.stm (January 16, 2002).

63. Otite, *Ethnic Pluralism*.

64. BBC News, "Nigerian Ethnic Fighting Flares," September 28, 1999, http://news.bbc.co.uk/2/hi/africa/460004.stm (February 9, 2000).

65. Maier, *This House Has Fallen*.

66. Quoted in OMCT and CLEEN, *Hope Betrayed*, 78.

67. OMCT and CLEEN, *Hope Betrayed*.

68. Under the revenue allocation formula, local governments are guaranteed a certain percentage of the national revenue. Communities can also claim compensation for their lands.

69. Otite, *Ethnic Pluralism*.

70. Isumonah and Gaskia, *Ethnic Groups*.

71. BBC News, "More Bloodshed in Delta," November 15, 1999, http://news.bbc.co.uk/2/hi/africa/521424.stm (March 2, 2000).

72. BBC News, "New Violence in Niger Delta," May 27, 2001, http://news.bbc.co.uk/2/hi/africa/1354055.stm (June 1, 2001).

73. Isumonah and Gaskia, *Ethnic Groups*.

74. OMCT and CLEEN, *Hope Betrayed*, and BBC News, "'Nigeria Clashes Kill Ninety' Says Report," May 21, 2000, http://news.bbc.co.uk/2/hi/africa/757986.stm (May 27, 2000).

75. BBC News, "Land Clash in Central Nigeria," November 26, 2001, http://news.bbc.co.uk/2/hi/africa/1676925.stm (November 27, 2001).

76. BBC News, "Villagers 'Massacred' in Nigeria," June 28, 2001,

http://news.bbc.co.uk/2/hi/africa/1412289.stm (July 3, 2001).

77. Otite, *Ethnic Pluralism*.

78. At the time, the Modakeke area was part of Oyo state. After the creation of Osun state in 1991, it became part of Osun.

79. OMCT and CLEEN, *Hope Betrayed*.

80. BBC News, "Six Killed in New Ethnic Clashes in Nigeria," December 31, 1997, http://news.bbc.co.uk/2/hi/africa/43794.stm (June 2000).

81. BBC News, "30 Dead in New Nigeria Clashes," March 6, 2000, http://news.bbc.co.uk/2/hi/africa/667075.stm (March 8, 2000), and BBC News "Violence Re-Ignites in South-West Nigeria," March 16, 2000, http://news.bbc.co.uk/2/hi/africa/679760.stm (Mach 16, 2000).

82. Interview with Dr. Olutayo Adesina in Ibadan, August 2002.

83. Donald Horowitz, *Ethnic Groups in Conflict* (Berkeley: University of California Press, 1985), 86.

84. Mackintosh, *Nigerian Government*.

85. Mackintosh, *Nigerian Government*.

86. Otite, *Ethnic Pluralism*.

87. As stated in Article 14(3) of the 1979 Constitution, "the composition of the government of the federation or any of its agencies and the conduct of its affairs shall be carried out in such manner as to reflect the Federal Character of Nigeria and the need to promote national unity, and also to command national loyalty thereby ensuring that there shall be no predominance of persons from a few states or a few ethnic or other sectional groups in the government or in any of its agencies."

88. The Kanuri are a big minority group in northern Nigeria, which is mainly concentrated in Borno, Nasarawa, Jigawa, Taraba, and Yobe states.

89. Those five seats went to the NPN.

90. Aminu Kano represented the radical PRP and Waziri Ibrahim led the Kanuri-dominated GNPP.

91. While the 1979 election was conducted by the departing military regime, the 1983 election was conducted by the Federal Electoral Commission, which was effectively under the control of the ruling NPN.

92. Interview with Moshood Erubami, president of Campaign for Democracy, in Ibadan, August 2002.

93. BBC News, "Nigerian Party Backs Obasanjo," January 6, 2003, http://news.bbc.co.uk/2/hi/africa/2625877.stm (January 8, 2003).

94. Interview with Dr. John Ademola Yakubu in Ibadan, August 2002.

95. Quoted in Tom Mbeke-Ekanem, *Beyond the Execution: Understanding the Ethnic and Military Politics in Nigeria* (Lincoln, NE: Writer's Showcase, 2000), 8.

96. Alli, *Federal Republic of Nigerian Army*, 212.

97. Alli, *Federal Republic of Nigerian Army*, 215.

98. Quoted in Mbeke-Ekanem, *Beyond the Execution*, 35.

99. International IDEA, *Democracy in Nigeria*.

100. Reprinted in Ken Saro-Wiwa, *Genocide in Nigeria: The Ogoni Tragedy* (Port Harcourt, Nigeria: Saros International Publishers, 1992), 94-95.

101. Mbeke-Ekanem, *Beyond the Execution*, 100.

102. These were Leton, Saro-Wiwa, E. N. Kobani, and A. T. Badey.

103. Mbeke-Ekanem, *Beyond the Execution*.

104. Mbeke-Ekanem, *Beyond the Execution*.

105. Quoted in Mbeke-Ekanem, *Beyond the Execution*, 108.

106. Mbeke-Ekanem, *Beyond the Execution.*

107. The victims were: Albert Badey (a former government chief secretary), Edward Kobani (a former commissioner); Samuel Orange (a former commissioner for health), and Theophilus Orange.

108. Quoted in Mbeke-Ekanem, *Beyond the Execution,* 161.

109. Article 162(2) of the 1999 Constitution.

Chapter 4

Nation-State Building in Postcolonial Nigeria

In Nigeria, a variety of institutional arrangements and policies have been undertaken to promote nation-state building. With the frequent regime changes, however, these arrangements and policies have made only modest success. Given the frequent changes of government and strategies to promote the nation-state, it is important to identify the objectives of nation-state building, map out the varieties of approaches that have been pursued, and evaluate their relative rates of success. By doing so, we can have a better sense of the achievements and difficulties in establishing a democratic and stable nation-state in Nigeria.

Objectives of Nation-State Building

Though the objectives of nation-state building in Nigeria have not been systematically outlined, the constitutions tend to enumerate certain principles that generally reflect the wishes of the Nigerian people for stability, liberty, and improvement in their living conditions. Paying close attention to the principles that have been outlined in the various constitutions of Nigeria, I will argue that the fundamental objectives of nation-state building in Nigeria are to foster: (a) integration and unity, (b) representation and diversity, (c) fair and equitable distribution, (d) peace and stability, (e) economic and social development, and (f) democratic legitimacy and constitutionalism.

Integration and unity is the main and most general objective of all Nigerian constitutions. The desire for unity is well expressed in the Nigerian motto: Unity and Faith, Peace and Progress. So urgent is the need for integration that both the 1979 and 1999 Constitutions called upon the Nigerian state to encourage "intermarriage among persons from different places of origin, or different religious, ethnic or linguistic association or ties" and "the formation of associations that cut across ethnic, linguistic, religious or other sectional barriers," so as to foster national integration.[1] Indeed the preoccupation with this problem in itself is recognition of the fact that Nigeria is still not yet a "united nation."

The need for fair representation and respect for the cultural diversity of Nigeria is well expressed in the constitutions. It is summed up in what Nigerians call the Federal Character principle. As all post-Biafra constitutions, most notably the 1979 Constitution, maintain: "the composition of the government of the federation or any of its agencies and the conduct of its affairs shall be carried out in such manner as to reflect the Federal Character of Nigeria and the need to promote national unity, and also to command national loyalty thereby ensuring that there shall be no predominance of persons from a few states or a few ethnic or other sectional groups in the government or in any of its agencies."[2] The Federal Character principle also applies at the state and local levels of government.[3] The 1999 Constitution further adds, "The state shall—protect, preserve and promote the Nigerian cultures which enhance human dignity" and "encourage [the] development of technological and scientific studies which enhance cultural values."[4] While the Federal Character principle sets out the vision for unity in diversity, the real problem has been to put in place concrete institutional arrangements and policies to materialize that vision.

Nation-state building in Nigeria also aims at ensuring fairness and equity in the distribution of resources. The key barrier in achieving this goal is discrimination. As such, the principles of equity, justice, and non-discrimination are stated in the various constitutions. Both the 1979 and 1999 Constitutions maintain: "the state social order is founded on ideals of Freedom, Equality and Justice." Furthermore, "national integration shall be actively encouraged, whilst discrimination on the grounds of place of origin, sex, religion, status, ethnic or linguistic association or ties shall be prohibited."[5] As we shall see, the real dilemma has been how to balance the principles of derivation and need, and thereby ensure that each group within the federation gets its due share of the national pie.

Furthermore, nation-state building in Nigeria is preoccupied with the question of peace and stability. Given the bitter lessons of the Nigerian Civil War and the recurring communal violence, it is not surprising that all Nigerian constitutions have stressed the importance of maintaining peace. This is constantly reaffirmed in the motto: Unity and Faith, Peace and Progress. Such is the concern for stability that all Nigerian constitutions reaffirm that "Nigeria is one indivisible and indissoluble Sovereign State."[6] The problem is that successive Nigerian governments have conducted themselves in ways that undermine peace and stability.

In Nigeria, it is well understood that there can hardly be a meaningful nation-state without some form of economic and social development. To this end, the constitutions mandate the state to "harness the resources of the nation and promote national prosperity and an efficient, a dynamic and self-reliant economy." In addition, the state is to ensure that "suitable and adequate shelter, suitable and adequate food, reasonable national minimum living wages, old age care and pensions, and unemployment and sick benefits are provided for all citizens."[7] The state is also required to provide universal free education as much as possible, and to protect the environment.[8]

Finally, it is widely agreed that the nation-state should be based on democracy and constitutionalism. As Article 14(1) of the 1979 and 1999 Constitutions states, "the Federal Republic of Nigeria shall be a State based on the principles of democracy and social justice." Furthermore, the constitutions emphasize: "sovereignty belongs to the people of Nigeria from whom government . . . [and the] Constitution derives all its powers and authority."[9] While there is a consensus that Nigeria should be a democracy, the troublesome question has been how to design a democracy that is stable and inclusive of the various ethnic groups in the country.

Approaches to Nation-State Building in Nigeria

The question for Nigerians is how to realize the principles outlined in the constitutions and thereby promote a democratic and stable multiethnic nation-state. Ehiedu Iweriebor has identified six criteria for mapping out the progress toward nation-state building in Nigeria.[10] These are: leadership, countrywide transport and communication networks, economic development, national education, pedagogical nationalism, and civil society. Based on these indicators, he narrated the successes and failures of successive regimes in promoting the nation-state. According to Iweriebor, the First Republic was mostly characterized by the promotion of regional consciousness. As for the Second Republic, it was plagued by excessive economic mismanagement, corruption, and ethnic favoritism. While it is too early to pass a verdict on the Fourth Republic, judging from past experiences and the current level of communal violence, one may wonder whether the current civilian government can realize the goals of nation-state building. The failures of these regimes require us to look into the nature of the institutional arrangements under which elected civilian governments operate as well as the conduct of their leaders. In so doing, we should not forget that elected civilian government can be designed or behave in ways that undermine the principles of democracy.

As for the military regimes, Iweriebor's evaluations are mixed. Overall, he sees the Gowon and the Mohammed/Obasanjo governments as positive contributors to nation-state building in Nigeria. Yakubu Gowon has been given credit for creating a centripetal federal government and a relatively balanced federation, mobilizing the youth, building infrastructure, and promoting postwar reconciliation. The Mohammed/Obasanjo government is remembered for establishing and strengthening national institutions. In contrast, both the Buhari and Babangida governments failed to promote the nation-state. The Buhari regime was so insensitive to Nigeria's ethnic diversity that its policies wittingly and unwittingly further divided the country. While initially the Babangida government made positive contributions through liberal populism, General Ibrahim

Babangida virtually undid them by switching to manipulative populism. As such, the regime became one of the most divisive forces in Nigeria.[11]

Though Iweriebor's study narrates the successes and failures of the various governments, it does not properly explain why a particular government failed or succeeded in promoting the nation-state. It is important to look for the underlying differences among the various regimes so as to understand better the twists and turns as well as the reactionary and progressive developments in the process of nation-state building in Nigeria.

In his study of public policy in Nigeria, Rotimi Suberu presented nation-state building as a question of unity and integration.[12] He identified two dimensions to integration: territorial and political. Territorial integration refers to the horizontal links across the country that bridge the social distance among the various groups of people. It involves subordinating parochial cultural, regional, linguistic, and ethnic loyalties to the Nigerian nation at large. Political integration deals with the vertical linkages among Nigerians. It involves minimizing the political distance between the citizens and their political leaders and fostering the political participation of the masses.

In analyzing some of the public policies that have been pursued to promote national integration and curb ethnicity in Nigeria, Suberu cautioned: "It is important to make a distinction between specific functional public policies on national unity on the one hand, and the broad political regimes and ideologies that invariably shape, constrain or inspire such policies, on the other hand."[13] For Suberu, the effectiveness of national integration policies cannot be separated from the nature of the regime and the dominant ideology in the country. He categorized national integration policies into: regionalization, redistributive, symbolic, and regulatory policies.[14] However, Suberu is not convinced of the success of these policies. As he concludes, "these policies have been characterized variously as poorly conceived, contradictory, ineffective, counterproductive and repressive, even if often well-intentioned. The result is that today, by general agreement or acknowledgment, Nigeria is in the throes of a huge and staggering crisis of national unity."[15] Suberu attributes the failure of national integration policies in Nigeria to the scarcity and/or mismanagement of resources, group and elite interest, institutional and constitutional instability, and the flawed ideological framework for unity, which is essentially domination.[16] Most recently, Suberu has focused on the pathologies of Nigerian federalism. While recognizing that there is no viable alternative to federalism in Nigeria, Suberu expressed deep worries about the institutionalization of a largely distributive and conflictive system of federalism.[17]

While Suberu's sensitivity to the varieties of regimes and ideologies and their impact on the success or failure of specific national integration policies is commendable, his analysis fails to differentiate the levels of success or failure associated with the various governments. He generalizes failure and marginalizes successful cases. As such, he neglects the vital learning processes in the ongoing struggle to build a democratic nation-state. It is best to identify the various approaches to nation-state building, evaluate their effectiveness, and try to account for the underlying causes for the differences in their performance. This will enable us to overcome some of the limitations of the previous studies.

In order to distinguish the various approaches to nation-state building in Nigeria, one must take into account the nature of the regime's mandate, the design of the institutions under which the regime operates, and the conduct of the leaders.[18] Regimes can illegitimately obtain their mandate through military takeover (i.e., military regimes) or legitimately obtain their mandate through multiparty election (i.e., elected civilian governments). By their very nature, the institutions of military regimes are antithetical to democracy. As for elected civilian regimes, while their institutions are intended to promote democratic values, poor designs tend to undermine those values. In terms of conduct, it is important to note that a government may conduct itself in a manner that is not compatible with the nature of its mandate. A democratically elected government may act in a way that undermines democracy, while a military regime may to some degree respect human rights, promote national integration, allow grassroots political participation, and even restore democracy. Given the fact that nation-state building in Nigeria has been heavily burdened by the problem of ethnicity, it seems to me that the most insightful question is whether the conduct of the various regimes and the institutions under which they operate are discriminatory toward certain ethnic groups or promote inclusion. On the one hand, discriminatory institutional designs as well as discriminatory conduct are likely to undermine democratic values in a multiethnic country. On the other hand, institutional designs as well as regime conduct that promote inclusion tend to support democratic values. Based on these assumptions, we can identify four main approaches to nation-state building in Nigeria: *authoritarian, inclusionary, exclusionary,* and *democratic.* Table 4.1 below illustrates this model:

Table 4.1: **Approaches to Nation-State Building in Nigeria**

Mandate of the Government	Institutional Designs	Conduct of the Government	Approach to Nation Building
Military Takeover	Undermine Democratic Values	Undermines Democratic Values	**Authoritarian**
	Undermine Democratic Values	Supports Democratic Values	**Inclusionary**
Multiparty Election	Undermine Democratic Values	Undermines Democratic Values	**Exclusionary**
	Undermine Democratic Values	Supports Democratic Values	
	Support Democratic Values	Undermines Democratic Values	
	Support Democratic Values	Supports Democratic Values	**Democratic**

As indicated in table 4.1, military regimes are most likely to pursue either an authoritarian or an inclusionary approach to nation-state building. The authoritarian approach is typical of military regimes that conduct themselves in ways that are discriminatory toward certain groups and generally oppressive. Such an approach tends to leave negative institutional legacies, and in the worst cases contributes to the disintegration of the nation-state. In cases wherein the military regime conducts itself in ways that support democratic values, I call the approach to nation-state building inclusionary. This approach is typical of progressive military regimes that help to promote national integration and restore democracy.

Despite the recurring allegations of electoral fraud, all the civilian governments in postcolonial Nigeria derived their mandate from competitive multiparty elections. Their institutional designs as well as the conduct of their leaders, however, do not necessarily support democratic values. In Nigeria, elected governments often function as quasi-democracies. Not surprisingly, their approach to nation-state building has mostly been exclusionary. The exclusionary approach can range from cases in which the civilian government is poorly designed and at the same time the leaders conduct themselves in ways that undermine democratic values to cases in which the regime is either deficient in its design or the conduct of its leaders. The democratic approach to nation-state building refers to cases in which elected civilian governments operate under inclusive institutions and the leaders conduct themselves in a way that strengthens democratic values. Potentially, the democratic approach is the best way to promote a stable and democratic multiethnic nation-state. Unfortunately, Nigerians have not yet successfully pursued this approach.

The political history of postcolonial Nigeria indicates clear differences in the mandate and performance of the various governments that have ruled the country. The first major distinction is between elected civilian (the governments of the First, Second, and Fourth Republic) and military (the governments of Johnson Ironsi, Yakubu Gowon, Murtala Mohammed/Olusegun Obasanjo, Muhammadu Buhari, Ibrahim Babangida, Sani Abacha, and Abdulsalam Abubakar) regimes.[19] Though the institutions of all the military regimes tend to undermine democratic values, there are marked differences in their conduct. Much of the evidence shows that despite their shortcomings, the governments of Gowon, Mohammed/Obasanjo, and Abubakar conducted themselves in ways that promoted inclusion and democratic values. To a large degree, their approach to nation-state building came close to the inclusionary model. In contrast, the Ironsi, Buhari, Babangida, and Abacha governments further divided the nation and undermined democratic values. To a large degree, they pursued the authoritarian approach.

As for the elected civilian governments, one can further distinguish them by their design. The First Republic was a parliamentary system with strong regions and a relatively weak center. On the other hand, the Second Republic was a presidential system with a strong central government. Although the Fourth Republic was intended to be a presidential system with more autonomy granted to the states, in reality it is still a centralized federation. Overall, the First Republic was structurally biased both in terms of its territorial division as well as in terms of representation in the federal government. Despite the federal restructuring, the Second Republic was structurally biased toward minorities, especially in terms of the distribution of resources. The Fourth Republic also falls short of the kind of decentralized arrangement that would improve the position of the marginalized minorities. Finally, all three republics have been plagued by some kind of leadership problems. Without prejudging the Fourth Republic, what is missing so far is an elected civilian government that would operate under inclusive institutions and be led by people whose conduct promotes democratic values. Thus, I will argue that the exclusionary approach has been the path of nation-state building pursued by the various civilian governments in Nigeria.

Authoritarian Approach: Integration and Unity

The regimes that pursued the authoritarian approach failed to promote integration and unity in Nigeria. Ironsi's Unification Decree of May 1966, for example, dissolved the federation, degraded the autonomous regions to provinces, nationalized the various regional civil services, and transformed Nigeria into a unitary state. Ultimately, the decree was highly divisive and antagonistic to the Hausa-Fulani. What made the decree even more dangerous was the fact that the government lacked a democratic mandate. In addition, it was ethnically biased: a purely Igbo government inaugurated in a bloody coup that left the key Hausa-Fulani leaders dead.

Buhari's drive to foster integration and unity focused mainly on the personality of Nigerians, which was deemed to be inherently undisciplined. As such, in 1984 the government launched a "War Against Indiscipline" on the citizens of Nigeria. War Against Indiscipline (WAI) was both a character and nation-state building program aimed at instilling discipline and self-reliance, discouraging corruption and criminal practices, and strengthening national unity. The most crucial part of the campaign was the phase of "nationalism and patriotism," launched in Jos in August 1984. It called upon Nigerians to appreciate the national symbols (such as the anthem, flag, and coat of arms) and to serve their country. Unfortunately, the program was conducted in a draconian manner, frequently resorting to compulsory participation, flogging, fines, and arbitrary imprisonment.[20] In fact, the acronym "WAI," by which the campaign was commonly known, actually mimics the way many Nigerians cry to express physical pain. Though initially WAI generated significant civic enthusiasm for Nigerian nationhood, it was plagued by the regime's lack of democratic mandate, excessive militarism, and bias toward non-Hausa-Fulani people. Far from achieving its aims, WAI actually intensified ethnic animosities and violated civil rights.

In July 1987, Babangida launched a national integration campaign known as Mass Mobilisation for Self-Reliance, Social Justice and Economic Recovery (MAMSER). As outlined in the Directorate of Social Mobilisation Decree (Decree No. 31) of 1987, MAMSER was intended to promote a new cultural environment, positive attitudes, and active citizenship. Among other things, MAMSER was to combat ethnic and religious bigotry, promote national integration, and spread the virtues of patriotism and positive participation in national affairs. As stated by the Directorate for Social Mobilisation, MAMSER was committed to "educating and mobilizing Nigerians to identify with the Nigerian nation and to reject manipulations or acts which threaten the identity, integrity and solidarity of the nation."[21] The directorate organized rallies and workshops and published a political education manual aimed at promoting political awareness.[22]

Despite the great ambitions, MAMSER did not achieve much. It was an elite affair that left out the very masses it wanted to educate. Most importantly, the campaign was contradicted by the divisive activities of the government, such as enlisting Nigeria in the Organization of Islamic Conference (OIC), manipulating the democratization process, corruption, and Hausa-Fulani favoritism. In fact, MAMSER was a typical example of Babangida's laborious and never-ending projects that were intended to engage Nigerians in complicated debates so as to distract them from what was actually going wrong. While the rhetoric was in line with the objectives of nation-state building, the government's lack of democratic mandate, corruption, and bias undermined the program. By 1992, the program was virtually dead.

By the time Abacha came to power, Nigeria was in such political chaos that one could hardly talk of a national integration program. If there was anything that could have integrated Nigeria at the time, it would have been the restoration of democracy. By incarcerating Mashood Abiola (winner of the annulled 12 June 1993 presidential election), executing Ken Saro-Wiwa, and terrorizing pro-democracy and minority activists, the government made it clear that it was not ready to restore democracy. Abacha adopted a brutal form of dictatorship that was deeply resented by most Nigerians, especially southerners and minority groups across the country. Ironically, while the government was working toward the disintegration of the country, the struggle against the worst dictatorship in postcolonial Nigeria became a unifying force that held the country together. It was like the rebirth of the nationalist movement. Nigerians were once again united against a common enemy—their own Abacha. The problem with this kind of unity is what happens after the disappearance of the common foe.

Authoritarian Approach: Representation and Diversity

In Nigeria, boundary adjustment and the Federal Character principle have been the two most outstanding mechanisms for promoting adequate representation and diversity. However, both the Ironsi and Buhari governments refused to create new states or LGAs. In fact, Ironsi tried to turn Nigeria into a unitary state. Buhari banned all movements that campaigned for the creation of new states and abolished the LGAs that were created during the Second Republic. Though there may be good reasons for stopping the abuse of state and LGA creation, what is disturbing is the fact that these governments had no viable alternatives for addressing the genuine grievances of the underrepresented groups.

From the outset, the Ironsi government was pro-Igbo and anti-Hausa-Fulani. So too Buhari's Supreme Military Council was overwhelmingly dominated by northerners. It consisted of twelve members from the North and seven from the South. Much more disturbing was the fact that his deputy, though a Yoruba, was a Muslim and from Kwara state, which was part of the North. By so doing, Buhari "violated one of the sacred, unspoken but understood rules of national political leadership . . . that the two main leaders—the President and his deputy should come from the two great geopolitical and religious divides . . . North and South."[23]

In contrast, both the Babangida and Abacha governments hypocritically created states and LGAs and reaffirmed the Federal Character principle. Under the States Creation and Transitional Provisions Decree of 1987 (Decree No. 24), Babangida created two new states, Katsina and Akwa Ibom, from Kaduna and Cross River respectively.[24] In August 1991, the government went against its word and created nine more states (see tables A.11 and A.12 and figures A.1-A.7). It argued that creating states would help promote decentralization and a more balanced federation. Indeed, there were strong pressures for new states, especially among minorities and the Igbo who were disgruntled by previous boundary adjustments. However, the new changes, which were seen as manipulative acts in favor of the Hausa-Fulani North, failed to redress their grievances.

In May 1989, the Babangida government created 149 LGAs, bringing their total to 449 (excluding the four areas of Abuja). However, this was against the recommendations of both the 1984 Dusaki Committee and a majority of the members of the Political Bureau, who recommended that the number of local government areas remain at 301.[25] Between August and September 1991, the government further increased the number of LGAs to 589 (excluding those in Abuja). It argued that the new arrangement would bring the government closer to the people, increase political participation and awareness, ensure no state has less than ten LGAs, and reduce ethnic conflict.[26] However, the government's bias and manipulative tactics undermined the potential benefits of boundary adjustment. Bias was so evident that the Yoruba state of Lagos, the most populous state, initially had only fifteen LGAs, while the Hausa-Fulani state of Kano, the second most populous state, had thirty-four LGAs. Given the fact that LGAs were the basis for carving out electoral districts, the new arrangement openly violated the population principle for electing members of the House of Representatives. Not surprisingly, it led to resentment and violent protest by the Yoruba. Most importantly, boundary adjustment was an effective way of derailing the democratic transition process. Though the government claimed that it was responding to popular demands, in essence it was disrupting the establishment of political parties and undoing the primaries, which required candidates to first seek nomination from their LGA before they could advance to the state or national level.[27]

The Abacha government followed in the manipulative footsteps of Babangida. On December 13, 1995, the government established a committee, led by Chief Arthur Mbanefe, to look into the issue of state and LGA creation. In October 1996, the government added one state in each of the six geopolitical zones, increasing the total number of states to thirty-six.[28] It argued that creating states would ensure a fair spread and balance within the geopolitical zones of the country. In addition, Abacha announced the creation of 183 new LGAs. However, the whole process was chaotic and shady which led to numerous contradictory changes.[29] As had happened during the Babangida government, state and local government creation during the Abacha government was more of a manipulative device to derail the democratization process and a populist endeavor to defuse resentments against the government rather than a genuine attempt to address the problem of representation and diversity. As such, it made very little positive contribution to nation-state building.

The Babangida government extended the Federal Character principle to the composition of the National Revenue Mobilization, Allocation, and Fiscal Commission (NRMAFC), the Public Complaints Commission, and the governing councils of higher institutions of learning, statutory institutions, companies in which the federal government had a controlling share, and admission to Unity Schools. However, the application of the principle did not reflect the ideals it envisioned. In practice, it became a form of institutionalized favoritism. In January, 1991, for example, the government altered the quotas for admission into Unity Schools from its original formula (national merit 20 percent, equality of states quota 50 percent, environment—state of location—quota 30 percent) to the following: national merit 15 percent, environmental quota 30 percent, equality of states quota 40 percent, discretion 15 percent.[30] While in principle the discretionary quota was supposed to address complicated situations wherein highly qualified students were edged out because of the tight competition and low quotas in their home states, in practice it gave the government extra resources to use as it wished—usually favoring one group against the other and promoting patronage.

General Abacha engineered the Draft Constitution of 1995 which called for the creation of a Federal Character Commission.[31] Furthermore, it proposed a rotational system of power sharing to ensure better political representation at the top of government. Initially, this was presented as rotating the presidency between the North and South (or among the six geopolitical zones). However, following Babangida's tactic of complicating arrangements to make them impossible to realize, the Abacha government redefined rotation to mean rotating six national positions (president, vice president, prime minister, deputy prime minister, senate president, speaker of House of Representative) among the six zones. Given the bias of the Babangida and Abacha governments it is safe to say that their commitment to the Federal Character principle was only on paper.

Authoritarian Approach: Fair and Equitable Distribution

The problem of resource distribution in Nigeria centers mainly on the details of the two revenue allocation systems—vertical and horizontal revenue sharing. Vertical sharing refers to the reallocation of central revenues among the federal, state, and local governments. Horizontal sharing deals with the distribution of revenue among the states and regions. Ironsi's short-lived government did not make any changes to the reallocation formula it inherited from the previous government. In 1984, Buhari altered the vertical revenue allocation formula (which was 55, 35, and 10 percent of the federal account to the federal, state, and local governments, respectively) by creating two funds which the federal government could use to solve ecological problems in any part of the country and develop the mineral producing areas. In practice, this enabled the federal government to increase its share by 2.5 percent at the expense of the states, dropping their real share to 32.5 percent. Given the biased nature of the government, the new arrangement further shortchanged the groups that were underrepresented in the federal government.

In 1989, Babangida established the National Revenue Mobilisation, Allocation, and Fiscal Commission (NRMAFC) as a permanent body to deal with the issue of fair and equitable distribution of national revenue. However, the commission's effectiveness was undermined by the political nature of its composition, inconsistencies in its mandate, and its ambiguous relation with the Federal Account Allocation Committee (FAAC). In 1992, Babangida introduced changes to the vertical revenue allocation formula that further reduced the share of the states and gave the federal government more room for manipulation. The June 1992 amendment set up the following formula: federal government 48.5 percent, states 24.0, local governments 20.0, and federally controlled special funds (including derivation, federal capital territory, mineral producing areas, general ecology, and stabilization) 7.5.[32] This formula practically weakened the states vis-à-vis both the federal government and the local governments. We should also not forget that embezzlement, manipulation of the Dollar-to-Naira exchange rate, and the federal government's practice of making deductions from the federal account before the sum was distributed further undermined the NRMAFC's effectiveness. Overall, the changes worked against groups that were not well represented in the federal government. Given the government's lack of democratic mandate and its bias, the changes further antagonized ethnic relations and undermined nation-state building.

Following long-standing complaints from people in the South about the revenue allocation formula and the composition of the NRMAFC, in January

1990 the Babangida government introduced some changes to the horizontal revenue allocation formula. The new arrangement was based on: equity 40 percent, population 30 percent, social development factor (based on education, health, and water need) 10 percent, land mass and terrain 10 percent, and internal revenue effort 10 percent. However, the change did not really improve equity or fairness in the distribution. In essence, it just maintained the status quo.[33] Though the South was pleased to see population and social development factors slashed by 10 percent and 5 percent respectively, and the internal revenue efforts factor increased to 10 percent, the Hausa-Fulani North was indirectly compensated by the introduction of the 10 percent for land mass and terrain. Here again we see the government maintaining a biased revenue sharing formula while pretending to genuinely address the concerns of the marginalized ethnic groups.

Under the Abacha government, Nigeria was in such chaos that hardly any of the rules were applied. Revenue allocation became arbitrary and corrupt—mostly allocating to the foreign bank accounts of Abacha and his favorites. Moreover, the government came up with new mechanisms to reduce the revenue of the states. In 1994, it replaced the sales tax, administered by the states, with the value added tax (VAT). The idea was to boost tax collection and return the revenue to the states, with the federal government retaining 20 percent to cover the cost of collecting the taxes. However, in 1995, the federal government increased its share to 50 percent and divided the other 50 percent among the states and localities. Given the government's Hausa-Fulani bias, this was seen as another attempt to shortchange the people in the South. After bitter opposition by southerners, in February 1996, the federal government altered the distribution to 40 percent, 35, and 25 for the states, federal government, and localities respectively. In 1998, it further reduced its own share to 25 percent.[34] For the government, VAT was a convenient way of extending patronage and quelling political opposition. One should not forget the Petroleum Special Task Fund (PTF), headed by General Buhari, into which the government pumped millions of petroleum dollars. With the huge amount of money under its controlled, the PTF became a parallel government at the disposal of the Hausa-Fulani. Not surprisingly, the Obasanjo government quickly eliminated the PTF. Instead of contributing to nation-state building, the Abacha government intensified the mistrust of those groups that were excluded from holding the reins of power.

Authoritarian Approach: Peace and Stability

The ethnic composition of Nigeria and the manner in which it came into being have always rendered the country vulnerable to communal violence. Governments that have pursued the authoritarian approach to nation-state building have tended to engage in activities that further encourage the outbreak of communal violence, and at the same time have dealt with the problem of order heavy-handedly. Under the public order decree, for example, the Ironsi government banned eighty-one political and ethno-cultural organizations. In February 1966, it sentenced Isaac Boro, Sam Owonaro, and Nottingham Dick to death for proclaiming the Delta Peoples Republic.[35]

Under the Civil Disturbances (Special Tribunal) Decree No. 2 of 1987, Babangida set up tribunals to deal with ethnic and religious violence in states such as Kaduna, Bauchi, and Rivers. One of the worst incidents of violence in the North was the May 1992 Zango-Kataf disturbances. It left 471 people dead, 518 injured, 229 houses, and 218 vehicles destroyed in Kaduna City, Zaria, and Ikara. Two tribunals were set up to deal with the incident, one headed by Justice Benedit Okadigbo and the other by Emmanuel Adegbite. Together, they sentenced fourteen people to death—including the former governor of Rivers state, retired General Zamani Lekwot—and imprisoned many more people. The sentences triggered huge demonstrations and litigation that forced the government to reduce the death sentences to prison terms. The problem with the tribunals was that they included serving members of the armed forces and the courts could not control the activities of the tribunals. Furthermore, they were more a witch-hunt and showed little concern for finding the root causes of the violence. As such, the whole exercise left the minorities even more embittered. The Babangida government responded to the Ogoni demands for a fair share of the oil revenue from their territory, ecological rehabilitation, and political autonomy by promulgating the Treason and Treasonable Offences Decree (Decree No. 29, May 4th 1993). Instead of promoting peace and stability, the decree amounted to a declaration of war against ethnic minorities who were campaigning for their social and political rights. It is worth noting that its wording was so open that one could be put to death even for exercising basic freedoms of expression.[36]

The Abacha government implemented and intensified the oppressive policies of Babangida and led a reign of terror against all sections of the Nigerian civil society—such as journalists, human rights groups, minorities, and pro-democracy activists. Ultimately, the government brought Nigeria to the verge of a civil war. More than any other single incident, the government demonstrated its will to suppress ethnic minorities by executing Ken Saro-Wiwa and his fellow MOSOP activists. From the perspective of maintaining peace and unity, the activities of the Abacha government were counterproductive. The government isolated itself from the international community. Most importantly, it further alienated the minorities and raised their political consciousness and determination to fight back. In response to the execution of the Ogoni activists, the National Congress of the Ijaw community declared:

> We wish to state for the umpteenth time that Nigeria as a multiethnic, pluralistic country, cannot in any way close her doors to the ravaging fires of ethnic nationalism the world over. The only answer to the problem lies in . . . dialogue, the spirit of give-and-take, and certainly not the use of terror and intimidation. If hangings were, therefore, intended to intimidate the oil-bearing minority nationalities of the Niger

Delta from (continuing) their legitimate agitation for justice, equity and fair play, it is (sic) obviously misplaced.[37]

Authoritarian Approach: Economic and Social Development

In terms of promoting economic development, the records of the governments that pursued the authoritarian approach are depressing. The Ironsi government did not last long enough to make any significant impact on Nigeria's economic development. As for the Buhari government, it was overwhelmingly preoccupied with discipline. It seems that its main strategy for solving Nigeria's economic problems was to discipline Nigerians and root out corruption in the country. Despite the heavy-handed approach of the government, corruption persisted.

The Structural Adjustment Program (SAP), engineered by the International Monetary Fund, formed the core of the Babangida government's economic development plan. Overall, SAP was an economic disaster for Nigeria.[38] Worst of all, while the government required the masses to make big sacrifices in their material well-being, the northern-dominated political elite were embezzling huge sums of government money. Initially, the Babangida government engaged in numerous populist programs which were portrayed as efforts to reach out to the rural masses. In early 1986, the government set up the Directorate of Food, Roads, and Rural Infrastructure (DFRRI). Its main objectives were to promote rural community development and encourage participation in the development process. It undertook some road construction, water, sanitation, electricity, and literacy projects. Though these were essential ingredients of economic and social development, the program was undermined by high-level corruption, favoritism, government manipulation, and false claims about accomplishments.

In 1987, First Lady Maryam Babangida, established a semi-official program known as the Better Life for Rural Women Programme (BLP). Its main objective was to encourage female participation in the mainstream development process of the nation. It encouraged the formation of commercial and craft associations and cooperatives, and provided technical aid. In addition, it constructed roads, sanitation facilities, and schools. In 1989, the government also established the People's Bank of Nigeria (PNB). According to Decree No. 22 of 1990, the bank was to give loans to underprivileged Nigerians, especially small-scale farmers, entrepreneurs, and tradespeople. These populist activities of the Babangida government were threaded in-between wider policies that favored the Hausa-Fulani, sophisticated manipulation of the political process, and abuse of power. As such, the overall contribution to nation-state building was either minimal or even counterproductive.

During the Abacha era, Nigeria became so chaotic that one could only talk of the level of economic and social regression. With a virtual monopoly over the oil revenues, the government used oil dollars to terrorize Nigerians, secure its hold on power, and set up huge personal bank accounts in foreign countries, notably Switzerland, for top government officials and their families. Currently, the Obasanjo government is trying to negotiate with international financial institutions and the Abacha family to work out a deal under which the government can recover some of the stolen money.[39]

Authoritarian Approach: Democratic Legitimacy and Constitutionalism

By the very nature in which the regimes that pursued the authoritarian approach came to power, it is clear that they are violators of the constitutions and therefore illegitimate governments. Even though these governments promised to restore democracy, they consistently failed to keep their promises. This is best exemplified by Babangida's manipulation of the democratic transition process and the terror that Abacha unleashed on the pro-democracy activists. Even more disturbing is the way in which regimes that pursued the authoritarian approach undermined the rule of law. Under such regimes, the constitution was more or less irrelevant. What mattered were the decrees that they arbitrarily imposed on the people. Far from promoting democracy and constitutionalism, the authoritarian approach further destroyed whatever remained of such institutions.

Exclusionary Approach: Integration and Unity

During the First Republic, the guiding principle of Abubakar Tafawa Balewa's government toward Nigerian integration was "unity in diversity." As the first government of independent Nigeria, the Balewa government created the initial symbols to promote the nation-state—such as the national flag, coat of arms, anthem, and public holidays. It also initiated the Unity Schools program. The schools were intended to encourage interaction among young Nigerians from various ethnic and cultural backgrounds, instill a sense of patriotism, and motivate them for achievement and self-improvement. The project envisioned the establishment of two Unity Schools in each state, including the Federal Capital Territory. Admission to the schools was based on a quota system—national merit 20 percent, equality of states 50 percent, and state of location 30 percent.[40] Certainly, these schools were a positive social development and a vital tool for national integration. However, their success was undermined by the structural imbalances of the federation. By design, the federation was highly unbalanced to the advantage of the North dominated by the Hausa-Fulani.

The government of Shehu Shagari was inaugurated at a time when there was a relatively high spirit for "unity in diversity," thanks to the bitter memories of the Nigerian Civil War and the conduct of the previous military regime. In addition, the government had a democratic mandate and a constitution that was negotiated by Nigerians. As such, the real task of the government was to build upon these achievements. However, the level of government corruption, the controversies surrounding the elections and the fact that the National Party of Nigeria (NPN) was essentially a Hausa-Fulani dominated party undermined whatever sense of unity that was built over the previous years.

Exclusionary Approach: Representation and Diversity

As far as promoting fair representation among Nigeria's diverse ethnic groups is concerned, the Balewa government took a significant step in 1963 to adjust the federal structure. It created one more region, Mid-Western Nigeria (Mid-West), out the Western Region. However, the restructuring did not create a balanced federation. Instead of being a genuine attempt to improve the representation of the minorities, the creation of the Mid-West region was mostly an attempt to weaken the Western Region vis-à-vis the Northern and the Eastern Regions. In particular, the boundary adjustment exercise failed to reduce the hegemonic position of the North. Furthermore, it ignored the grievances of the minorities in the North and the East.

Following the spirit of the Federal Character principle laid out in the 1979 Constitution, the NPN, led by Shagari, devised some structural arrangements aimed at making the government more representative of the country's diversity. As stated in Article 21 of the NPN Constitution: "zoning shall be understood by the party as a convention in recognition of the need for adequate geographical spread."[41] The party created four zones: (a) all the Northern states, (b) all the states of the former Western Region, (c) all the states of the former Eastern Central state, and (d) the states of the southern minorities: Bendel, Cross River, and Rivers (see figures A.2-A.4). The zoning principle was to be applied to offices such as the national chairman, president, vice-president, president and deputy president of the Senate, national secretary, speaker and deputy speaker of the Federal House of Representatives and majority leader of the House, federal ministers, and officials of parastatal agencies. The concept of zoning was also extended to the state level. Unfortunately, the NPN government failed to support this arrangement with practices that could promote national integration. Despite the attempt to ensure that Nigerians from all parts of the country would have someone in the government, the government failed to win the hearts of most Nigerians from the South because it was characterized by corruption, embezzlement of public funds, and above all Hausa-Fulani favoritism.[42] As it turned out, zoning was merely a strategy to win the election rather than a genuine commitment to fair representation and diversity.

Exclusionary Approach: Fair and Equitable Distribution

The struggle to devise a fair and equitable revenue allocation formula in Nigeria goes back to the period of colonial rule. The 1946 Phillipson Commission recommended that revenue allocation should be based on the principles of *derivation* and *even progress*. While the principle of derivation allocated revenue to the regions in proportion to the revenue they generated, even progress gave more support to poorer regions to bring them up to par with the rest of the federation. This meant that the North, which was economically less developed and presumably much more populated, would get a bigger share of the federal revenue. At the Ibadan Constitutional Conference of 1950, a bitter argument broke out among the regional leaders over revenue allocation. In trying to maximize their comparative advantage, northerners demanded that revenue allocation should be based on population size, easterners argued for the need principle, while leaders of the western region favored the principle of derivation.[43] The Hichs-Phillipson Commission, which was a product of the Ibadan Constitutional Conference, recommended a compromise solution based on independent revenue, need, national interest, and special grant. In 1953, Sir Louis Chick was called upon to review the revenue allocation system. He endorsed the derivation principle, but recommended that the federal government be empowered to make grants to regions that were in serious difficulties.[44]

The post-independence government of Balewa inherited the formula that was designed by the Raisman Commission and approved at the 1957 Constitutional Conference. It de-emphasized derivation and took into consideration: (a) the population size, (b) the basic responsibilities of each regional government, (c) the need for continuity in regional public service, and (d) the importance of balanced development. A distributive pool account (DPA) was created out of which the North would receive 40 percent, the East 31 percent, the West 24 percent, and Southern Cameroon 5 percent. Mining revenues were divided as follows: 50 percent for the region of origin, 30 percent for the DPA, and 20 percent for the federal government.[45] The Balewa government set up the Binn Commission in 1964, which substantially increased the DPA and provided for an annual block grant.[46] The shift from the derivation to the even progress revenue allocation principle under the Balewa government further embittered the people in the South, who believed that they were contributing more and getting far less in return.

The Shagari government set up a revenue allocation commission led by Dr. Pius Okigbo and passed the 1981 Revenue Allocation Act. The 1981 Revenue Allocation Act assigned 58.5, 31.5, and 10 percent of the national revenue to the federal government, the states, and the localities, respectively. In October 1981, the Supreme Court nullified the act after it was challenged by the states in the South. The January 1982 Revised Revenue Allocation Act reduced the federal share to 55 and increased that of the states to 35 percent. The government also altered the horizontal revenue sharing formula. Under the 1981 Act, the government maintained the 50 percent weight for the equality principle, reduced the population share to 40 percent, and allocated 10 percent for land mass. The 1982 Revised Act reduced equality to 40 percent and eliminated the land mass share. However, it allocated 15 percent for social development (calculated from

Direct Inverse Primary School Enrollment) and 5 percent for internal revenue generation effort.[47] The changes brought to light two kinds of struggles: one between the federal and state governments and the other between the people in the South and those in the North. The states, those in the South in particular, wanted to stop a trend toward the concentration of revenue in the hands of the federal government. Southerners were also trying to uphold the derivation principle which would allow them to retain a bigger share of the oil revenues. The Hausa-Fulani dominated federal government wanted to concentrate more revenue at the center. Given the disproportionate concentration of oil in the southern part of the country, northern states were also pushing the federal government to give more weight to the principle of even progress in the allocation of revenue. Though the 1981 Act reduced the population share, which has traditionally favored the North, the loss was made up for by the introduction of land mass and social development factors.

Exclusionary Approach: Peace and Stability

Even before the coup of January 1966, Nigerian democracy was virtually dead. As Diamond points out: "The surface manifestations of democratic decay were apparent . . . [in] two lines of historical development—the secular deterioration through corruption, profligacy and waste, and the episodic deterioration through the sequence of exhausting and unresolved crises."[48] These episodic crises not only contributed to the breakdown of democracy, but also threatened the survival of the nation-state. Notwithstanding the political skills of Prime Minister Balewa, the government's record was far from satisfactory. On several occasions, the ability of the Balewa government to maintain peace in Nigeria was stretched to the limit. Some of the most crucial cases were the 1962-1963 crisis in the Western Region and the 1963-1964 census crisis. To get a better sense of the Balewa government's approach to peace and stability, it will be helpful to look at some of the episodes that raised the stakes in the tense ethnic and regional conflicts.

The 1962-1963 crisis in the Western Region began as an internal problem within the Action Group (AG), which was divided between the Awolowo and Akintola factions. In an attempt to oust Chief Samuel Akintola, the Awolowo faction mounted charges of mal-administration, anti-party activities, and indiscipline against him. On May 19, 1962, they passed a resolution demanding Akintola's resignation as deputy party leader and premier of the Western Region. Two days later, the Regional Council elected Alhaji O. S. Adegbenro to replace Akintola. The governor dismissed Akintola who refused to accept the decision. Akintola challenged his dismissal in the courts and his supporters vowed to disrupt the meetings of the Regional Council.[49]

The disorder that erupted in the Western Region gave the federal government—NPC and NCNC coalition—a chance to fully intervene in the conflict.

As violence escalated, the Awolowo factions asked Prime Minister Abubakar Tafawa Balewa for police protection within the Chamber to ensure a peaceful forum. The prime minister granted police protection on condition that the federal government would not accept any decision reached during such proceedings in the Chamber.[50] Furthermore, he instructed the police not to recognize any of the rival premiers and to close the chamber if violence erupted. As anticipated, the May 25, 1962 meeting of the Regional Council, intended to pass a vote of confidence on Alhaji O. S. Adegbenro, ended in a fight.

On May 29, 1962, the federal government declared a state of emergency in the Western Region and dismissed the governor, premier, ministers, and other executive and legislative officials of the region. The prime minister replaced them with an administrator, Senator M. A. Majekodunmi, who was given sweeping powers to appoint commissioners, command the police and civil service, maintain order, imprison anyone spreading misleading reports, prohibit public processions and meetings, detain or restrict any person in the interest of public order, and search premises without warrant.[51] The administrator restricted most of the politicians, especially those on the Awolowo camp, to places outside of Ibadan. As a mark of the federal government's bias, Akintola was tacitly allowed to reorganize his faction into a new party—the United People's Party. Furthermore, the government lifted his ban. In addition, the federal government appointed the Coker Commission, which ended up being a witch-hunt aimed at discrediting the AG. The commission blamed Obafemi Awolowo for the crisis and exonerated Akintola, opening the way for his reinstatement as premier on January 1, 1963—against the wishes of the majority of the people in the Western Region. Already, the federal government had backed away from its promise to hold a fresh election in the Western Region. In return, Akintola agreed to give the NCNC a generous share of political positions in the West and to the creation of the Mid-Western Region, which he had bitterly opposed in the past.[52]

The most critical aspect of the turmoil in the Western Region was the trial of Awolowo and his colleagues. On September 22, 1962, he was placed under house arrest for allegedly plotting a coup. In November, charges of treasonable felony were filed against Awolowo and thirty of his colleagues. Even though the police discovered a small collection of weapons, it was not clear whether they were intended for a coup.[53] According to the defense, the weapons were kept for the purpose of self defense. After the appeal, Awolowo was cleared of the charges of a coup plot but found guilty of arms importation and possession for which he was sentenced to ten years in prison.[54] Though the government refrained from using outright force to eliminate the opposition and politically weaken the Yoruba, the whole incident undermined peace and stability in Nigeria. As Diamond argued, "in decimating the federal opposition, thwarting the will of the western people, and harshly curtailing political liberties," the government "made the system distinctly less democratic. And in so doing so, the federal coalition also undermined the legitimacy of the regime among the opposition's committed supporters."[55] Furthermore, it embittered the Yoruba, who saw the whole incident as politically engineered to weaken them.

Thanks to the bitter lessons of the Nigerian Civil War and the activities of the previous military regime, the Shagari government inherited a country that was relatively peaceful. However, Shagari's failure to convincingly win the 1979 presidential election, the high levels of corruption within the government, and the violence that characterized the 1983 elections showed that the government was not keen on promoting peace in Nigeria.[56] As early as 1981, the NPN demonstrated that it was not willing to abide by the rule of law. The NPN-controlled State Assembly in Kano went all out to impeach the reformist Peoples Redemption Party (PRP) governor, Alhaji Abdualkadir Balarabe Musa. The Nigerian opposition forces saw his removal from office in June 1981 as undemocratic and unconstitutional. It is also believed that the NPN instigated the July 1981 violence in Kano to intimidate the new PRP governor, Mohammed Abubakar Rimi, and derail his reforms. During the violence, Rimi's political advisor was killed and government property destroyed. Even before the 1983 election, political violence was already rampant.[57] By May 1981, for example, thirty-nine people had been killed, ninety-nine injured and 376 arrested in Borno state alone.[58]

The conduct of the NPN government during the 1983 election further undermined peace and democracy. The voter registration process was marred by irregularities that mostly favored the NPN. In addition, the Federal Electoral Commission (FEDECO) refused to register the newly formed Progressive Peoples Party (PPP). Through various forms of electoral fraud, the NPN secured the presidency, thirteen gubernatorial positions, and two-thirds of the seats in the National Assembly.[59] In the Yoruba states, this led to violent protest that left one hundred people dead and $100 million worth of property destroyed.[60] Given its conduct, it is clear that the Shagari government actually undermined democracy and peace in Nigeria. So bad was the direction of government that the Hausa-Fulani understood that the government could not be sustained for too long. Not surprisingly, General Buhari toppled the government without much resistance.

Exclusionary Approach: Economic and Social Development

The Balewa government has been credited for creating a unified national education system to replace the regional systems. This represented the first step toward promoting a solid education in all parts of Nigeria. Furthermore, the government constructed new roads, expanded the rail, postal, and communication networks, and constructed the Kainji Hydroelectric Dam and a national power grid.[61] However, the positive effects of some of these economic and social development projects were undermined by bias in their distribution, which tended to favor the North.

The Shagari government did expand some of the infrastructure developments initiated by the preceding military government. It started a national housing program that aimed to build 2,000 houses a year in each of the nineteen states and in the Federal Capital Territory. Out of the 40,000 units that were started in 1980, 24,584 were completed by 1981.[62] However, the Shagari government's ability to promote economic and social development was undermined by rampant corruption at all levels of government. In 1983 alone, for example, the minister of commerce misused $2.5 billion. In the same year, the thirty-seven story building, headquarters of the Nigerian External Telecommunications in Lagos, burned. Many Nigerians believe that the building was deliberately set afire to cover up government corruption and embezzlement in the company.[63]

Exclusionary Approach: Democratic Legitimacy and Constitutionalism

Both the Balewa and Shagari governments gained their mandate to govern through competitive multiparty elections. However, they operated as quasi-democracies and violated the provisions of the constitution with impunity. In particular, these governments rigged elections and intimidated opponents to the point that the multiparty elections became virtually meaningless. Apart from rigging elections, these governments violated the constitutions. Contrary to the spirit of the 1960 Constitution, the Balewa government intervened in the Western Region and imposed a government against the wishes of the people. So too the Shagari government tried to bypass the federal legislature in its attempt to alter the revenue allocation formula to the advantage of the North. Overall, both governments failed to uphold the rule of law. As such, they undermined the development of a democratic multiethnic nation-state.

Inclusionary Approach: Integration and Unity

In 1973, the Gowon government initiated the National Youth Service Corps. The goal of the program was to instill discipline, patriotism, and a sense of common experience and to promote labor mobility within the country. According to Decree No. 24 of 1973, all university, college, and polytechnic graduates below the age of thirty-one were required to serve the country for one year in a state outside of their place of birth and ethnic origin before pursuing further studies or careers. They were to be assigned in areas that corresponded to their training, especially in the teaching field, and they were required to participate in community development services. They were also required to engage in language, civic, leadership, and physical-fitness training. The scheme, which began with 2,264 participants, is estimated to have recruited more than a million people.[64]

By exposing the youth to the country's cultural diversity and facilitating interaction among them, it was hoped that they would be more prepared to unite and respect their country's heterogeneity. Unfortunately, the adoption of the "state-of-origin" rule in the hiring of state and local government employees and the discriminatory practices of successive regimes have undermined some of the symbolic and practical benefits of the program. Despite allegations that the scheme was a disguised form of forced labor and the bureaucratic bungles that characterized it, it seems to me that Gowon's idea was an ingenious one for Nigerians to build upon.

The Mohammed/Obasanjo government relocated the Federal Capital Territory from Lagos to Abuja, which is considered the geographical center of the country.[65] Abuja was intended to be ethnically neutral, easily accessible from all parts of the country, and most of all, a symbolic home for all Nigerians. As Mohammed argued, "The area is not within the control of any major ethnic group in the country. We believe that a new federal capital created on such a virgin land will be for all Nigerians, a symbol of their oneness and unity."[66] Unfortunately, one has to face the fact that successive governments have undermined the symbolic benefits of the project through corruption and favoritism in allocating land and jobs in Abuja. Nevertheless, the project of itself was an innovative effort to promote the nation-state.

On October 1, 1978, the Mohammed/Obasanjo regime introduced a new national anthem and pledge. The anthem eliminated the reference to tribes and stressed the shared experience of Nigerians, patriotism, unity, and determination to build a nation where peace and justice shall reign. The pledge also emphasized commitment to Nigerian territorial integrity and the will to defend Nigerian unity. Furthermore, the government created a register of national heroes. The register was opened with the names of four Nigerian forefathers: Herbert Macaulay, Alhaji Abubakar Tafawa Balewa, Alvan Ikoku, and General Murtala Mohammed.[67] The aim was to create a powerful symbol of Nigerian nationhood and provide a leadership reference point for all Nigerians.

Inclusionary Approach: Representation and Diversity

In 1967, the Gowon government tried to address the unbalanced nature of the federation by dividing the country into twelve states—six in the North and three each in the West and East (see tables A.11 and A.12). The aim was to prevent the Nigerian Civil War and in the long run ensure that no state would dominate the federal government. In particular, the program aimed at making states into compact geographical areas that would be sensitive to the history and wishes of the peoples concerned. Indeed, the reorganization did place the federal government in a much stronger position vis-à-vis the states—previously referred to as regions. Furthermore, it addressed some of the grievances of the minorities, especially in the North and East.

Boundary adjustment continued during the Mohammed/Obasanjo era. The main aim was to further strengthen the center and at the same time decentralize the federation by directly reaching out to more of the underrepresented communities.[68] In 1976, the government increased the number of states to nineteen and divided the country into 301 LGAs. The reform standardized the system of local government across the country and transformed it into a distinct layer of government. While there is a consensus that the original three-region federation was grossly imbalanced, there is no agreement as to the right number of states or localities to adequately represent all the contending groups. As a mechanism for promoting representation, boundary adjustment has been applauded and criticized as well. In particular, the new states and LGAs have helped to improve the representation of minorities in the federal government as well as their share of the national revenue. However, boundary adjustment can be abused to enhance patronage and derail democratic reforms. The question then is when does boundary adjustment cease to be a positive development in the nation-state building process? Much will depend on the general character of the government that is redrawing the boundaries and its social legitimacy among the citizens. Indeed boundary adjustment under the governments that pursued the inclusionary approach to nation-state building is different from those that followed the authoritarian path. Notwithstanding the shortcomings of boundary adjustments under the Gowon and Mohammed/Obasanjo governments, they were largely seen as genuine attempts to solve a very complex problem. As Rotimi Suberu summed it up:

> The creation of states was a very critical institutional design, which was very useful. You have to historically contextualize it. The military made that change not because they wanted to or had the imagination, but because it became an act of desperation. They had to save the federation and the only way they could with the imminence of the Biafra secession was to divide Nigeria into several states. By giving the minorities in the proposed Biafra states their own state, it was hoped that they would defect from the Biafran project. So it was a strategy of desperation rather than of imagination and choice—nevertheless, it played a very positive role in maintaining Nigerian unity.[69]

Another significant development in the attempt to ensure proper representation and respect for Nigeria's diversity is the introduction of the Federal Character principle. In the 1979 Constitution, Federal Character was understood as the distinctive desire of the peoples of Nigeria to promote national unity, foster national loyalty, and give every citizen of Nigeria a sense of belonging. The concept was introduced by Murtala Mohammed during his October 1975 address to the Constitutional Drafting Committee. He urged the members to adopt an executive presidential system in which "the President and Vice-President are elected . . . in such a manner so to reflect the Federal character of the country."[70] The idea was to devise an institutional arrangement that would ensure that all ethnic and sectional groups were properly represented in the federation. Despite the constraining features associated with consociational arrangements, the Federal Character principle has been crucial for ensuring unity in diversity. The problem is the actual application of the idea. As I have argued, it is important to take into account the general nature of the government in question. Though governments that pursued the authoritarian and exclusionary approaches frequently abused the Federal Character concept, and have actually turned it into institutionalized discrimination, one can still expect the Federal Character principle to be a positive tool for governments that want to pursue the inclusive or democratic approach to nation-state building.

Inclusionary Approach: Fair and Equitable Distribution

Both the Gowon and Mohammed/Obasanjo governments addressed the problems of revenue allocation and appointment to government offices. Gowon introduced a quota system for employing civil servants, awarding scholarships, and admission into educational institutions. Though it was a genuine attempt to divide the Nigerian pie as fairly as possible, the quota system actually became an end in itself, generating numerous controversies. Perhaps the most vivid manifestation of this problem was the increasing use of the state of origin rule (i.e., indigene or non-indigene) in hiring and access to public services. However, the Gowon government further watered down the principle of derivation in the horizontal distribution of revenue and strengthened the position of the federal government vis-à-vis the states. It expanded the distributive pool account (DPA) and reduced the proportion of the DPA allocated on the basis of derivation. Under Decree No. 13 of 1970, for example, half of the excise duties on tobacco and petroleum products, and 40 percent of export duties were allocated to the DPA. Furthermore, the proportion of mining rents and royalties paid into the DPA was increased from 35 percent to 50 percent, while the corresponding shares of the states of derivation was reduced from 50 to 45 percent. Decree No. 6 of 1975 further increased the share of the DPA from mining rents and royalties to 80 percent.[71]

Under Decree 31 of 1970, the federal government undercut the states by taking a 50 percent share from tax revenues that formerly had fully belonged to the states, such as excise duties on tobacco and petroleum products. In 1971, Gowon passed the Off-Shore Oil Revenue Decree, which deprived the oil producing states of their off-shore oil revenues. As the decree stated: "all royalties, rents and other revenues derived from or relating to the exploration, prospecting or searching for or the winning or working of petroleum . . . in the territorial waters and the continental shelf shall accrue to the Federal Military Government."[72] In an attempt to get the economy under control, the federal government took over the marketing boards, reduced the poll tax, standardized personal income tax, introduced a uniform fuel price, and eliminated export duties and sales taxes on agriculture, betting, casinos, and gambling—all of which had been collected by the state governments.

To the extent that there was a need for greater interregional integration, fiscal uniformity, and reducing the gap between the North and South, the Gowon government's revenue allocation policies could be seen as a positive step in nation-state building. Indeed, the government made good use of the money by promoting the post-war reconciliation effort and undertaking vital economic and social development projects. However, it also left a pattern of fiscal centralization that biased and mischievous governments could easily abuse. Fiscal centralization continued during the Mohammed/Obasanjo era. The 1977/78 Aboyade Committee recommended that all federally collected revenue should be placed into a single account, 60 percent of which should go to the federal government, 30 to the states, and 10 to the localities.[73] The recommendation, which was incorporated into the 1979 Constitution, further strengthened the federal government and at the same time weakened the position of the states vis-à-vis the localities.

Inclusionary Approach: Peace and Stability

The biggest challenge for the Gowon government was how to deal with the Biafra secessionists. The Nigerian Civil War did succeed in preserving the territorial integrity of the country, but failed to bring about Nigerian unity. In fairness to the Gowon government, it is important to note that the causes of the war lay fully within the activities of the previous regimes—colonial as well as postcolonial. Gowon tried to prevent the war by restructuring the federation. However, the creation of eight more states did not heal the deep wounds that had already been created. Despite the devastation of the East and the human rights violations during the war, Gowon has been commended for his post-war reconciliation policies. Driven by a "no victor, no vanquished" philosophy, Gowon pursued a generous post-war reconciliation policy, which included a general amnesty, prohibited retaliation against the Igbo, rehabilitated some of the areas that were destroyed—spending about 120 million Nairas—and reintegrating the secessionists into the civil service.[74] The Mohammed/Obasanjo government's greatest contribution to the promotion of peace was the 1979 Constitution, which they engineered. The constitution was a creative attempt to correct the institutional deficiencies that led to the civil war. Given the fact that the Mohammed/Obasanjo government was a transitional one, what they actually did was to set a positive vision and guidelines for Nigerians to follow in their drive to build a peaceful and democratic nation-state.

Inclusionary Approach: Economic and Social Development

The Gowon and the Mohammed/Obasanjo era (1966-1979), commonly referred
to as the first military interregnum, was a period of significant economic and
social development. Thanks to the oil boom, these governments were able to
improve the infrastructure and promote education. Under Gowon's 1970 to
1974 development plan, 7,000 kilometers of roads were completed, and by 1979
the available roads had been increased to 95,374 kilometers (half of which were
paved). In September 1976, the government implemented the Universal Primary
Education program, raising the primary schools' population from 3,515,827 to
8,260,189. The secondary school population also rose from 310,054 in 1970 to
826,926 in 1976. In April 1976, the first national television system was set up
with a station in each state.[75]

Inclusionary Approach: Democratic
Legitimacy and Constitutionalism

It is clear that both the Gowon and Mohammed/Obasanjo governments were
unconstitutional and lacked a democratic mandate. It is important to remember
that Nigerians had many good things to say about these governments, however,
especially in comparison to others. Of the two governments, the most difficult to
assess is the Gowon government which lasted for eight years. Indeed the manner in which Gowon came to power was problematic—a bloody coup that was a
revenge against the Igbo. Right from the beginning, Gowon's task of winning
the sympathy of the Igbo seemed remote. Added to this was the effect of the
civil war. Above all, Gowon stayed too long in power and actually backed away
from his promise to restore civilian rule. The Mohammed coup became a step
toward forging the much more balanced and democratic federation that Nigerians were expecting from Gowon. By handing over power to an elected civilian
government, the Mohammed/Obasanjo government became a truly transitional
government. So too was the nine-month government of General Abubakar.
Though it did not stay long enough to engage in a substantive nation-state building project, Abubakar had the wisdom to know that Nigerians were sick and
tired of Hausa-Fulani-dominated military rule. It is widely believed that his decision to speedily restore civilian rule saved Nigeria from sliding into a civil
war.

Conclusion: The Democratic Option

As I have argued before, the democratic approach is the best path to nation-
state building. Alas, lack of democratic mandate, poor institutional designs, or
bad leadership has made it nearly impossible for successive governments in

Nigeria to pursue the democratic approach to nation-state building. Even though it may be too soon to lose hope in the current government of Olusegun Obasanjo, I am afraid that we can only be modestly optimistic. To begin with, many Nigerians are not satisfied with the 1999 Constitution of the Fourth Republic. As we shall see, it failed to address the fundamental stateness question. Given his resistance to the call for a National Conference, it is not even clear whether Obasanjo really wants to address the stateness question. Furthermore, he has not made any commitment to the recommendations of the Presidential Committee on the Review of the 1999 Constitution. Even more troublesome is the lack of accountability, the poor state of the economy, and the ethnicization of the government. As Suberu observes, "one of the biggest problems with the Obasanjo government is the lack of accountability. It is a serious problem. We have not been able to impose enough restraint on those who rule us—and this has aggravated the ethnic question. There is lack of pressure on the political leadership to behave in a responsible manner. So you have high levels of corruption in the local, state, and even federal government level." In a chilling reminder of the fate of the Second Republic, Suberu warns, "If we continue to have these same levels of corruption and the economy is mismanaged, the sustainability of democracy will be reduced. The country's survival will be endangered."[76] The problem is not with the government alone, but what one can call the democracy deficit. As Adigun Agbaje said, "It is unfair to score this government because both government and the people do not have the experience in the management of differences in a democratic context. However, if I have to score it, I will put it close to zero. There are all kinds of intrigues from ministers, governors and police personnel. Most importantly, the government is brutal on the people and it has failed to learn."[77]

Notes

1. Article 15(3)(c) and (d) of the 1979 and 1999 Constitutions.
2. Article 14(3).
3. "The composition of the government of a state, a local government council, or any of the agencies of such government or council, and the conduct of the affairs of the government or council or such agencies shall be carried out in such manner as to recognize the diversity of the peoples within its area of authority and the need to promote a sense of belonging and loyalty among all the peoples of the federation" (Article (14)(4) of the 1979 and 1999 Constitutions).
4. Article 21.
5. Articles 17(1) and 15(2).
6. Article 2(1) of the 1979 and 1999 Constitutions.
7. Article 16 of the 1979 and 1999 Constitutions.
8. Article 20 of the 1999 Constitution.
9. Article 14(2)(a) of the of the 1979 and 1999 Constitutions.
10. Ehiedu Iweriebor, "Nigerian Nation Building since Independence," *Nigerian Journal of Policy and Strategy* 5, no. 1 and 2, (June/December 1990): 1-38.

11. Iweriebor, "Nigerian Nation Building."

12. Rotimi Suberu, *Public Policy and National Unity in Nigeria* (Ibadan, Nigeria: Development Policy Center, 1999).

13. Suberu, *Public Policy*, 7.

14. *Regionalization*: creation of new states, LGAs, and chiefdoms, boundary adjustments, and the relocation of the federal capital; *redistributive*: revenue allocation and Federal Character principle; *symbolic*: integrative national symbols, National Youth Service Corps, Unity Schools, national language, direct political education; and *regulatory*: the War of National Unity and the proscription of ethnic political associations and ethnic activists. See Suberu, *Public Policy*.

15. Suberu, *Public Policy*, 83.

16. Suberu, *Public Policy*.

17. Rotimi Suberu, *Federalism and Ethnic Conflict in Nigeria* (Washington, D.C.: United States Institute of Peace Press, 2001).

18. Abu Bah, "Approaches to Nation Building in Post Colonial Nigeria," *Journal of Political and Military Sociology* 32, no. 1 (Summer 2004): 45-60.

19. I should also note the odd case of the short-lived interim national government of Ernest Shonekan.

20. Suberu, *Public Policy*.

21. Quoted in Suberu, *Public Policy*, 69.

22. Interview with Professor J. A. A. Ayoade in Ibadan, August 2002.

23. Iweriebor, "Nigerian Nation Building," 22.

24. This increased the number of states to twenty-one and resolved the bitter wrangling about what constitutes two-thirds of the states in the federation, as occurred during the 1979 presidential elections.

25. The Political Bureau was set up by Babangida in 1986 to provide an objective and in-depth critique of the nation's past political experience and to design a political model for the democratic transition program.

26. Suberu, *Public Policy*.

27. To advance to the national level, a candidate must have also secured nomination at the state level.

28. Bayelsa (South-South), Ebonyi (Southeast), Ekiti (Southwest), Gombe (Northeast), Nasarawa (Middle Belt), and Zamfara (Northwest).

29. Suberu, *Public Policy*.

30. Suberu, *Public Policy*.

31. Also see Federal Republic of Nigeria (FRN), "Federal Character Commission (Establishment, etc.) Decree 1996" (Decree No. 34), Supplement to Official Gazette Extraordinary, No. 70, Vol. 83, December 27, 1996—Part A.

32. Suberu, *Public Policy*.

33. The revised 1981 formula was: equity 40 percent, population 40, social development factor (calculated from direct and inverse primary school enrollment) 15, and internal revenue effort 5.

34. Suberu, *Public Policy*.

35. They were later pardoned by Gowon.

36. Under the Treason and Treasonable Offences Decree, "any person who utters any word, displays anything or publishes any material which is capable of breaking up Nigeria or any part thereof or causing a community or section of thereof to engage in violence against a section of that community or another community, is guilty of treason and liable on conviction to be sentenced to death."

37. Quoted in Suberu, *Public Policy*, 82.

38. Eghosa Osaghae, *Structural Adjustment and Ethnicity in Nigeria* (Uppsala, Sweden: Nordiska Afrikainstitutet, 1995).

39. BBC News, "Nigeria Recovers 'Stolen' Money," November 27, 2003, http://news.bbc.co.uk/2/hi/business/3244092.stm (December 2, 2003).

40. Iweriebor, "Nigerian Nation Building."

41. Quoted in Iweriebor, "Nigerian Nation Building," 20.

42. Richard Joseph, *Democracy and Prebendal Politics in Nigeria: The Rise and Fall of the Second Republic* (New York: Cambridge University Press, 1987).

43. At the time, most of Nigeria's revenue came from the cash crops grown in the Western Region. However, with the discovery of oil in the East, the West started to back away from the derivation argument. The Eastern Region became the new champion of the derivation principle.

44. Nigeria, "Report of the Fiscal Commissioner on Financial Effects of Proposed New Constitutional Arrangement" (Nigeria: Government Printer, 1953).

45. Joint Action Committee of Nigeria (JACON), *Way Forward for Nigeria: Revolution Not Transition*, Publication No. 4 (Lagos, Nigeria: JACON, 1999), 90-91; Federation of Nigeria, *The Constitution of the Federation, 1960*; Federation of Nigeria, "Report by the Resumed Nigeria Constitutional Conference" (held in London, September and October 1958) (Lagos: Federal Government Printer); and Federation of Nigeria, "Report by the Nigeria Constitutional Conference" (held in London, May and June 1957) (Lagos: Federal Government Printer).

46. Federal Republic of Nigeria (FRN), "Report of the Fiscal Review Commission" (Lagos, Nigeria: Federal Ministry of Information Printing Division, 1965).

47. Suberu, *Public Policy*.

48. Larry Diamond, *Class, Ethnicity and Democracy in Nigeria: The Failure of the First Republic* (Syracuse, New York: Syracuse University Press, 1988), 289.

49. Diamond, *Class, Ethnicity and Democracy*.

50. Implicitly, the government made it clear that it would not recognize the election of Alhaji O. S. Adegbenro. Instead, the government committed itself to holding an election in the Western Region—a promise that was later broken.

51. Diamond, *Class, Ethnicity and Democracy*.

52. Diamond, *Class, Ethnicity and Democracy*.

53. The weapons seized were two machine guns, twenty-four tear-gas pistols, several revolvers with some 3000 rounds of ammunition, twenty gas and automatic pistols, fifty cases of explosives, and forty-eight special torchlights. See Diamond, *Class, Ethnicity and Democracy*.

54. Diamond, *Class, Ethnicity and Democracy*.

55. Diamond, *Class, Ethnicity and Democracy*, 125.

56. During the 1979 presidential election, Shagari won a plurality of votes and at least 25 percent of the votes in twelve of the nineteen states. However, to avoid runoff elections, Articles 125 and 126 of the 1979 Constitution required that a candidate must gain a plurality of votes and at least 25 percent of the votes in two-thirds of the nineteen states of the federation. To Awolowo, and the opposition at large, it seemed that Shagari had stolen the election.

57. Joseph, *Democracy and Prebendal Politics*.

58. Larry Diamond, "Nigeria: Pluralism, Statism, and the Struggle for Democracy," in *Democracy in Developing Countries: Africa*, eds. Diamond et al. (Boulder, Colorado: Lynne Rienner Publishers, 1988), 33-91.

59. As expected, these gains were contested in the courts, but very few were overturned.

60. Diamond, "Nigeria."

61. Iweriebor, "Nigerian Nation Building."

62. Iweriebor, "Nigerian Nation Building."

63. Diamond, "Nigeria."

64. Federal Republic of Nigeria (FRN), "National Youth Service Corps Decree 1973" (Decree No. 24), Supplement to Official Gazette Extraordinary, No. 28, vol. 60, May 22, 1973—Part A, and Suberu, *Public Policy*.

65. The decision to create Abuja and make it the new capital of Nigeria was made in 1976. However, Abuja was not opened until 1991.

66. Quoted in Suberu, *Public Policy*, 31. Also see: Federal Republic of Nigeria (FRN), "Report of the Committee on the Location of the Federal Capital of Nigeria" (Lagos, Nigeria, December 1975), and Federal Republic of Nigeria (FRN), "Government Views on the Report of the Panel on the Location of the Federal Capital" (Lagos: Federal Ministry of Information, 1976).

67. Alvan Ikoku was a prominent educator from eastern Nigeria.

68. See: Federal Republic of Nigeria (FRN), "Federal Military Government's View on the Report of the Boundary Adjustment Commission" (Lagos: Federal Ministry of Information Printing Division, 1976) and "Federal Military Government Views on the Report of the Panel on Creation of States" (Lagos: Federal Ministry of Information Printing Division, 1976).

69. Interview with Dr. Rotimi Suberu in Ibadan, August 2002.

70. See Appendix II to the 1979 Constitution.

71. Federal Republic of Nigeria (FRN), "Constitution (Distributive Pool Account) Decree 1970" (Decree No. 13), Supplement to Official Gazette No. 12, vol. 57, March 12, 1970-Part A, and Suberu, *Public Policy*.

72. Federal Republic of Nigeria (FRN), "Off-Shore Oil Revenue Decree 1971" (Decree No. 9), Supplement to Official Gazette Extraordinary, No. 15, vol. 58, March 31, 1971—Part A.

73. See Federal Republic of Nigeria (FRN), "Government View on the Report of the Technical Committee on Revenue Allocation" (Lagos: Federal Ministry of Information, 1978).

74. Suberu, *Public Policy*, and Iweriebor, "Nigerian Nation Building."

75. Iweriebor, "Nigerian nation building."

76. Interview with Dr. Suberu in Ibadan, August 2002.

77. Interview with Professor Adigun Agbaje in Ibadan, August 2002.

Chapter 5

Varieties of Institutional Designs in Postcolonial Nigeria

Nigerians have been preoccupied with designing institutions that would make democracy work and hold their multiethnic country together. These efforts are evident in the numerous constitutions that have been designed since independence. Though the constitutions tend to repeat most of the provisions of the previous ones, each constitution is characterized by new institutional arrangements aimed at promoting democracy and the nation-state. The first of these arrangements can be traced to the shift from a parliamentary system of government and federalism with strong regions during the First Republic to a consociational presidential system of government and a centralized federation during the Second Republic. The second major shift is between the party system of the aborted Third Republic and the previous constitutions. While the First and Second Republics were multiparty systems, the aborted Third Republic was supposed to be a state sponsored two-party system. As for the Fourth Republic, there were strong pressures to zone the country and rotate the top political offices at each level of the federation. If rotation had been institutionalized, it would have been a major shift from all the previous constitutions.[1] Nigerians are still calling for a national conference to negotiate the basis of their mutual co-existence. As Oyeleye Oyediran passionately states:

> I hold a very strong view on the National Conference. Unlike some of my colleagues and many Nigerians, I am not talking of a Sovereign National Conference. I do not want the question of "sovereignty" to be the stumbling block. All I want is representatives of the various groups in Nigeria—whether it is representatives of local government areas, ethnic groups, senatorial units or zones, it does not matter to me. Whatever we decide should be the basis for representation. I want Nigerians to sit together and talk. With the exception of the Constituent Assembly of 1978, I do not think we have had anything like this, Nigerians sitting together and deciding. This is what many of the people from the Northern areas are unhappy about. If people want to say, we have had it and let each group go it alone, then so be it. It might be unfortunate, but if the majority of people say that is what they want, so be it.[2]

There are strong campaigns, especially from the minorities, for a political structure that would give greater autonomy to states and ethnic groups. For them, the national conference should not only be an opportunity to talk. It should also ensure that each group gains "control over its resources, whether they exist on land or offshore. Each group must be able to govern itself according to its customs and the wishes of its people, and should be able to secede from the federation if the group so mandates. Police and military must be decentralized, with each ethnic group or political region having control over its own force."[3]

Looking at the postcolonial history of Nigeria, it is clear that *constitution making* and *constitution breakdown* have become a never-ending and problematic endeavor. As Ibrahim Babangida himself acknowledges, "The persistent, destabilizing interruption and disruption of . . . [the] orderly political evolution by bad politics, bad governments and reactive military interventions is a form of national self-defeat."[4] In her study of the dynamics of constitution making in Nigeria, Mottoh-Migan attributed the cycle of constitution breakdown to the conduct of the military, constitution makers, and operators of the constitution.[5] I argue that the cycle of constitution breakdown and constitution making brings to light the two dimensions in Nigeria's political development—the failures and the creativity of Nigerians in addressing the complex problem of democratization and nation-state building. Very often, constitutions are made in bad faith. Equally, constitution making has been used as a mechanism to prolong dictatorship. Many Nigerians have come to the cynical conclusion that constitution making is a way to outmaneuver other Nigerians in the struggle for power and resources. As I. B. Bello-Imam laments, "The whole idea of constitution making in Nigeria is simply to decide who gets what and how much of it."[6] Sadly, like Babangida, Nigerians eventually outwit themselves by plunging the whole country into chaos. From a more positive point of view, however, Nigerians have shown courage and creativity in their effort to live together. They have recognized that the classical model of liberal democracy and the notion of the nation-state need to be modified to fit the multiethnic character of the postcolonial multiethnic nation-state. As I have argued before, democratization and nation-state building are intertwined processes that have been plagued by the problem of ethnicity. Indeed, the pioneers of the Nigerian constitutions have taken into account this interconnection. Though an adequate solution to ethnicity has not yet been found, all the Nigerian constitutions have tried to come up with institutional arrangements to mitigate the negative effects of ethnicity on multiparty democracy and the nation-state.

The First Republic: Regionalism and the Making of the War of National Unity

The First Republic was associated with two of the most remarkable moments in the history of Nigeria. First, it marked the inception of Nigeria as a sovereign democratic nation-state. Second, and ironically, its demise also set the scene for the prolonged involvement of the military in politics and the virtual collapse of the nation-state during the Nigerian Civil War. Even before independence, Nigerians had foreseen the war and the breakdown of democracy. The question then was how to sustain democracy and avoid a war.

Features of the 1960 and 1963 Constitutions

As is evident in the 1960 and 1963 Constitutions, the pioneers of the First Republic saw a parliamentary democracy and federalism with autonomous regions as the main strategy for promoting democracy and peace in Nigeria.[7] Notwithstanding the increased significance of the central government, it was hoped that regionalism would maintain the balance of power and peace among the three major ethnic groups. The 1960 Constitution defined Nigeria as a federation consisting of "regions" and a federal territory; namely: Northern Nigeria, Western Nigeria, Eastern Nigeria, and the Federal Territory of Lagos.[8] Mid-Western Nigeria was created (out of Western Nigeria) in 1963, in accordance with Article 4 of the 1960 Federal Constitution, which made provision for the creation of new regional units.[9]

Both the 1960 and 1963 Federal Constitutions guaranteed the fundamental human rights that are essential for the operation of a democratic regime. As outlined in chapter III of the 1960 and 1963 Constitutions, these rights included freedom of expression, freedom of conscience, freedom of assembly and association, freedom of movement, and freedom from discrimination. The 1960 and 1963 Constitutions also called for a democratically elected legislature and a parliamentary system of government at both the federal and regional levels of government, independent from one another. At the federal level, executive powers were exercised by the prime minister and his council of ministers, which were collectively responsible to Parliament.[10] Parliament consisted of a House of Representatives, which was the real law making body, and a weak Senate. There was also a governor general, who was the ceremonial head of state representing the British Monarch. The 1963 Republican Constitution replaced the governor general with a ceremonial president, who was directly elected by the people of Nigeria. In the regions too, executive power was exercised by the premier and the executive council, which were collectively responsible to the legislative houses of the regions. The governors were required to act according to the advice of the premier and the executive council of their respective regions. The governor was responsible for appointing the premier and other members of the executive council from members of the legislative house, who commanded majority support in the House of Assembly.[11]

The constitutions of the First Republic also delineated the legislative powers of the federal and regional governments into an exclusive and a concurrent legislative list. Although the regions could not legislate on items in the exclusive list, the regional legislatures were given residual legislative powers. As stated in Article 64(5) of the 1960 Federal Constitution and Article 69(5) of the 1963 Constitution: "subject to the provisions of subsection (4), nothing in this section shall preclude the legislature of a Region from making laws with respect to any matter that is not included in the Exclusive Legislative List."[12] The exclusive list consisted of around forty-three items such as archives, aviation, bills of exchange, copyright, customs, defense, immigration, certain higher educational institutions, mines, shipping, railways, trunk roads, measurements, and federal constitutional matters.[13] The concurrent legislative list, which was open to both the federal and regional governments, included around twenty-eight items such as arms, bankruptcy, census, fingerprinting, higher education, labor, prisons, public order, scientific research, statistics, and traffic. Some of the residual issues included important subjects such as agriculture, primary and secondary education, local government, and water supply. In general, the regions had the power to make laws for the peace, order, and good government of their respective territories. Essentially, this gave the regions a significant degree of autonomy in running their affairs. The central government was granted the power to make laws for the peace, order, and good government of Nigeria (or any part of the country) on issues outlined in the two legislative lists. With respect to the federal territory, the central government could legislate on any matter, whether or not it was included in the legislative lists.[14]

As a symbol of their autonomy during the First Republic, each of the regions had a constitution, separate from the federal constitution. The regional constitutions had the full force of law within their respective territories. As stated in Article 5(1) of the 1960 and 1963 Federal Constitutions, "the constitution of each Region shall have the full force of law throughout that Region and if any other law is inconsistent with that constitution, the provisions of that constitution shall prevail." Article 5(2) further stated, "the constitution of a Region may be altered only by a law enacted by the legislature of that Region." It is also interesting to note that while the 1960 Federal Constitution failed to emphasize Nigerian identity, each of the three regional constitutions began with a preamble that asserted their regional identity. The 1963 Constitution tried to correct this by introducing a preamble to the federal constitution that took some note of Nigerian unity and slightly modified the preambles of the regional constitutions.[15]

Furthermore, each region had an independent judiciary, civil service, police force, and constitutionally guaranteed sources of revenue.[16] The regional High Courts were vested with the powers of a superior court. As stated in Article 51(3) of the 1963 Constitution of Eastern Nigeria, for example, "the High Court of the Region shall be a superior court of record and, save as otherwise provided by any law in force in the Region, shall have all the powers of such a court." Regions were also allowed to establish regional courts of appeal to hear certain kinds of cases from their High Courts. The Federal Supreme Court was mainly charged with adjudicating disputes between the federation and the regions or between regions, and hearing appeals from the High Court of a region.[17] The

1960 Constitution also reaffirmed the regionalization of the civil service, which was introduced in the 1954 Constitution. The independence of the regional civil service was clearly demonstrated during the period of emergency rule in the Western Region in 1962. Even though the administrator was directly responsible to the prime minister, the civil service of the Western Region was not accountable to the federal civil service commission. The management of the regional civil service was under the control of the regional service commission as stipulated in the regional constitution. Although numerous bodies were set up to facilitate the harmonious implementation of policies, they were only forums for consultation between the central and the various regional governments.[18]

Another mark of regional autonomy was the existence of the local government police force and the role of the regions in the organization of the Nigerian police force. Despite the creation of a unified Nigerian police force, the regions were still allowed to maintain local police forces. According to Article 98(7) of the 1960 Federal Constitution and Article 105(7) of the Federal 1963 Constitution, "nothing . . . shall prevent the legislature of a region from making provision for the maintenance by any native authority or local government authority established for a province or any part of a province of a police force for employment within that province." In fact, both the Northern and Western Regions maintained their own local government police forces, which were responsible for enforcing local by-laws and regulations.[19] The existence of such forces greatly strengthened the powers of the regional government.[20] At the national level, the regions were also given a significant say in the organization of the police force. The 1963 Federal Constitution, for example, called for the establishment of the Nigerian Police Council, which was to consist of a minister of the federal government (serving as a chairman), a minister from each region, and the chairman of the federally appointed Police Service Commission.[21] Under this arrangement, the regions could collectively out-vote the federal government.[22] The council was empowered to make recommendations to the federal government. In turn, the federal government was required to pay serious attention to the recommendations of the council and furnish it with any information pertaining to matters under its supervision. Most importantly, Article 108 stipulated, "the organization and administration of the Nigerian Police Force and all other matters relating thereto (not being matters relating to the use and operational control of the force or the appointment, disciplinary control and dismissal of members of the force) shall be under the general supervision of the Nigerian Police Council." The regional governments also had a say in the appointment as well as dismissal of the police commissioner in their regions.[23]

Another important area for regional autonomy was revenue allocation. Both the 1960 and 1963 Federal Constitutions guaranteed the financial autonomy of the regions by giving them the right over certain kinds of taxes, mining royalties, and a specified share of the distributive pool account (DPA). The taxes included certain kinds of income and property taxes, import duties on motor oils, import and excise duties on tobacco, and export duties from produce, hides, and skins.[24] The federal government was empowered to collect the taxes and return the revenue to the regions, in proportion to their individual contribution.[25] Furthermore, 50 percent of mining royalties and rents were paid back to the region where the minerals (including oil) were extracted, while 30 percent was deposited into the distributive pool account, and the federal government retained just 20 percent.[26]

The 1960 and 1963 Constitutions further guaranteed the autonomy of the regions by entrenching the clauses that underpinned the federal arrangement, most notably the clauses dealing with the legislative powers of the central and regional governments, the executive authority of the regions, the exercise of executive authority of the federation, the office of the president, Parliament, the electoral commission, the Supreme Court, the High Court of the Federal Capital Territory, human rights, public funds, the police, revenue allocation, and boundary adjustment. Under Article 4 of both the 1960 and 1963 Federal Constitutions, an amendment to any of the entrenched clauses would require a two-thirds majority in both houses of the federal legislature and the consent of a majority of the regions.[27]

Finally, the autonomy of the regions was enhanced by their size, and the political strength of their leaders and the parties associated with them. Each of the three major regions, dominated by one of the major ethnic groups, comprised huge populations and territories. Each of the regions successfully established a major political party that was capable of effectively challenging the central government.[28] These parties had full grip over the political, economic, and socio-cultural resources in their regions and were very instrumental in promoting the interests of the dominant ethnic group in their region. The regions were also governed by some of the most powerful political leaders in Nigeria. This is most evident in northern Nigeria where the long-time leader of the NPC, Ahmadu Bello, chose to lead the regional government and sent his deputy to head the central government. So too in eastern Nigeria the NCNC president, Michael Okpara, remained premier of the region instead of taking part in the central government. Also in western Nigeria, notwithstanding his position as the official federal opposition leader, Obafemi Awolowo was strongly involved in the political developments of the region, as evident during the Western Region crisis.

Limitations to Regional Autonomy during the First Republic

Even though the strength of the regions was unquestionable during the First Republic, there were ways in which the central government was able to increase its influence and undermine the autonomy of the regions. To begin with, according to Article 1 of both the 1960 and 1963 Federal Constitutions, the federal constitution "shall have the force of law throughout Nigeria." Furthermore, "if any other law (including the constitution of a region) is inconsistent with . . .

[the federal] constitution . . . [the federal] constitution shall prevail and the other law shall, to the extent of the inconsistency, be void." Federal laws on any issue on the concurrent legislative list were also superior to regional laws. As Article 69(4) of the 1963 Federal Constitution stated, "If any law enacted by the legislature of a Region is inconsistent with any law validly made by Parliament, the law made by Parliament shall prevail and the regional law shall, to the extent of the inconsistency, be void." Parliament was also empowered to legislate on any matter that was incidental or supplementary to items mentioned in the two legislative lists. Together, these provisions indirectly increased the legislative power of the federal government at the expense of the regions.

The 1960 and 1963 Constitutions also required the regions "not to impede or prejudice the exercise of the executive authority of the federation or to endanger the continuance of the federal government in Nigeria."[29] The regions were not allowed to secede, and the federal government was empowered to take temporary action against the regions whenever they endangered the federation. As stated in Article 70 of the 1963 Federal Constitution, "Parliament may at any time make such laws for Nigeria or any part thereof with respect to matters not included in the Legislative Lists as may appear to Parliament to be necessary or expedient for the purpose of maintaining or securing peace, order and good government during any period of emergency." The constitution defined "emergency" as periods when: (a) the federation is at war, (b) each house of Parliament declared that a state of public emergency exists, or (c) each house of Parliament, supported by votes of not less than two-thirds of all the members of the house, declares that democratic institutions are threatened by subversion.[30] However, the constitution did not specify what conditions are deemed subversive to democracy or could lead to a situation of public emergency. Given the volatile nature of politics in Nigeria, this provision compromised the autonomy of the regions and opened the way for mischievous intervention by the federal government, as occurred during the Western Region crisis.

The Collapse of the First Republic and the Making of the Nigerian Civil War

The fundamental problem of the First Republic was that the federation was plagued by structural imbalances that made it unstable. With the exception of Mid-Western Nigeria, the regions were too big and politically powerful. Due to their size and political weight, they saw themselves as self-sufficient units that could do without the rest of the federation. At various points in the history of Nigeria, each of these regions has threatened to secede from the federation. Regional consciousness was further strengthened by the development of a strong regionally based political party in each of the regions. This is well demonstrated by the level of support which the three major parties were able to garner in their respective regions. During the 1961 regional elections, for example, the NPC gained 69 percent of the votes and 94.1 percent of the seats in the North. In the East, the NCNC won 79.2 percent of the votes and 86.2 percent of the seats. Even the internally divided AG was able to win 53 percent of the votes cast and 62.9 percent of the seats in western Nigeria.[31] The problem is that these parties bred a strong sense of regional consciousness and loyalty at the expense of national unity, and thereby opened the way for intense competition among the three dominant ethnic groups for the control of the federal government. As Gowon lamented in his speech marking the end of the civil war, "the collision of three giant regions with pretensions to sovereignty created distrust and fear and led to the tragic conflict now ending."[32]

Another interrelated problem was the size of the Northern Region, which was estimated to encompass 75 percent of the land mass and 60 percent of the population of Nigeria.[33] Accordingly, the North was given a bigger share of the distributive pool account and more than half of the seats in the House of Representatives. According to Article 135 of the 1960 Federal Constitution, 40 percent of the amount in the distributive pool account was allocated to the North, 31 percent to the East, and 24 percent to the West. Under the 1963 Federal Constitution, the North and the East maintained their respective shares; 18 percent went to the West and 6 percent to the newly created Mid-Western Nigeria.[34] Most significantly, the North was accorded 167 of the 312 seats in the House of Representatives, which was the real law-making body.[35] Though in the Senate the regions were equally represented, with twelve seats each, the Senate was not strong enough to check northern domination in the legislature. In fact, the Senate could only delay a bill for up to six months, but could not prevent it from becoming a law.[36] Essentially, this arrangement greatly empowered the Hausa-Fulani, who dominated the North. All they needed to control the federal government was to win the majority of seats in the North and form alliances with a few minorities in at least one of the other regions. They accomplished this with great success. During the 1959 federal elections, for example, the Hausa-Fulani dominated NPC won 60.8 percent of the votes cast and 77 percent of the seats in the North. The AG gained 14.3 percent of the seats, while the NEPU/NCNC alliance got only 4.6 percent of the seats in the North. Even more spectacular was the 1964 federal election in which the NPC won 82 percent of the votes cast and 97 percent of the seats in the North.[37] Consequently, the NPC ruled Nigeria throughout the First Republic. Southerners, who saw this disparity as the product of British gerrymandering, resented it. Awolowo consistently complained about the abnormal structure of the federation which enabled the Hausa-Fulani North to bend the will of the entire federation.[38] As the role of the central government, boosted by rising oil revenue, increased, the problem of uneven access to political power at the center became more acute, culminating in a civil war.

Furthermore, the federal structure did not properly represent the millions of Nigerians who belonged to relatively smaller ethnic groups. Contrary to the wishes of many Nigerians, each region was structured around one of the three major ethnic groups. For the numerous minorities clustered in these regions, access to political power and resources at the regional level of government was just as problematic as their marginalization at the federal level. Unlike the majority groups, the minorities were unable to develop strong political parties to defend their interests. The best attempt to create a minority-dominated party was the Tiv-spearheaded United Middle Belt Congress (UMBC). Despite its popularity in the Tiv areas of northern Nigeria, the party failed to make any significant gains in the northern or federal legislature. The first-past-the-post voting system grossly disadvantaged minority parties. As already noted, the majority parties were able to take far more seats than their actual percentage of the votes. The marginalization of minorities became the source of discontent that is still plaguing Nigeria. The first attempt to rectify this anomaly was the creation of the Mid-Western Region. However, the irony has been that as new states were created to accommodate the minorities, the center, dominated by the majority groups, became stronger.

Ethnically motivated wrangling between the president and the prime minister over their respective powers also plagued the First Republic. As Oyediran recalled, "In 1964, when we were close to breaking up, many people did not know whether to blame Prime Minister Balewa or President Azikewe because we had dual roles and interests. If the one leaned on one side, the other leaned on the opposite side."[39] While the exercise of executive powers was vested in the office of the prime minister and his cabinet, the president was directly elected. Furthermore, Article 34 of the 1963 Federal Constitution referred to the president as the commander-in-chief of the armed forces of the federation.[40] As he had sworn, the President was also expected "to preserve, protect and defend the constitution." President Nnamdi Azikiwe, an Igbo from eastern Nigeria, saw his position as more than a ceremonial one. He actively engaged in the political debates and tried to influence decisions. At times, he even tried to use his office to check the NPC government. Indeed, his office was the only federal arm of government that was not under the control of the NPC. Though he may have been acting as a genuine check to Hausa-Fulani domination, the problem was that the president was supposed to be above party politics (and by implication ethnic politics as well). Even though he gave up the presidency of the NCNC, he was the godfather of the Igbo-dominated NCNC. As Benjamin Nwabueze argued, "It cannot be claimed for Dr. Azikiwe that he was entirely free of tribal bias. Perhaps no one could be, given the emotionally charged tribal atmosphere of Nigerian politics during those years."[41] During the 1964 federal election crisis, Azikiwe sided with the NCNC. His initial refusal to reappoint Prime Minister Abubakar Tafawa Balewa of the NPC on the grounds of election irregularities led to a constitutional crisis during which each of them openly solicited the support of the armed forces.[42] As for Prime Minister Balewa, he was a skillful NPC politician, dedicated to the promotion of Hausa-Fulani interests. Both men called for fundamental constitutional changes that would have effectively eliminated the other. While Azikiwe argued that the president should be accorded executive powers, Balewa advocated the adoption of a one-party system of government in the hope that the NPC would be the main force behind the one-party state.[43]

In terms of sustaining democracy, the emergency powers of the federal government undermined Nigerian democracy. Because the powers were broad and undefined, it was easy for the central government to exploit political crises in the regions, as happened in the Western Region, for the selfish interest of the party and ethnic group in power. Such interventions undermined democratic institutions in the regions, violated human rights, and unknowingly invited the security forces to interfere in political matters. Most importantly, the ease with which the federal government trampled the government of western Nigeria pointedly demonstrated the strength of the federal government. The intervention made it clear to the other dominant ethnic groups that control over their region alone was not enough to protect their interests within the Nigerian federation.

The First Republic manifested two conflicting features that contributed to its breakdown. On the one hand, the regions were centers of enormous power and loyalty which bred a deep sense of autonomy. On the other hand, there were loopholes in the constitutions that made it possible for the central government to undermine the autonomy of the regions and assume a greater role for itself. Because the First Republic was conceptually framed as a federation in which the regions were autonomous, attempts to boost the powers of the federal government were easily seen as encroachment on regional autonomy. Given the fact that the North controlled the federal government, such moves were easily interpreted as attempts to impose Hausa-Fulani domination. The structural imbalance of the federation became the source of animosity among the three dominant groups as well as between the dominant groups and their respective minorities. The animosity accumulated over the years was well manifested during the Major Chukwuma Nzeogwu coup of January 1966 that toppled the First Republic and the counter-coup that ensued in July. Both coups were inspired by ethnicity. Not surprisingly, not only did they end Nigerian democracy, but also contributed to the collapse of the nation-state.

The new military government, led by Major General Ironsi, saw a unitary state as the way to rectify the structural imbalances of the First Republic. The Unification Decree (No. 34) of 1966 stated: "Nigeria shall on 24th May 1966 . . . cease to be a federation and shall accordingly as from that day be a republic, by the name of the Republic of Nigeria, consisting of the whole territory which immediately before that day was comprised in the federation."[44] The decree abolished the regions and downgraded them to provinces under the command of the central government. So too the regional services were replaced with a unified public service under the control of the National Public Service Commission. The military government ended regionalism and initiated a process of centralization in Nigeria. The hope was that centralization would "unite" Nigerians. However, as Sulemanu Takuwa argued in the *New Nigerian* in April 1966, "a Nigerian unitary government does not necessarily unite the people of Nigeria. Especially if one views critically the events that led to the introduction of that desired unitary government." He went on to argue, "Nothing short of 'federal- ism' is good for Nigeria. The federation may be modified, but it must remain."[45]

While the January 1966 coup marked the breakdown of democracy, the vir- tual collapse of the nation-state began with the declaration of Biafran indepen- dence. Both events had their roots in the anomalies of the First Republic. The Biafran Declaration of Independence took particular note of the injustices that had been suffered by easterners at the hands of northerners, and the inability of the federation to do justice to them. The allegations, as articulated in the proc- lamation of Biafran independence, included the "the premeditated murder of over 30,000 . . . innocent men, women and children by Northern Nigerians, the calculated destruction of the property . . . the shameless conversion of 2,000,000 Eastern Nigerians into refugees in their own country."[46] It was further alleged, "the Federation of Nigeria has failed, and has given . . . [easterners] no protec- tion."[47] In his declaration of Biafran independence, Lieutenant Colonel C. Odu- megwu Ojukwu referred to easterners as a people who have been "unfree part- ners" and victims of tribalism and nepotism. Though in his victory speech Gowon attributed the outbreak of the war to the conduct of the Ironsi govern- ment and the opportunistic and exploitative behavior of Ojukwu, it seems to me that the seeds of the war lay in the anomalies of the First Republic and the form of colonial rule that was imposed on Nigeria.

Consociational Presidentialism and the Making of the Second Republic

The breakdown of the First Republic reinvigorated the debate about the federal arrangement. The central question was how to overcome the deficiencies of the First Republic without breaking up the country. Ironsi hoped to solve the prob- lem by simply abolishing regionalism and imposing a unitary state. But as Gowon argued upon his assumption of office on August 1, 1966, Nigerians could not "honestly and sincerely continue in this wise, as the basis of trust and confidence in our unitary system of government has not been able to stand the test of time . . . putting all consideration to test—political, economic, as well as social—the base for unity is not there or is so badly rocked, not only once but several times."[48] In Gowon's view, because of its size and diversity, Nigeria could not be ruled under a unitary form of government, except if it was a dicta- torship. In his address to the ad hoc constitutional conference in September 1966, he presented the delegates with three versions of federalism: "a federation with a strong central government," "a federation with a weak central govern- ment," or "a confederation." Short of these, he challenged them to devise "an entirely new arrangement which will be peculiar to Nigeria and which has not yet found its way into any political dictionary."[49] Gowon strongly promoted the idea of centralized and inclusive federalism. By 1975, when the Constitutional Drafting Committee (CDC) was set up by his successor, federalism was already taken for granted.[50] In his October 18, 1975 inaugural address to the committee, Murtala Mohammed reminded the members that his government was "committed to a federal system of government." The new arrangement, he emphasized, should "eliminate cut-throat political competition based on a system or rules of winner-takes-all." Instead, it should "develop consensus politics and government, based on a community of all interests rather than the interest of sections of the country," even if it meant doing away with political parties.[51]

Features of the 1979 Constitution

The 1979 Constitution replaced the parliamentary system of government with a presidential system and shifted from regionalism to a centralized federal arrangement.[52] To the exclusion of anyone else, the president was "the Head of State, the Chief Executive of the Federation and Commander-in-Chief of the Armed Forces of the Federation."[53] The tenure of the president and the governors of the states was limited to two four-year terms.[54] The House of Representatives was increased to 450 members, elected from single-member constituencies that were carved out on the basis of population criteria.[55] The Senate was to consist of five members from each state and its powers were greatly increased.[56] As stated in article 54(1) of the 1979 Constitution, "the powers of the National Assembly to make laws shall be exercised by bills passed by both the Senate and the House of Representatives." Both houses were empowered to initiate bills as well as to stop a bill from becoming a law. As mandated by the constitution, "where a bill has been passed by the House in which it originated, it shall be sent to the other House; and it shall be presented to the President for assent when it has been passed by that other House and agreement has been reached between the two Houses on any amendment made on it."[57] At the state level, the governor was the chief executive.[58] The constitution also replaced the House of Chiefs with the State Council of Chiefs that was only empowered to advise the governor.[59] At the local level, the constitution called for the establishment of elected local government councils.[60]

Even though federalism was maintained, the 1979 Constitution legitimized the centralization process established by the military regime. To begin with, the 1979 Constitution "legitimized" the division of Nigeria into nineteen states. In contrast to the regions during the First Republic, the states were not given separate constitutions. They were much smaller in size and equally represented in the reformed Senate. Though the constitution tried to discourage further division of the country, it did make provision for the creation of more states if there was a case commanding the overwhelming support of the rest of the nation.[61] The creation of more states not only addressed the structural imbalance in the federation, but also weakened the position of the states vis-à-vis the federal government.

The 1979 Constitution further weakened the states by creating a constitutionally independent third tier of government. Though the states were responsible for establishing local government councils and organizing local elections, the constitution guaranteed the system of local government by democratically elected local government councils.[62] The constitution defined the internal boundaries of the states, the size of their Houses of Assembly, and spelled out the functions of local government councils. Part I of the First Schedule of the 1979 Constitution explicitly listed the state headquarters and local government areas (LGAs) of each of the nineteen states. Article 104 also empowered the Federal Electoral Commission to "divide every state in the federation into such number of state constituencies as is equal to three times the number of federal constituencies within that state."[63] In principle, this meant that the internal boundaries of a state as well as the composition of the House of Assembly could not be altered by the states themselves. Furthermore, the constitution gave local government councils significant duties such as making recommendations on the economic development of their states, collecting rates, issuing radio and television licenses, and constructing and maintaining roads and other public facilities. They were also allowed to participate in the provision of vital social services, such as primary education and health care, and the development of agriculture.[64] Most importantly, Article 149 of the 1979 Constitution guaranteed the local government councils a share of the revenue in the federation account. The creation of an independent third tier of government made it easy for both the federal government and local government councils to sideline the state governments.

In terms of the division of power between the federal and state governments, the 1979 Constitution drastically increased the legislative powers of the federal government at the expense of the states. In fact, the Constitutional Drafting Committee (CDC) recommended a single legislative list with seventy items exclusive to the federal government.[65] The Second Schedule of the 1979 Constitution enumerated no less than sixty-five items in the exclusive legislative list.[66] Among other things, the list included issues of arms, defense, banking, customs, export, external affairs, insurance, railways, taxation, marriages (other than marriages under Islamic and customary law), and traffic on federal trunk roads. It also empowered the federal government to legislate on any matter that was incidental or supplementary to the items in the exclusive list. In contrast, the concurrent legislative list was reduced to twelve items.[67] As in the 1963 Constitution, federal law was superior to state laws with regard to any matter in the concurrent legislative list.[68]

The 1979 Constitution centralized the judicial system. It established a Federal Court of Appeal and a Federal High Court. Furthermore, it did not allow the states to establish their own appeals courts. In addition, it reduced the powers of the state High Courts. However, the state High Courts were given "original jurisdiction to hear and determine any question whether any person has been validly elected to any office or to the membership of any legislative house, or whether the term of office of any person has ceased or the seat of a person in a legislative house has become vacant."[69] The only exceptions to this were cases involving the office of the president or vice-president of the federation, which were left to the Federal High Court. The states were also responsible for appointing the judges of the state courts. According to Article 235 of the 1979 Constitution, "the appointment of a person to the office of Chief Judge of the High Court of a State shall be made by the Governor of the State on the advice of the State Judicial Service Commission subject to the approval of such appointment by a simple majority of the House of Assembly of the State." Furthermore, judges of the state High Courts were to be appointed by "the Governor of the State acting on the recommendation of the State Judicial Service Commission."

The 1979 Constitution also brought the police under the total control of the federal government. It eliminated the Nigerian Police Council as well as the local police. It terminated the advisory role of regional governments and fully empowered the federal government to appoint the chief executives of the Nigerian police force at both the federal and state level. As stated in Article 195(1), "the Inspector-General of Police . . . shall be appointed by the President, and a Commissioner of Police for each State . . . shall be appointed by the Police Service Commission."[70] While the constitution empowered the president to give binding orders to the inspector-general "with respect to the maintenance and security of public safety and public order," the directives of a state governor toward the commissioner of police of the same state were subject to the approval of the federal government. Article 195(4) allowed the commissioner of police of a state to "request that the matter be referred to the President or such Minister of the Government of the Federation as may be authorized in that behalf by the President for his direction."

In terms of revenue generation and allocation, the 1979 Constitution greatly strengthened the position of the federal government vis-à-vis the states. As stated in the exclusive legislative list, the 1979 Constitution granted the federal government exclusive control over the major sectors of the economy such as mines and mineral resources, exports and imports, fishing and fisheries (other than inland waters), and taxes on incomes, profits, and capital gains. Though the federal government was obliged to maintain a distributable pool account (i.e., the federation account) and share the revenue with the states and local government councils, the constitution empowered the National Assembly to prescribe the terms and manner for distributing the revenue.[71] As stated in Article 149(2), "any amount standing to the credit of the Federation Account shall be distributed among the Federal and State governments, and the local government councils in each State, on such terms and manner as may be prescribed by the National Assembly." Practically, this allowed the federal government to take a bigger share of the revenue. In what might be seen as an unconstitutional attempt to delegate the legislative function of the National Assembly, for example, the government of Shehu Shagari established the Presidential Commission on Revenue Allocation, chaired by Dr. Pius Okigbo, to recommend a revenue allocation formula. The commission was asked to examine whether the "federation has adequate revenue to enable it to discharge its functions as laid down in the constitution, [and to] examine the present formula for revenue allocation having regard to such factors as national interest, derivation, population, even development, equitable distribution and the equality of states."[72] The commission allocated 53 percent to the federal government, 30 to the state governments, 10 to local government councils, and 7 to the special fund (i.e., 2.5 percent for the initial development of the Federal Capital Territory [FCT], 2 percent for the special problems of mineral producing areas, 1 percent for continuous ecological problems, and 1.5 percent for the revenue equalizing fund). In terms of the allocation of revenue among the states, 40 percent was on the basis of the minimum responsibility, 40 on population, 15 on social development factor (measured in terms of direct and indirect primary school enrollment), and 5 for internal revenue efforts.[73] Even though the commission greatly increased the share of the center, the federal government tried to take an even bigger slice of the revenue. Under the 1981 Revenue Allocation Act, the federal government took 58.5 percent of the federation account and passed on 31.5 and 10 percent to the states and local government councils, respectively. Not surprisingly, the Bendel state government took the federal government to court. The Supreme Court nullified the 1981 Revenue Allocation Act. The January 1982 Revised Revenue Allocation Act reduced the federal share to 55 and increased the share of the states to 35 percent.[74] Despite the objections of the states, especially those in the oil-producing region, the 1979 Constitution allowed the federal government to drastically increase its share of revenue.

The 1979 Constitution also incorporated the Obasanjo military government's Land Use Decree, which nationalized all the mineral land of Nigeria. According to Article 41(3) of the 1979 Constitution, "the entire property in and control of all minerals, mineral oils and natural gas in, under or upon any land in Nigeria or in, under or upon the territorial waters and the Exclusive Economic Zone of Nigeria shall vest in the government of the Federation and shall be managed in such manner as may be prescribed by the National Assembly." For the minorities, this was a gross violation of their natural right to property. The nationalization policy opened their land to unprecedented exploitation without adequate compensation. Many communities, such as the Ogoni, have been deprived of their farmland and fishing waters, and left without a viable source of living.

The 1979 Constitution and Its Implications for Democracy and the Nation-State

Despite the concentration of power at the center, the states were still significant in the Nigerian federal arrangements. To a large degree, they incarnated the various ethnic groups that were struggling for representation at the center. In

addition, some of them have also been the "oil" that still keeps the Nigerian corporation running. Not surprisingly, the Second Republic was designed as a consociational system. The most significant institutional arrangement of the Second
Republic was the introduction of the Federal Character principle and its application to the election of the president of the federation and the governors of the
states, the composition of the government, political parties, the army, executive
bodies, and the distribution of resources. Given the bitter ethnic rivalry in Nigeria, it was logical that as power shifted from the regions to the federal government so too was it imperative to make the center more inclusive. The Federal
Character principle was meant to ensure that no ethnic or regional group would
be marginalized in the new political arrangement—at the federal, state, or local
government levels. As stated in Article 14(3) of the 1979 Constitution: "the
composition of the government of the federation or any of its agencies and the
conduct of its affairs shall be carried out in such manner as to reflect the Federal
Character of Nigeria and the need to promote national unity, and also to command national loyalty thereby ensuring that there shall be no predominance of
persons from a few states or a few ethnic or other sectional groups in the government or in any of its agencies." Article 14(4) further stated: "The composition of the government of a state, a local government council, or any of the
agencies of such government or council, and the conduct of the affairs of the
government or council or such agencies shall be carried out in such manner as to
recognize the diversity of the peoples within its area of authority and the need to
promote a sense of belonging and loyalty among all the peoples of the federation."

     In order to realize the Federal Character principle, Articles 125 and 126 of
the 1979 Constitution required a presidential candidate to obtain a majority of
votes with "not less than one-quarter of the votes cast at the election in each of
at least two-thirds of all the States in the federation" in order to be elected. Article 135(3) of the 1979 Constitution required the president to "appoint at least
one Minister from each State, who shall be an indigene of such state." Furthermore, Article 203(2)(b) stipulated that members of the executive committee or
other governing body of political parties should "belong to different States not
being less in number than two-thirds of all the States comprising the Federation." Political parties were also required to maintain a physical presence in all
parts of the country and avoid displaying ethnic or regional symbols. According
to Article 197 of the 1979 Constitution, "The composition of the officer corps
and other ranks of the armed forces of the Federation shall reflect the Federal
Character of Nigeria." The constitution empowered the National Assembly to
establish a body "which shall have power to ensure that the composition of the
armed forces of the Federation . . . reflect the Federal Character of Nigeria."[75]
The Federal Character principle also applied to the composition of the federal
executive bodies.[76] Overall, the 1979 Constitution created structural arrangements to ensure that the governing institutions would reflect the ethnic and regional diversity of the country.

If it had been properly applied, the Federal Character principle could have greatly promoted democracy and national integration in Nigeria. On the side of democratization, it could have eliminated the winner-takes-all fear that is associated with multiparty politics in divided societies. By recognizing that the country is an amalgamation of numerous ethnic groups and making them feel a sense of belonging in the country, Nigerians would have also created an environment that was much more conducive to national integration. By building it into the constitutions, the Federal Character principle gave Nigerians a vision of tolerance and committed them to inclusive politics. In this sense, the Federal Character principle simultaneously contributed to democratization and nation-state building.

Apart from the Federal Character principle, the 1979 Constitution also outlined certain political, economic, social, and educational objectives aimed at promoting democracy, social justice, and national integration. Article 14(1), for example, committed the Nigerian state to the principles of democracy and social justice. Article 15(2) required the state to actively encourage national integration and prohibit "discrimination on the grounds of place of origin, sex, religion, status, ethnic or linguistic association." Article 16(1)(a) of the constitution also called for the control of the "national economy in such a manner as to secure the maximum welfare, freedom and happiness of every citizen on the basis of social justice and equality of status and opportunity." The Nigerian state was also required to ensure suitable employment for the citizens, humane conditions of work, health care, and equal pay for equal work. The 1979 Constitution committed the state to the eradication of illiteracy and called on the government to provide, whenever possible, free education at all levels.

The 1979 Constitution also introduced a code of conduct for public officers and established the Code of Conduct Bureau. Public officers were prohibited from placing themselves in a position where their personal interest would conflict with their duties. Furthermore, they were forbidden from taking bribes, keeping foreign bank accounts, or abusing their offices. They were also required to declare their assets and liabilities.[77] Given the abuse of power that characterized the First Republic, it was hoped that the code of conduct would instill some discipline in Nigerian leaders.

Shortcomings of the 1979 Constitution and the Collapse of the Second Republic

Despite the vision of integration and democratic governance embodied in the 1979 Constitution, it would be naïve to ignore the shortcomings of the Second Republic. The irony is that the Federal Character principle, which was intended to be a shield against marginalization, was actually transformed into an institutionalized form of discrimination against other Nigerians, who happened to be living away from their ancestral homes. The application of the principle in the distribution of socially valuable resources meant that Nigerians could only enjoy full citizenship in their own part of the country—in their ancestral homes where they were accorded the status of an indigene.[78] The anomalies in the application of the Federal Character principle became even more evident in the growing campaigns for the creation of new states and LGAs, especially in areas dominated by the majority ethnic groups, all with the aim of maximizing their access to federal revenue (see tables A.11, A.12, and A.13). In addition to this institutionalized form of discrimination, corruption and lack of good faith on the part of the political leadership during the Shagari government transformed the Federal Character principle into a divisive force—contrary to what it was intended to be. To begin with, the election that brought Shagari to power was marred by fraud and irregularities that violated the spirit of consociationalism embodied in the Federal Character principle. Even worse was his reelection for a second term in 1983.

The breakdown of the Second Republic can be traced to institutional deficiencies of the 1979 Constitution and the conduct of the political leaders, which promoted ethnic and political violence. By the time the military intervened, the Shagari government had lost its legitimacy in the eyes of many Nigerians, especially in the South. Rightly, Awolowo predicted that the NPN's 1983 election victory would only last for a short time. Indeed, the 1983 elections were fraudulent and the Federal Electoral Commission (FEDECO) was controlled by the Hausa-Fulani dominated NPN. Consequently, the courts were overwhelmed and incapable of properly dealing with the numerous cases of election irregularities brought before them. Worst of the all, the judges too were drawn into the partisan struggles, as reflected in the contradictory rulings handed down. In addition, corruption, misappropriation of government money, and neglect of the economy reached a new height under the Shagari government. Given the tradition of military rule, these were inviting conditions for a coup.

Two-Party Democracy and the Aborted Third Republic

The 1989 Constitution, which was intended to lead to the Third Republic, came into being against the backdrop of a bitter experience with multiparty democracy as well as military rule. As noted earlier, both the First and Second Republics were plagued by political violence that pitted one ethnic group against another. While Nigerians were eager to restore democracy, they were also concerned about the violence associated with multiparty politics. The desire to prevent sectional violence became a central consideration in the designing of the 1989 Constitution.[79] The foundation of the 1989 Constitution was laid by the Political Bureau, which was set up by General Babangida to recommend a political program for Nigeria. As Babangida noted during the bureau's inauguration on January 13, 1986, "in addition to guiding, monitoring, analyzing and documenting the national political debate," the bureau was charged with providing "an objective and in-depth critique of . . . [the country's] past political experience in order to serve as background information for the debate . . . [and a] blueprint of a new political model (or models) for the consideration of the administration."[80] The bureau, however, redefined its functions to include a far more encompassing review of the Nigerian political order.[81]

In its report, the Political Bureau ruled out the idea of dyarchy or triarchy, as suggested by some who sympathized with military rule.[82] In particular, it rejected the argument that military participation in government would put an end to coups. It also recommended that the role of traditional leaders should be confined to local government affairs alone. Even at the local government level, chiefs should not be given legislative, executive, or judicial functions. As for the form of government, the bureau noted that many Nigerians supported the presidential system, but cautioned that this "may be due to the fact that Nigerians have forgotten or do not know what [the] parliamentary form of government is."[83] On the issue of state creation, the bureau was divided on whether to maintain the existing nineteen states or add a few more states (anywhere between two to six). The Political Bureau reaffirmed the merits of federalism. As it argued, "although we appreciate the expression of the sense of structural alienation, and the manifest need to correct the ills of certain aspects of the existing system, we do not find any compelling merit in the case for confederalism or in the case for a unitary system of government for Nigeria. In fact, we do not see any other accommodating and healthier arrangement for Nigeria than the continuation of the system of federalism."[84] However, the bureau argued for the introduction of a unicameral legislature at all levels of the federation. In its view, the legislature should also be informed of the ways in which the laws are executed. It argued that a unicameral assembly would be more likely to act as a check on the powers of the executive. It recommended that the federal legislature should consist of 301 deputies, one from each of the recommended 301 LGAs. The state assemblies were to consist of three representatives from each of the LGAs within each state. Essentially, this meant the rejection of the population criterion for representation in the legislative bodies. The bureau also recommended the establishment of a National Commission on Political Parties and Elections, which would act as neutral umpire and oversee elections and the activities of the parties. Most significantly, the bureau favored a two-party system in which membership would be open to all Nigerians. It recommended a single five-year term for the executive and members of the legislature at both the federal and state levels, and three years for local government councils.

In July 1987, the federal military government announced a detailed program for transition to democratic civilian rule. Among other things, the program called for the establishment of a National Electoral Commission, a Constitutional Review Committee, and the holding of non-partisan local government elections in 1987. In 1988, the program envisaged the establishment of a National Population Commission, a Code of Conduct Bureau, a Code of Conduct Tribunal, a Constituent Assembly, and termination of the Structural Adjustment

Program. In 1989, the constitution was to be promulgated, the ban on party politics lifted, the two registered political parties unveiled, and partisan local government elections conducted. In 1990, elections for state legislative and executive offices were to be held, and the elected officials were to assume their duties. A census and local government elections were to be held in 1991. In 1992, the military was to hand over power to an elected president, after the National Assembly election, the convening of the National Assembly, and the presidential election.[85]

In September 1987, the government set up a Constitutional Review Committee (CRC) to reexamine the 1979 Constitution. The CRC submitted its report in February 1988. The Constituent Assembly was established in April 1988 to deliberate on the draft constitution and make recommendations to the ruling Armed Forces Ruling Council (AFRC). However, even before the Constituent Assembly had the chance to deliberate on the draft constitution, the Babangida government had already predetermined the basic framework of the 1989 Constitution. As Babangida categorically pointed out during his May 11, 1988 inaugural address to members of the Constituent Assembly:

> The Assembly should not indulge itself in the fruitless exercise of trying to alter the agreed ingredients of the Nigerian political order, such as federalism, presidentialism, the non-adoption of any religion as [a] state religion, and the respect and observance of fundamental human rights . . . the two party system, the ban or disqualification placed on certain persons from participation in politics and belief in basic freedoms. . . . Your job is to improve on these agreed political issues and not to change them.[86]

As such, areas with the best possibilities for significant and novel arrangements in the 1989 Constitution were "no-go areas" for the Constituent Assembly. By adopting such a position, the Constituent Assembly was reduced to a discussion group and a rubber-stamp body for what the military had already decided.

Features of the 1989 Constitution

The 1989 Constitution retained most of the features of the 1979 Constitution. The most significant difference between the 1989 Constitution and the 1979 Constitution was the party system. While the 1979 Constitution did not limit the number of political parties, the 1989 Constitution allowed only two political parties. As article 220(1) of the 1989 Constitution stated: "There shall be only two political parties in the Federation." These parties were to be created and monitored by the National Electoral Commission. The 1989 Constitution empowered Parliament to set the maximum amount of money any individual could contribute to a political party.[87] The two-party system was a radical structural change aimed at de-emphasizing ethnic and other sectional differences in Nigerian politics. Essentially, it created a framework that forced Nigerians to embrace other Nigerians.[88]

Apart from the party system, the 1989 Constitution only made modest changes to the overall institutional arrangement. Like the previous constitution, it incorporated the states and LGAs created by the military regime. The constitution also created an additional five federal executive bodies.[89] In some ways, the constitution increased the powers of the president. For example, it empowered the president to appoint members of federal executive bodies. However, the 1989 Constitution did not require the approval of the Senate.[90] The 1989 Constitution also allowed the president, in consultation with the National Defense Council, to deploy the armed forces for combat duties outside the country whenever he believed that the national security was endangered.[91] The 1989 Constitution raised the bar for the Federal Character requirement for the election of the president and governors. In addition to a majority vote, Articles 132 and 177 of the 1989 Constitution now required a candidate to obtain "not less than one-third of the votes cast at the election in each of at least two-thirds of all the states of the federation."[92]

The composition of the National Assembly and control over local government was also modified. The Senate was to consist of three members from each state and one person from the Federal Capital Territory (FCT); and the House of Representatives was increased to 453 members.[93] Unlike the 1979 Constitution, the federal government was now responsible for the establishment of LGAs and the conduct of local government council elections.[94] The 1989 Constitution also called for an elected chairman and vice-chairman of local government councils.

The 1989 Constitution permanently disqualified persons convicted of any crime that involved dishonesty from seeking elected office.[95] According to Article 64(1)(d), for example, "no person shall be qualified for election to the Senate or House of Representatives—if he has been convicted and sentenced by a court of law or tribunal established by law for an offense involving dishonesty or he has been found guilty of a contravention of the code of conduct." In terms of the political objectives, the 1989 Constitution added a few more, such as requiring the Nigerian state to protect civil liberties, ensure efficient functioning of government services, and promote national prosperity. Among other things, Article 24 of the 1989 Constitution required citizens to abide by the constitution, protect and preserve public property, help enhance the good name of the country, respect the dignity and religion of other Nigerians, contribute to the well-being of the community where they reside, abstain from any activity detrimental to the general welfare of other citizens, ensure proper upbringing of children, participate in the democratic process, render assistance in the maintenance of law and order, and pay their taxes.

The 12 June 1993 Presidential Election and Its Implications for Democracy and the Nation-state

Since the 1989 Constitution was not fully implemented, the most important legacy of the aborted Third Republic was the impasse surrounding the 12 June 1993 presidential election. The 1989 Constitution was abandoned at the very end of the transition program. Rightly, the period dating from the local government elections of December 12, 1987, to the annulment of the 12 June 1993 presidential election has been dubbed the "aborted Third Republic." In a way, this is to recognize the existence of some democratic institutions and lament their abrogation. Even though the military regime was in full control of the federal executive arm of government and the country at large, there were elected officials at all other layers of government. As Babangida boasted at the time of his withdrawal from power on August 17, 1993:

> Under the platform of the two national political parties, Nigeria established democratic government in 593 Local Government Areas in order to bring government closer to the vast majority of our population. With that grass-roots level of government established, we confidently moved on to the State level. After successful governorship primaries, we conducted the elections of the Governors and the members of the State Assemblies. These representatives of their respective constituencies have been, for the past two years, wrestling with the intricate process of democratic governance in the 30 States of the federation. . . . On 4 July 1992, successful nationwide elections were conducted into the National Assembly (Senate and House of Representatives). . . . Accordingly, this esteemed Assembly came into being after its inauguration on 5 December, 1992. . . . We have . . . achieved well over 95 percent of our democratic project.[96]

The would-be Third Republic remained a project that failed to mature precisely because the Hausa-Fulani dominated military government was not honest in conducting the transition program. To begin with, the 12 June 1993 presidential election took place in an environment of deceit and confrontation. While the civic groups, supported by the international community, were determined to see the restoration of civilian rule, the military government was reluctant to hand over power. On several occasions, Babangida made numerous promises loaded with deceitful qualifications. In 1986, for example, he vowed that his "administration will not stay a day longer than it is absolutely necessary." In 1987, he promised Nigerians that the military would disengage in 1992, "all things being equal." Even after annulling the August 1, 1992 presidential primaries, Babangida promised, "it is still the resolve of this military administration to fully make good its promise" of handing power to a democratically elected civilian government.[97] Contrary to the promises, Babangida tried to stay in power for as long as he could. In fact, it is believed that he masterminded the Association for a Better Nigeria (ABN), led by Arthur Nzeribe, which on June 4, 1993, sought a court injunction from the Abuja High Court to postpone the presidential election until 1997. On June 10, 1993, the Abuja High Court, presided over by Justice Bassey Ikpeme, ordered the National Electoral Commission (NEC) to cancel the presidential election scheduled for June 12, 1993 on the grounds of corruption. However, the NEC ignored the injunction and went ahead with the election as scheduled. Even after counting got underway, attempts were made to use the judicial system to halt the process. This led to conflicting court rulings to suspend the vote counting and others that called for the continuation of counting. On June 15, 1993, the ABN obtained a court order from the Abuja High Court prohibiting the NEC from releasing further election results. On June 16, the NEC suspended the announcement of election results. The Abuja court order was countered by the High Courts of Lagos, Ibadan, and Benin, which ordered NEC to immediately publish the results; and the NEC took the case to the Kaduna Court of Appeal.[98]

The biggest blow came on June 23, 1993, the day the hearing on the NEC's appeal was to begin at the Kaduna Court of Appeal. Instead of allowing the appeal to go ahead, the military government suspended the NEC, nullified all judicial proceedings on the presidential election and revoked all relevant decrees relating to the transition program. During his national broadcast on June 26, 1993, Babangida defended the annulment of the presidential election. He accused the parties of using an excessive amount of money, over 2.1 billion Nairas, during the elections and alleged that the presidential candidates would have a conflict of interest with the government. He concluded: "to continue action on the basis of the 12 June 1993 presidential election, and to proceed to proclaim and swear in a President who encouraged a campaign of divide and rule amongst our various ethnic groups, would have been detrimental to the survival of the Third Republic."[99] To further complicate the transition process, Babangida immediately lifted the ban on all those previously banned from participating in politics, with the exception of those with criminal records.[100] He also stipulated new requirements for contesting the presidency.[101] Babangida was immediately slapped with condemnations and sanctions from western powers. At home, he was confronted by the Campaign for Democracy (CD), which brought together forty pro-democracy and human rights organizations under the leadership of Beko Ransome-Kuti, president of the Committee for Defense of Human Rights (CDHR). The CD engaged in civil disobedience and mass action intended to make the country ungovernable, and thereby force the government to respect the election results.

Despite the sanctions and protests, Babangida managed to deny Nigerians their well-deserved democracy. As the stalemate continued, some of the civilian politicians came to accept the military verdict on the 12 June 1993 presidential election. In fact, a tripartite committee comprising representatives of the military government, the National Republican Convention (NRC), and Social Democratic Party (SDP) agreed that Babangida should instead hand over power to a civilian-dominated Interim National Government (ING) no later than August 27, 1993. While the civilian politicians rationalized the ING as a pragmatic nonviolent means of ousting the military, the pro-democracy movement rightly saw it as a de facto continuation of military dictatorship. The installation of the ING on August 26, 1993 provoked more demonstrations.

Notwithstanding the failure of the aborted Third Republic, from the perspective of institutional design, the 1989 Constitution was a significant lesson in the political development of Nigeria. Though the North-South regional divide did not totally disappear, the two-party system weakened the tie between ethnic/regional affiliation and political parties. For the first time, Nigerians had no options but to vote in significant numbers for candidates and parties that were not strongly affiliated with their ethnic groups. Despite the low turnout during the 12 June 1993 presidential election, both parties gained votes that were fairly spread across the country.[102] In fact, only 62 percent of the votes gained by the SDP, which was perceived to be a southern party, came from the South. So too for the NRC, which was considered a northern party, only 56 percent of its total votes came from the North. Chief Moshood Abiola, the SDP candidate, secured at least one-third of the votes in all but two states (Sokoto and Kebbi). Even the NRC candidate, Bashir Tofa, who lost in most states, was able to win northern as well as southern states, especially in the minority areas. In fact, the NRC scored its highest votes in Rivers state, which is in the South-South zone (see tables A.8 and A.9). Compared to previous elections this was a remarkable shift in the voting pattern of Nigerians.[103] In addition to the distribution of votes, Abiola's background as a Yoruba from the South and a Muslim provided a golden opportunity to bridge the regional, ethnic, and religious divides in Nigeria.

The 1989 Constitution was a failure because it was grossly violated by the very government that created it. Among other things, the breakdown of the 1989 Constitution can be attributed to the dishonesty associated with the Babangida transition program, the politicization and corruption of the military, the divisions among the civilian politicians, ethnicity, and the materialistic nature of Nigerian politics. The conduct of the 12 June 1993 presidential election not only dealt a blow to Nigerian democracy but also reinvigorated ethnic rivalry and raised new doubts about national integration. As *Africa Watch* pointed out in August 1993:

> The tragedy of the present crisis is that Nigerian citizens, who in the election seemed to have overcome a legacy of ethnic conflict by crossing ethnic and regional barriers to vote for Mr. Abiola have been forced once again to narrow their sights and put their ethnic identities first, rather than their citizenship as Nigerians. . . . In the past few weeks, tens of thousands of Nigerians have fled the cities for their home villages, fearing the outbreak of widespread ethnic violence. Southern rage has been ignited, and anti-Hausa sentiments are increasingly given [voice]. In the North, Hausa who supported Mr. Abiola have been stung by the recent anti-Hausa backlash and withdrawing back to their ethnic and regional identities.[104]

The annulment of the election and the different reactions of the various ethnic groups around the country showed that ethnicity was still a very thorny issue in Nigeria. Even though Abiola gained a majority of votes in nearly all parts of Nigeria, opposition to the annulment of the election was mainly restricted to the Yoruba-dominated southwestern states (Lagos, Ogun, Ondo, Osun, and Oyo states).[105] In addition, many non-Yoruba politicians, including Abiola's running mate, Baba Kingibe, withdrew their support for the restoration of the 12 June 1993 presidential mandate. In his March 21, 1994, letter to Abiola, Kingibe wrote: "For the vast majority of our country men and women, the restoration of 'June 12' is no longer on the cards."[106] He alleged that Abiola's crusade for the restoration of the 12 June 1993 presidential mandate had more a personal, at best limited sectional, character. He went on to remind Abiola that the nationwide party machinery and movement that had won them the 12 June 1993 presidential election was no longer in place. In fact, Kingibe himself as well as other SDP figures, such as Jonathan Zwingina, Lateef Jakande, Ebenezer Babotope, Jim Nwobodo, Abubakar Rimi, and Solomon Lar were already involved with the Abacha government. The Yoruba within the NRC, who were willing to concede victory to Abiola, were quickly accused of promoting ethnicity. Governors of the NRC from the North and East denounced Abiola and tried to mobilize ethnic and regional opposition against him. At the same time, Abiola and his fellow Yoruba became very open about the ethnic nature of the conflict. The Western Leaders Forum categorically stated that the Yoruba people "have been governed by others in a united Nigeria" and "should not be denied the right of governance in an undivided Nigeria."[107] Abiola himself accused Babangida of annulling the 12 June 1993 presidential election because he was not from the North.

Rotational Presidency and the Birth of the Fourth Republic

The Fourth Republic emerged at a time of heightened ethnic conflicts in Nigeria. To many Nigerians, the death of General Sani Abacha was a divine intervention that saved their country from disintegrating into a civil war. In particular, the ethnicization of the 12 June 1993 presidential election led to fierce demands for the renegotiation of the Nigerian federation and power sharing. Even before the 12 June 1993 presidential election, there were growing calls for a national conference to reconsider the basis of cohabitation among the various groups that constitute the Nigerian federation. This idea was strongly supported by Chief Anthony Enahoro, chairman of the Movement for National Reformation (MNR). At the meeting of the Eastern Progressives in Owerri, Imo State, leaders from the East also called for a "national dialogue through a national conference to be organized by the incoming democratically elected government immediately after being sworn in on August 27."[108] The secretary general of the Ethnic Minorities of Africa, Alfred Ilenre, also added his voice to the growing calls for a national conference. One of the central questions that the pioneers of the Fourth Republic had to deal with was how to ensure that power would shift from one region to another, and by implication from one ethnic group to another as well. Southerners, Yoruba in particular, insisted that it was their turn to rule Nigeria.[109] With the high population growth and huge oil deposits in the territories belonging to relatively smaller groups, ethnic minorities also became very vocal about power sharing.

While the 1989 constitutional arrangement tried to force Nigerians to circumvent ethnicity and sectionalism in their political calculations, the post-12 June 1993 presidential election debate recognized ethnic and regional identities as strong organizing principles and called for their incorporation in an institutionalized and transparent arrangement. Not surprisingly, most of the debates surrounding the 1995 Draft Constitution as well as the 1999 Constitution focused on devising a formula that would give all regions (and more ethnic groups) a fair chance to rule the country. To this end, rotational presidency was seen as the best formula for ensuring political stability and equity among the various ethnic groups.

The idea of power sharing can be traced back to the Federal Character principle and the zoning policy of the NPN during the Second Republic. In 1986, rotation was suggested to the Political Bureau. However, the bureau argued: "a constitutional provision for rotation . . . amounts to an acceptance of our inability to grow beyond ethnic or state loyalty."[110] It was assumed that the two-party system would significantly minimize ethnicity and sectionalism in Nigerian politics. As such, there would not be any need for zoning. As it turned out, the two-party system failed to reduce ethnic or regional bigotry. Not surprisingly, the call for rotation among the various regional groupings became even stronger after the annulment of the 12 June 1993 presidential election. Already, Abacha had carved Nigeria into six geopolitical zones.[111] Abacha convened a constitutional conference in 1994 where it was agreed that the presidency should rotate between the North and South. This was a compromise between southern delegates, who argued that the principle of rotational presidency among the six geopolitical zones should be written into the constitution, and northern delegates who opposed such a move. Northern delegates argued that the application of the principle of rotation should be left to the political parties, which should be responsible for rotating their presidential candidates.[112] Article 229 of the 1995 Draft Constitution accordingly stated: "the office of President shall rotate between the North and South." At the state level, "the office of the Governor shall rotate among the three senatorial districts in that state." The office of the chairman of the Local Government Council was to also rotate within the local government area.[113] In order to be registered, a political party was required to reflect the principle of rotation in its constitution.[114] To further enhance power sharing, Article 142 of the 1995 draft constitution provided for three federal vice-presidents. Article 143(1) required a presidential candidate to nominate one person from his/her region and two persons from the other region as running mates, who would occupy the offices of vice presidents should they win the election.

Features of the 1999 Constitution

Like the 1989 Constitution, the 1995 draft constitution was suppressed by the military government. In fact, the 1995 draft constitution was not even promulgated. To complicate the process, General Sani Abacha demanded that six key national positions should be rotated among the six geopolitical zones. As soon as Abacha started to request unreasonable changes to the draft constitution, it became clear to Nigerians that he was not going to hand over power to a civilian government. At best, he sought to transform himself into a civilian dictator against the wishes of the majority of Nigerians. Luckily for Nigerians, Abacha's sudden death in 1998 opened a new window of opportunity for resolving the impasse that began with the annulment of the 12 June 1993 presidential election. A month later, the situation became even more urgent after Moshood Abiola suddenly died in prison, shortly before his scheduled release. Ethnic tensions were so high in the country that General Abdusalam Abubakar clearly understood that it would be suicidal to attempt to continue Hausa-Fulani military rule. It was against this political impasse that the 1999 Constitution was rushed through by the Provisional Ruling Council, marking the birth of the Fourth Republic.

The 1999 Constitution did not introduce any major structural changes to the 1979 Constitution. As noted in Decree No. 24 of 1999, the Constitutional Debate Coordinating Committee concluded that there was a general consensus for the restoration of the 1979 Constitution with some amendments.[115] As in the 1979 Constitution, the 1999 Constitution called for federalism, presidentialism, a bicameral legislature, a multiparty system, a strong central government, and the Federal Character principle. The 1999 Constitution also incorporated the states and LGAs already created by the military regime. Some of the changes introduced in the 1999 Constitution included the right to recall members of the legislature, at the federal as well state level, whenever they lost the confidence of the electorate. According to Article 69 of the 1999 Constitution, a member of the National Assembly can be recalled if a petition is "signed by more than one-half of the registered voters in that member's constituency alleging their loss of confidence in that member." However, the petition must be approved by a simple majority in a referendum conducted by the Independent National Electoral Commission within three months of the petition date.

The 1999 Constitution introduced two new federal executive bodies, the Federal Character Commission and the National Judicial Commission. It retained all the federal executive bodies established under the 1979 Constitution and three of those introduced in the 1989 Constitution (i.e., the Code of Conduct Bureau, the Nigerian Police Council, and the Revenue Mobilization, Allocation, and Fiscal Commission). In terms of control over the police force, the reintroduction of the Nigerian Police Council and the Police Service Commission was arguably an attempt to replicate some parts of the model of the First Republic. However, the 1999 Constitution gave the federal government full control over the police force. In terms of appointment and command over the force, at both the federal and state levels, there is not much difference between the 1979 and the 1999 Constitutions.[116]

The 1999 Constitution further centralized the judiciary.[117] It expanded the jurisdiction of the Court of Appeal and the Federal High Court, and took away the powers of the High Courts of the states to hear election petitions. These powers were passed on to the election tribunals, namely the National Assembly Election Tribunal at the federal level and the Governorship and Legislative Houses Election Tribunal at the state level. The 1999 Constitution gave the federal government a strong role in the appointment of members of these tribunals as well as the judges of the federal and state courts. In particular, the federally dominated National Judicial Council was empowered to "recommend to the Governors from among a list of persons submitted to it by the State Judicial Service Commissions persons for appointments to the offices of the Chief Judges of the States and Judges of the High Courts of the States, Grand Kadis and Kadis of the Sharia Courts of Appeal of the States and the Presidents and Judges of Customary Courts of Appeal of the States." The council was empowered to exercise disciplinary control over such judges and recommend their removal.[118]

Under the 1999 Constitution, the Revenue Mobilisation, Allocation, and Fiscal Commission was empowered to monitor the federation account and "review, from time to time, the revenue allocation formulae and principles in operation to ensure conformity with changing realities."[119] Article 162(2) of the 1999 Constitution requires the president to seek the advice of the commission before submitting a revenue allocation proposal to the National Assembly. To address the touchy issue of a just revenue allocation formula, Article 162(2) also requires the National Assembly to "take into account, the allocation principles especially those of population, equity of states, internal revenue generation, land mass, terrain as well as population density." However, the principle of derivation must "be constantly reflected in any approved formula as being not less than thirteen percent of the revenue accruing to the Federation Account directly from any natural resource." Given the fact that each state is represented in the commission, this was an attempt to moderate the powers of the federal government.[120] While this may help the states influence vertical revenue allocation in their favor, it does not necessarily help oil-producing states to increase their share of horizontal revenue allocation beyond the mandatory thirteen percent for derivation. This is because the majority of states heavily depend on the oil revenue from the oil-producing areas.

The 1999 Constitution also incorporated the principles of social justice, democracy, economic development, and responsible citizenship introduced in the 1989 Constitution. In addition, Article 20 of the 1999 Constitution required the Nigerian state to "protect and improve the environment and safeguard the water, air and land, forest and wild life of Nigeria."

The 1999 Constitution and the Future of the Fourth Republic

Though the 1999 Constitution is structurally similar to the 1979 Constitution, Nigerians have a different reaction to it. The 1979 Constitution, which went through a relatively strong Constituent Assembly, has largely been seen as the people's constitution. In contrast, the 1999 Constitution was simply given to the people by the military.[121] Most importantly, the 1979 Constitution was introduced against the backdrop of skepticism about the merit of strong regional autonomy. As such, the concentration of power in the hands of the federal government was not too problematic. In contrast, the 1999 Constitution came into being at a time when many Nigerians were calling for greater autonomy for the states and power sharing at the federal level of government. Contrary to the wishes of many Nigerians, the 1999 Constitution failed to dilute the powers of the federal government and the dominance of the major ethnic groups. As the Presidential Committee on the Review of the 1999 Constitution (PCRC) concluded, "the process that culminated in the Constitution ignored both structural issues that have bedeviled the country's ability to enthrone a truly accountable, transparent, and democratic order." Furthermore, "it did not directly address the nationality or ethnic question." To the contrary, it "has actually deepened primordial contradiction."[122] One of the central problems of the 1999 Constitution, I will argue, is that it failed to decentralize the federation and promote power sharing. As Bello-Imam complained, "the constitution is a unitary constitution for a federal state."[123] To many people, the arrangement is federal only in name. As such, the current debates call for *true federalism*, and by that many Nigerians, especially in the South, mean decentralization.

Nigerians accepted the 1999 Constitution on the understanding that it would be revisited under a democratically elected government. Not surprisingly, it has been undergoing intense scrutiny. Various committees have been set up by the president, the National Assembly, and civic organizations to review the 1999 Constitution and make proposals for a new one. On October 19, 1999, President Olusegun Obasanjo inaugurated the Presidential Committee on the Review of the 1999 Constitution (PCRC).[124] The committee was asked to: (a) coordinate and collate the views and recommendations of Nigerians for the review of the constitution, taking into account the need to maintain the unity of the nation; (b) identify the defects in the constitution and make appropriate recommendations; (c) make proposals for the review of the constitution and suggest ways of making the constitution an expression of the will of the people; and (d) address the lingering issue of power sharing between the federal and state governments and between states and local governments.[125] On March 30, 2001, the Citizens' Forum for Constitutional Review (CFCR) submitted a memorandum to the National Assembly Committee on the Review of the 1999 Constitution, stating its tentative position and recommendations.

Both the PCRC and the CFCR criticized the 1999 Constitution for concentrating too much power in the hands of the central government, and inadequately protecting the rights of individuals and minority groups.[126] As the PCRC summed it up, "submissions across the country called for the restructuring of Nigeria into a true federation with the component units granted fiscal autonomy."[127] The commission itself recommended that "Nigeria should continue to remain a federation, clearly recognizing states as the federating units and Abuja as Federal Capital Territory, but with much more power devolved to the federating units with the federal government enjoying a minimum of important powers transcending state jurisdiction."[128] The committee also recommended that the concurrent legislative list should be expanded and more functions passed to local governments. In its memorandum, the CFCR criticized the limitations placed on the powers of the state judiciary and its dependence on the federal government.

To promote true federalism and address the grievances of the minorities, both the PCRC and the Citizens' Forum agreed that the principle of derivation should be given significant consideration in the allocation of revenue. According to the CFCR, "the federating units should have control and ownership of the resources in their area. They should, however, pay taxes to the Federal Government. . . . The rate may, however, not be more than 50%, considering that states would take on more spending responsibilities under true federalism."[129] In order to make it easy for minorities to form political parties to defend their interests, especially at the state level, the Citizens' Forum also called for the elimination of the stringent Federal Character requirements for registering political parties.

Both the PCRC and the CFCR called for greater protection of the civil, political, and social rights of the citizens, and of women in particular. The Citizens' Forum argued that such rights should not just be mentioned in the constitution, but should also be legally enforced. The 1999 Constitution was also criticized for making the judiciary heavily dependent on the federal executive organ in a way that undermined its independence. Given the disturbing tradition of military intervention, it is argued that the constitution should have stipulated the punishment for coup makers.

Conclusion

Despite decades of constitution making, Nigerians are still calling for a national conference and a new constitution.[130] From the outset, this is a clear indication of the failures of the attempts to design a democratic and integrated nation-state. Indeed, Nigerians are not just worried about the current constitution, but also the performance of the current civilian government as well. To many Nigerians, the current government has failed to promote integration. Perhaps the only reason why Obasanjo is still in power is because of the fear that any power vacuum may lead to a catastrophic battle among the various ethnic groups. Yet, despite the numerous challenging moments since the end of the civil war, Nigeria is still intact. This in itself may be a sign of political maturity and a dividend of the collective learning that may have resulted from the process of institutional design. Nigeria's attempt to manage ethnicity and design a stable and integrated democratic nation-state points to the dual character of ethnicity. The very ethnicity that has been contributing to the breakdown of the democracy and threatening the nation-state is also the force behind the persistent calls for a more representative democracy and integrated nation-state. Furthermore, the Nigerian case also illustrates the link between democratization and nation-state building as well as the cyclical nature of institutional design.

Notes

1. Though rotation was not written into the 1999 Constitution, the principle was informally applied during the 1999 presidential election.

2. Interview with Professor Oyeleye Oyediran in Ibadan, July 2002.

3. Tom Mbeke-Ekanem, *Beyond the Execution: Understanding the Ethnic and Military Politics in Nigeria* (Lincoln, Neb.: Writer's Showcase, 2000), 291.

4. Quoted in Vivian Roli Mottoh-Migan, *Constitution Making in Post-Independence Nigeria: A Critique* (Ibadan, Nigeria: Spectrum Books Limited, 1994), 173.

5. The other factors are: low level of (political) development in Nigeria; the contents of the constitution; the way federalism is operated; and the dormant Nigerian citizenry. See Mottoh-Migan, *Constitution Making*, 79.

6. Interview with Professor I. Bello-Imam in Ibadan, August 2002.

7. Both the 1960 Constitution and the 1963 Constitution consisted of a federal constitution and separate constitutions for each region of the federation.

8. Articles 2 and 3 of the 1960 Federal Constitution.

9. According to Article 4 of the 1960 Federal Constitution, such an amendment required a two-thirds majority in the federal legislature, the approval of the legislative assemblies of a majority of the regions, or the consent of the legislative houses of all the regions involved in the transaction. Furthermore, the Act could not come into effect until (a) "a resolution has been passed by each legislative house of at least two Regions signifying consent to its having effect"; and (b) a referendum upon the question whether the Act should have effect has been held in every part of Nigeria that would be affected by the boundary change, and supported by at least three-fifths of the persons entitled to vote in those areas.

10. As stated in Article 84(1) of the 1963 Federal Constitution, "The executive authority of the federation shall be vested in the President and, subject to the provisions of this Constitution, may be exercised by him either directly or through officers subordinate to him." Article 84(2) further noted that "nothing in this section shall prevent Parliament from conferring functions on persons or authorities other than the President." Article 93(1) further noted that "in the exercise of his functions under this Constitution or any other law the President shall act in accordance with the advice of the Council of Minis-

ters or a Minister of the Government of the Federation acting under the general authority of the Council of Ministers except in cases where by this Constitution or the constitution of a Region he is required to act in accordance with the advice of any person or authority other than the Council of Ministers."

11. The Legislature consisted of a House of Assembly and a House of Chiefs.

12. According to subsection (4), "if any law enacted by the legislature of a Region is inconsistent with any law validly made by Parliament, the law made by Parliament shall prevail and the Regional law shall, to the extent of the inconsistency, be void."

13. The higher educational institutions were: the University College at Ibadan, the University College Teaching Hospital, the Nigerian College of Arts, Science and Technology, the School of Pharmacy at Yaba, the Forest School at Ibadan, and the Veterinary School at Vom.

14. Articles 64 and 69 of the 1960 and 1963 Federal Constitutions, respectively.

15. The 1963 Federal Constitution opened with the following words: "Having resolved to establish the Federal Republic of Nigeria, with a view to ensuring the unity of our people and faith in our fatherland, for the purpose of promoting inter-African cooperation and solidarity, in order to ensure world peace and international understanding, and so as to further the ends of liberty, equality and justice both in our country and in the world at large."

16. Though it was allowed, the East did not maintain a regional police force.

17. The Nigerian judicial system was regionalized in 1954, with the High Courts of the regions serving as the final court of appeal for many kinds of cases. Thus, the changes introduced during the First Republic, such as Article 107 and 110 of the 1960 Federal Constitution, could be seen as the first step toward centralization. See John Mackintosh, *Nigerian Government and Politics: Prelude to the Revolution* (Evanston, Ill.: Northwestern University Press, 1966).

18. Such as the National University Commission, the National Council on Establishment set up in 1957, and the National Economic Council established in 1955 on the recommendation of the World Bank. See: Sam Egite Oyovbaire, *Federalism in Nigeria: A Study in the Development of the Nigerian State* (New York: St. Martin's Press, 1984), and Mackintosh, *Nigerian Government.*

19. Mackintosh, *Nigerian Government.*

20. Unfortunately, the local police force was also used by regional governments to intimidate opposition parties.

21. The inspector-general of the Nigerian Police or his representative could attend the meetings of the Nigerian Police Council but could not vote (Article 107).

22. However, there was a strong tendency for the North to vote with the NPC-dominated federal government.

23. According to Article 110(2): "the Police Service Commission . . . before making appointment to the office of Commissioner of Police of a Region or removing the Commissioner from office the Commission shall consult with the Premier of the Region."

24. Articles 137, 138, and 139 of the 1963 Constitution.

25. Each region was required to cover the cost incurred by the federal government in collecting taxes on its behalf (Article 136 of the 1960 and Article 142 of the 1963 Constitution).

26. Under the 1960 Constitution, 40 percent of the amount in the distributive pool account went to the North, 31 to the East, and 24 to the West (Article 135). Under the 1963 Constitution, the North and the East maintained their respective shares; 18 percent went to the West and 6 percent to the newly created Mid-Western Nigeria (Article 141).

27. A majority meant two regions under the 1960 Federal Constitution and three regions under the 1963 Federal Constitution. In the case of boundary adjustment, the requirements for amending the constitution were far stricter.

28. The NCNC in the East, the AG in the West, and the NPC in the North.

29. Article 80 of the 1963 Federal Constitution and Article 86 of the 1963 Federal Constitution.

30. Article 70(3) of the 1963 Federal Constitution.

31. Mackintosh, *Nigerian Government*.

32. A. H. M. Kirk-Greene, *Crisis and Conflict in Nigeria: A Documentary Sourcebook 1966-1970; July 1967-January 1970*, Volume 2 (London: Oxford University Press, 1971), 459.

33. Benjamin Nwabueze, *A Constitutional History of Nigeria* (New York: Longman, 1982). Also see table A.2.

34. Article 141.

35. The constitution emphasized the population criteria in carving out constituencies. According to Article 51(2) of the 1963 Federal Constitution, "the boundaries of each constituency shall be such that the number of inhabitants thereof is as nearly as equal to the population quota as is reasonably practicable: provided that the number of inhabitants of a constituency may be greater or less than the population quota in order to take account of means of communication, geographical features, the distribution of different communities and the boundaries of territories." Also see Mackintosh, *Nigerian Government*.

36. According to Article 64(1) of the 1963 Federal Constitution: "where a money bill is passed by the House of Representatives and, having been sent to the Senate at least one month before the end of the session, is not passed by the Senate without amendment within one month after it is so sent, the bill shall, unless the House of Representatives otherwise resolve, be presented to the President for his assent." Article 64(2) further states, "where: (a) a bill that is not a money bill is passed by the House of Representatives and, having been sent to the Senate at least one month before the session, is not passed by the Senate before the end of the session or is passed by the Senate with amendments to which the House of Representatives does not before the end of the session agree; and (b) in the following session (whether of the same Parliament or not) but not earlier than six months after it was first passed by the House of Representatives, the same bill, with no other alteration than those . . . [certified by the Speaker of the House of Representatives as necessary owing to the time lapse since the bill was first passed or represented changes made by Senate] is passed again by the House of Representatives and sent to the Senate at least one month before the end of the session and is not passed by the Senate before the end of the session or is passed by the Senate with such amendments to which the House of Representatives does not before the end of the session agree, the bill shall . . . be presented to the President for his assent with such amendments, if any, as may have been agreed to by both Houses."

37. Mackintosh, *Nigerian Government*.

38. Obafemi Awolowo, *The Travails of Democracy and the Rule of Law* (Ibadan, Nigeria: Evans Brothers Limited, 1987).

39. Interview with Professor Oyeleye Oyediran in Ibadan, July 2002.

40. However, there are debates as to whether the constitution gave the president operational control over the force or simply referred to him as commander-in-chief in ceremonial terms. Nwabueze, *Constitutional History of Nigeria*.

41. Nwabueze, *Constitutional History of Nigeria*, 259.

42. Nwabueze, *Constitutional History of Nigeria*.

43. Mackintosh, *Nigerian Government*.

44. A. H. M. Kirk-Greene, *Crisis and Conflict in Nigeria: A Documentary Sourcebook 1966-1970; January 1966-July 1967*, Volume 1 (London: Oxford University Press, 1971), 169.

45. Kirk-Greene, *A Documentary Sourcebook 1966-1970*, Vol. 1, 163.

46. Though there were many horrible incidents of violence against Igbo people living in the North, the casualty figures are disputed.

47. C. Odumegwu Ojukwu, *Biafra: Selected Speeches and Random Thoughts of C. Odumegwu Ojukwu* (NewYork: Harper & Row, 1969), 192.

48. Kirk-Greene, *A Documentary Sourcebook 1966-1970*, Vol. 1, 197.

49. Kirk-Greene, *A Documentary Sourcebook 1966-1970*, Vol. 1, 219.

50. Oyovbaire, *Federalism in Nigeria*.

51. See Appendix II of the 1979 Constitution.

52. The 1979 Constitution eliminated the regional constitutions.

53. Article 122(2) of the 1979 Constitution.

54. Articles 128(1)(b) and 166(1)(b) of the 1979 Constitution.

55. Article 66 of the 1979 Constitution.

56. Under the 1960 Constitution, the Senate could only delay a bill for up to six months, but could not stop it from becoming a law.

57. Article 54(3) of the 1979 Constitution.

58. Article 162(2) of the 1979 Constitution.

59. The House of Assembly was now the only state legislative organ.

60. The State Electoral Commission was empowered to "organize, undertake and supervise all elections to local government councils within the State" (Third Schedule, Part II, 7(a) of the 1979 Constitution).

61. According to Article 8 of the 1979 Constitution, a request for the creation of a new state must be "supported by at least two-thirds majority of members (representing the area demanding the creation of the new state)" in both houses of the National Assembly, the House of Assembly of the affected states, and the local government councils of the areas concerned. Furthermore, the proposal must be "approved in a referendum by at least two-thirds majority of the people of the area where the demand for creation of the state originated." The result of the referendum must also be "approved by a simple majority of all the states of the federation supported by a simple majority of members of the Houses of Assembly." Finally, the proposal must be "approved by a resolution passed by a two-thirds majority of members of each House of the National Assembly."

62. According to Article 7(1), "the system of local government by democratically elected government councils is under this Constitution guaranteed; and accordingly, the Government of every state shall ensure their existence under a law which provides for the establishment, structure, composition, finance and functions of such councils."

63. Article 85 also pegged the number of seats in the House of Assembly of a state to "three times the total number of seats which that state has in the House of Representatives."

64. Fourth Schedule of the 1979 Constitution.

65. Oyovbaire, *Federalism in Nigeria*.

66. According to Article 4(3), "the power of the National Assembly to make laws for the peace, order and good government of the Federation with respect to any matter included in the Exclusive Legislative List shall, save as otherwise provided in this Constitution, be to the exclusion of the Houses of Assembly of States."

67. These were: allocation of revenue; antiquities and monuments; archives; collection of taxes; electoral laws for local government councils; electricity; exhibition of cinematograph films; industrial, commercial and agricultural development; scientific and technological research; statistics; trigonometrical, cadastral, and topographical surveys; and university, technological, and post-primary education (Second Schedule of the 1979 Constitution).

68. Article 4(6) of the 1979 Constitution.

69. Article 237(1).

70. Members of the Police Service Commission were appointed by the president and confirmed by the Senate (Article 141 of the 1979 Constitution).

71. According to Article 149(1) of the 1979 Constitution, "the Federation shall maintain a special account to be called 'the Federation Account' into which shall be paid all revenues collected by the Government of the Federation, except the proceeds from the personal income tax of the personnel of the armed forces of the Federation, the Nigeria Police Force, the ministry or department of government charged with responsibility for External Affairs and the residents of the Federal Capital Territory."

72. Federal Republic of Nigeria (FRN), "Report of the Presidential Commission on Revenue Allocation," Vol. 1, Main Report (The Federal Government Press, APAPA, 1980), 5.

73. Federal Republic of Nigeria (FRN), "Report of the Presidential Commission on Revenue Allocation," Vol. 1, Main Report (The Federal Government Press, APAPA, 1980), 86-102.

74. Rotimi Suberu, *Public Policy and National Unity in Nigeria* (Ibadan, Nigeria: Development Policy Center, 1999), and Oyovbaire, *Federalism in Nigeria.*

75. Article 199 of the 1979 Constitution.

76. The federal executive bodies established by the 1979 Constitution are: (a) Council of State; (b) Federal Civil Service Commission; (c) Federal Electoral Commission; (d) Federal Judicial Service Commission; (e) National Defence Council; (f) National Economic Council; (g) National Population Council; (h) National Security Council; and (i) Police Service Commission (Article 140(1)).

77. According to Part 1 (paragraph 11) of the Fifth Schedule, "every public officer shall within 3 months after coming into force of this Code of Conduct or immediately after taking office and thereafter—(a) at the end of every four years; and (b) at the end of his term of office; submit to the Code of Conduct Bureau a written declaration of all his properties, assets and liabilities and those of his spouse, or unmarried children under the age of 21 years."

78. Such as admission to university, employment within the civil service of the states, and obtaining government loans. See Daniel Bach, "Indigeneity, Ethnicity, and Federalism," in *Transition Without End: Nigerian Politics and Civil Society under Babangida*, eds. Larry Diamond et al. (Boulder, Colo.: Lynne Rienner Publishers, 1997).

79. One should not forget to note that the elaborate constitutional design and transition program was also used by Babangida to frustrate the transition to civilian rule.

80. Quoted in Oyeleye Oyediran, "The Political Bureau," in *Transition Without End: Nigerian Politics and Civil Society under Babangida*, eds. Larry Diamond et al. (Boulder, Colo.: Lynne Rienner Publishers, 1997), 83.

81. As listed by Oyediran, the redefined roles were: (1) Stimulating, coordinating, and guiding the national political debate through organizing grassroots participation and mobilizing the broad masses of people in the quest for a new political order; encouraging the contribution of professional, academic, economic, and social groups and organiza-

tions; seeking the views of people with experience in public affairs. (2) Collecting all relevant data for the work of the bureau and for possible use by the government. (3) Collating, analyzing, and summarizing the views expressed in the course of the national political debate. (4) Reviewing Nigeria's political history and identifying the basic problems therein and making recommendations for solving and coping with these problems. (5) Working out a basic philosophy of government for Nigeria. (6) Preparing a blueprint for a future political model or models for the country. (7) Providing a blueprint for an economic model consistent with the political order. (8) Providing guidelines for the implementation of the recommended model. (9) Providing a time sequence for political transition by 1990. (10) Deliberating on any other political matter that may be referred to the bureau by the government: See Oyediran, "The Political Bureau," 81-103.

82. Diarchy is a rule by mixture of military personnel and civilian politicians, and triarchy is rule by a mixture of military personnel, civilian politicians, and traditional rulers.

83. Quoted in Oyediran, "The Political Bureau," 91.

84. Quoted in Oyediran, "The Political Bureau," 93.

85. Mottoh-Migan, *Constitution Making*.

86. Quoted in Mottoh-Migan, *Constitution Making*, 177.

87. Article 226(e) of the 1989 Constitution.

88. I should note that such rigid structures also had the tendency to alienate many people, especially when they were not supported with the appropriate conduct on the part of the leadership. Not surprisingly, the voter turnout was very low during the 12 June 1993 presidential election.

89. These were: Code of Conduct Bureau, National Boundaries Commission, National Primary Education Commission, Revenue Mobilization, Allocation, and Fiscal Commission, and Public Complaints Commission. The Police Service Commission was replaced with the Nigerian Police Council (Article 151(1) of the 1989 Constitution).

90. Article 141(1) of the 1979 Constitution required the approval of the Senate.

91. While the 1979 Constitution required the approval of the Senate before the deployment, the 1989 Constitution required the approval of Senate "within seven days of actual combat management" (Article 5(5) of the 1989 Constitution).

92. Under the 1979 Constitution, a candidate was required to obtain no less than one-quarter of the votes cast at the election in each of at least two-thirds of all the states in the federation.

93. Under the 1979 Constitution, each state had five senators and the House of Representatives consisted of 450 members.

94. Article 7(2) of the 1989 Constitution called for 449 LGAs. According to Article 283(1): "There shall be a Local Government Council for each Local Government Area in the Federation." Article 284(1) further stated: "subject to the provisions of this Constitution, the National Electoral Commission shall divide each Local Government Council Area into such number of wards, not being less than ten or more than twenty, as the circumstance of each Local Government Area may require."

95. Under the 1979 Constitution, such persons were banned for a period of ten years.

96. Sam Oyovbaire and Tunji Olagunju, eds., *Crisis of Democratization: Selected Speeches of IBB*, Volume 3 (Lagos, Nigeria: Malthouse Press Limited, 1996), 158.

97. Oyovbaire and Olagunju, eds., *Crisis of Democratization*, 126.

98. Larry Diamond et al., eds. *Transition Without End: Nigerian Politics and Civil Society under Babangida* (Boulder, Colo.: Lynne Rienner Publishers, 1997), 485-92.

99. Oyovbaire and Olagunju, eds., *Crisis of Democratization*, 136-37.

100. On June 27, 1986, Babangida placed a ten-year ban on certain appointed and elected officials of the Second Republic. A year later, Decree 25 banned any official of the First or Second Republic found guilty of abuse of office, as well as many appointed civilian, military, judicial, and police officials who have held offices since January 15, 1966.

101. A candidate must: 1) not be less than 50 years old; 2) have not been convicted for any crime; 3) believe, by acts of faith and practice, in the corporate existence of Nigeria; 4) not possess records of personal, corporate, and business interests which conflict with the national interest; 5) have been a registered member of either of the two political parties for at least one year prior to the election. See Oyovbaire and Olagunju, eds., *Crisis of Democratization*, 138.

102. The highest turnout was in Ondo state with 59.2 percent. The lowest turnout was in Kano with 12.6 percent (see tables A.8 and A.9).

103. However, it is possible that the picture might have been different had the turnout rate not been so low.

104. Quoted in Rotimi Suberu, "Crisis and Collapse: June-November 1993," in *Transition Without End: Nigerian Politics and Civil Society under Babangida*, eds. Larry Diamond et al. (Boulder, Colo.: Lynne Rienner Publishers, 1997), 285-86.

105. These were also the areas with the highest voter turnout rate and the highest vote cast for Abiola. He scored anywhere between 83.52 to 87.78 percent of the votes in these states.

106. Quoted in Mbeke-Ekanem, *Beyond the Execution*, 64.

107. Quoted in Bola Akinterinwa, "The 1993 Presidential Election Imbroglio," in *Transition Without End: Nigerian Politics and Civil Society under Babangida*, eds. Larry Diamond et al. (Boulder, Colo.: Lynne Rienner Publishers, 1997), 275.

108. Quoted in Akinterinwa, "The 1993 Presidential Election Imbroglio," 262.

109. The Yoruba based their argument on the fact that the winner of the 12 June 1993 presidential election, Moshood Abiola, was a Yoruba. In addition, there had never been an elected Yoruba head of state or head of government.

110. Quoted in Anthony Akinola, *Rotational Presidency* (Ibadan, Nigeria: Spectrum Books Ltd, 1996), 13.

111. Southwest (Lagos, Oyo, Osun, Ogun, Ondo, Ekiti); Southeast (Abia, Anambra, Enugu, Imo, Ebonyi); South-South (Edo, Delta, Akwa Ibom, Cross River, Rivers, Bayelsa); Northeast (Kebbi, Sokoto, Katsina, Jigawa, Kano, Kaduna, Zamfara); Northwest (Yobe, Borno, Bauchi, Taraba, Adamawa); Middle Belt (Kwara, Kogi, Benue, Niger, Plateau, Abuja, Nassarawa).

112. Akinola, *Rotational Presidency*.

113. The State Electoral Commission was empowered to divide each LGA into three equal parts for the purpose of the rotation of the chairmanship.

114. Article 229(5) of the 1995 draft constitution.

115. The Constitutional Debate Coordinating Committee received large volumes of memoranda from Nigerians at home and abroad, and held public hearings, seminars, workshops, and conferences throughout the country.

116. Unlike the provisions of the 1963 Constitution, the police commissioner of a state can be appointed without consulting the governor of the state.

117. The constitution created a full set of courts for the Federal Capital Territory (FCT), namely: a High Court, a Sharia Court of Appeal, and a Customary Court of Appeal.

118. Part I (paragraph 21) of the Third Schedule of the 1999 Constitution.

119. However, any revenue allocation formula which has been accepted by the National Assembly will remain in force for a period of not less than five years (Part I (paragraph 23) of the Third Schedule).

120. The Revenue Mobilization Allocation and Fiscal Commission was first introduced by Babangida and incorporated into the 1989 Constitution.

121. Interview with Professor Oyeleye Oyediran in Ibadan, July 2002.

122. Federal republic of Nigeria (FRN), "Report of the Presidential Committee on the Review of the 1999 Constitution," Volume 1 (Lagos, Nigeria, February 2001), 3.

123. Interview with Professor I. Bello-Imam in Ibadan, August 2002.

124. The committee submitted its report in February 2001.

125. Federal Republic of Nigeria, "Report of the Presidential Committee," 26.

126. However, the PCRC report is conservative compared to the position of the Citizens' Forum. In contrast to the CFRC, the PCPC recommended the retention of some highly controversial elements of the 1999 Constitution such as the Land Use Act, the Federal Character restriction on the formation of political parties, and federal control over the police.

127. Federal Republic of Nigeria, "Report of the Presidential Committee," 8.

128. Federal Republic of Nigeria, "Report of the Presidential Committee," 9.

129. Citizens' Forum for Constitutional Reform, "Position of the CFCR on the Review of the 1999 Constitution of the Federal Republic of Nigeria" (Lagos, Nigeria: CFCR, 2001), 29.

130. Some people are even calling for a Sovereign National Conference (i.e. a conference in which delegates can also discuss the question of secession from the Nigerian federation).

Chapter 6

Conclusion: The Breakdown and Reconstitution of Democracy in a Postcolonial Multiethnic Nation-State

Since the end of colonial rule, African countries have been struggling to build stable and democratic nation-states. In nearly all the countries, the failure of the western model of liberal multiparty democracy led to the emergence of one-party and military regimes as alternative models of governance aimed at promoting stability and national integration. By the 1990s, however, it was evident that the non-democratic regimes have not only failed economically, but they have also undermined the stability of the very nation-states that they wanted to consolidate. With the fall of communism and the globalization of democracy, most African governments were pressured to restore multiparty democracy. Even though most of the non-democratic regimes in the continent capitulated to the pro-democracy forces, very often the leaders were skeptical about the feasibility of the neo-liberal model of multiparty democracy in a postcolonial multiethnic country. Despite the skepticism, very few countries tried to customize their democracies to meet the peculiar needs of the postcolonial multiethnic nation-state.[1] Not surprisingly, the democratic transitions of the 1990s have mostly led to the perpetuation of quasi-democracies in many parts of the continent. In other cases, such as in Sierra Leone, Liberia, Congo, and the Ivory Cost, democratization has contributed to the breakdown of law and order. Even though for most African countries the democratic restoration of the 1990s was their second experience with democracy, essentially it was their first chance to design it themselves.[2] Unlike most African countries, Nigeria was undergoing its third wave of democratization. Most importantly, the Nigerian democratization process has always been characterized by deliberate attempts to design institutions geared toward the peculiar character of the postcolonial multiethnic nation-state. The attempts to customize democracy and simultaneously address the question of stateness make the Nigerian experience unique and provide insights for building truly representative democracies and stable multiethnic nation-states in postcolonial Africa.

137

To say that Nigeria is a consolidated democracy or a well-integrated nation-state would be wishful thinking. Yet, the relentless struggles for democratic deepening and an inclusive nation-state are clear indications that Nigeria is on a progressive path. Despite the strong military involvement in Nigerian politics, military rule has never been acceptable. In fact, all the military regimes presented themselves as transitional governments. Furthermore, such regimes have always been bravely challenged and ultimately forced to hand over power to a civilian government. Even more impressive is the creativity in customizing democracy and the collective learning that has resulted from such an exercise. As I have demonstrated, the complexities of the Nigerian case are enormous. Notwithstanding its complexity, Nigeria is an archetypical postcolonial multiethnic nation-state. To begin with, the country is less than one hundred years old; and it has only existed for about fifty years as an independent nation-state. It has a huge and ethnically diverse population, enormous mineral resources, and a vast territory. Despite the huge oil resources, however, Nigeria is a poverty-ridden country that can hardly provide basic services for its citizens. This combination has made the Nigerian path to democratization and nation-state building a challenging case to deconstruct. Interestingly, these very complexities make the Nigerian case paradigmatic and insightful for understanding the problems associated with democratization and nation-state building in postcolonial multiethnic countries.

As I have endeavored to argue in this study, the democratization process in postcolonial multiethnic countries is inherently intertwined with the problems of forging a nation-state. With the emergence of the global village, it is neither desirable nor unproblematic to forge a nation-state without incorporating the basic principles of democracy. Unlike the absolute monarchies of Europe, contemporary dictatorships are under the watchful eye of a global community that expects basic standards of human rights and a humane treatment of people. Further, people in postcolonial developing countries themselves are aware of the political standards and the level of economic and social development in the consolidated democracies of the western world. Yet, democracy is difficult to sustain where there is no integrated nation-state. The challenge then for postcolonial multiethnic countries has been how to simultaneously promote multiparty democracy and forge a nation-state. The Nigerian case amply illustrates the synergy between democratization and nation-state building. Right from the dawn of independence, Nigerians had foreseen that the political relations among the various ethnic groups would be difficult. Given the fact that partition was not a realistic option, the task then was to find a democratic arrangement that would promote unity in diversity and give the various ethnic groups proper representation in the various institutions of power. The nation-state was supposed to promote a common identity and unity among Nigerians without undermining the existing ethnic identities. By doing so, it was hoped that the various ethnic groups would develop common ground rules that would allow them to compete for their respective interests in a democratic and peaceful environment. Nearly fifty years after independence, Nigerians are still struggling to sustain democracy and forge a nation-state. They have resorted to a variety of complex consociational arrangements aimed at promoting a democratic and inclusive multiethnic nation-state. However, the designs often tend to focus more on the distribution of power and national wealth than the inculcation of the values of tolerance, equity, fairness, liberty, and patriotism, which are essential for the development of democratic multiethnic nation-states. As such, democratization and nation-state building in Nigeria have been marred by deceit and grudges, frequently leading to breakdowns. Programs such as the Unity Schools, National Youth Service, War Against Indiscipline, and Mass Mobilisation for Self-Reliance, Social Justice, and Economic Recovery that were aimed at promoting tolerance and patriotism have mostly been unsuccessful.

In this study, I have specifically focused on ethnicity as the paradigmatic issue that Nigeria and other postcolonial multiethnic nation-states must address in their efforts to build stable democracies and integrated nation-states. The Nigerian case brings to light the complexities of ethnicity. On the larger political scale, ethnicity is essentially a struggle among the three major ethnic groups as well as a struggle between the dominant groups and the so-called minorities. At the sub-national level, ethnicity also entails struggles among disadvantaged ethnic groups. In Nigeria, ethnicity has been a prime cause of political instability and the breakdown of law and order. The implications of ethnicity, in its various forms and manifestations, have been very catastrophic to the consolidation of democracy and national integration. As in nearly all sub-Saharan African countries, ethnicity is part of the everyday world of Nigerians. Moreover, ethnicity is not just a simple social problem. Ethnicity is a political issue that has been further complicated by the emergence of an oil-based economy that is monopolized by the state. Not surprisingly, ethnicity goes hand-in-hand with the politics of distribution and the struggle to control the state at the various levels of government. Ethnicity has undermined the credibility of civilian regimes and effectively contributed to the breakdown of democracy. Furthermore, the high levels of violence associated with ethnicity have also undermined the stability of the nation-state, as evident in the numerous incidents of communal violence and demands for political autonomy and secession.

Despite the negative effects of ethnicity on the consolidation of democracy and national integration, the Nigerian case shows that ethnicity can also be a positive factor in the struggle to build a more representative democracy and inclusive multiethnic nation-state. In Nigeria, ethnicity has contributed to the reconstitution of democracy and the nation-state. In particular, it has forced Nigerians to search for alternative models of democracy and national integration. Unlike other studies that have demonized ethnicity, this work emphasizes the dual character of ethnicity and pays attention to the conditions under which ethnicity could become a negative or positive force. Ethnic grievances have prompted new debates about the nature of Nigerian democracy and the configuration of the nation-state. During the First Republic, for example, the institutions were generally designed to protect the interests of the three major ethnic groups. By the time of the second democratization exercise, ethnic grievances had prompted the restructuring of the federation and the introduction of the Federal Character principle. Later on, the continued marginalization of non-Hausa-Fulani people, minorities in particular, invigorated demands for an institutionalized system of power-sharing as well as political and fiscal autonomy. In their efforts to reconstitute democracy and the nation-state, Nigerians have had to factor ethnicity into the design of political institutions. In some cases, such as during the aborted Third Republic, the strategy was to suppress the manifestation of ethnic identities and the promotion of ethnic interests in the political arena. In other cases, the approach has been to recognize the inevitability of ethnicity and institutionalize ethnic balancing. During the First Republic, the interests of the three major ethnic groups were protected through regional autonomy. During the Second Republic, ethnic interests were supposed to be protected though the Federal Character principle and the restructuring of the federation. Currently, Nigerians are calling for the devolution of power from the center to the federating units as a way to protect the rights and interests of the various ethnic groups. It seems to me that by engaging in ethnic balancing, Nigerians are also inching toward a more representative democracy and inclusive nation-state. As I have argued, in divided societies, democracy is not just about the representation of individuals, but also about the representation of the relevant groups within the various institutions of power.

The cycle of breakdown and reconstitution of democracy in Nigeria raises questions about traditional notions of democratic transition and consolidation. As I have demonstrated, in Nigeria, democratic transitions actually begin with military intervention. Essentially, military intervention brings about the end of either quasi-democracies or military regimes and opens the way for further institutional design aimed at reconstituting a more representative democracy and inclusive nation-state. This is not to condone the atrocities committed by military governments. Simply, this is to highlight the intrinsic relation between the breakdown of democracy and its reconstitution in Nigeria. Apart from the immediate effect of ousting regimes that would not faithfully subjugate themselves to free and fair multiparty election, the breakdown of quasi-democracies may also serve as a vital lesson in the experimentation with democracy. Breakdowns may actually expose the deficiencies in some of the institutional arrangements of the multiethnic nation-state. In the Nigerian case, for example, the bitter memories of the First Republic have led to distaste for the parliamentary system of government and huge federating units. So too Nigerians have more or less ruled out a unitary state. Overall, one can argue that a breakdown is not necessarily a fatal regression in the process of democratization. A breakdown may prevent the perpetuation of quasi-democracy, which is often a recipe for future disaster. A breakdown can also provide a chance to experiment with new institutional arrangements aimed at building a more inclusive democracy and nation-state.

The Nigerian experience also raises questions about institutional design. Generally, we tend to think of institutional design as an effort to come up with a blueprint for democracy, based on models that have worked in other countries. We tend to assume that nothing is fundamentally wrong with the borrowed designs. As such, once implemented they should lead to a stable democracy. The Nigerian case challenges this linear and ahistorical approach to institutional design. As we have seen, each new design tried to incorporate the strengths of the previous design and avoid its weaknesses. However, because institutional designs are holistic arrangements, their durability has been undermined by the partial deficiencies of the designs. Evidently, the process of building a stable democracy and an inclusive nation-state has been neither linear nor necessarily a vicious cycle.

Furthermore, the cycle of breakdown and reconstitution in Nigeria shows that institutional design is a process that is interwoven with the development of the postcolonial multiethnic nation-state and it takes place within a historical context that is shaped by both external and internal forces. As an integral part of the Nigerian historical reality, institutional design has had a bearing on the field of action. Ethnic groups and their political leaders have linked institutional design to the distribution of power and resources, and adjusted their political demands accordingly. For instance, as the revenue distribution formula shifted from derivation to equity and even development, the dominant ethnic groups started to request the creation of more states and LGAs within their respective regions as a way to increase their share of the national wealth. Thus, boundary adjustment, which began as a progressive way of addressing minority grievances, has now become an instrument of manipulation in the struggle among ethnic groups for resources and power. I argue that institutional design entails a series of experimentations that come with partial successes and failures which serve as a collective learning experience for the political actors and the nation at large. Perhaps the true measure of the progress toward the development of a stable democracy and an inclusive multiethnic nation-state lies in the institutional capacity to defuse and manage crises that would have led to a breakdown. Despite the troubles with Nigeria, one can take consolation in the fact that the country has so far avoided another civil war and has not given up on democracy.

The irony in the Nigerian attempt to establish a stable democracy and an inclusive nation-state is that the military has been at the forefront of the breakdown as well as the reconstitution of democracy and the nation-state. Since the fall of the First Republic, the military has mainly engineered Nigerian political institutions. Successive military rulers have re-divided the country into numerous states and LGAs, centralized the federation, promulgated the constitutions, institutionalized the Federal Character principle, defined the criteria for forming political parties, and organized transitional multiparty elections. By terminating Nigeria's quasi-democracies and subsequently engaging in institutional design, the military has come to position itself as the custodian of the nation-state and the pioneer of a truly representative multiethnic democracy. Sadly, the military regimes have not always been sincere in their attempts to reconstitute democracy and the nation-state. In particular, the military regimes that pursued the authoritarian approach to nation-state building have caused more havoc than the troubles they actually inherited. They promoted ethnicity and undermined the autonomy of institutions such as the courts, the media, and the civil service that are crucial for the development of a democratic political culture. Furthermore, they engaged in prebendalism, brutalized minority and civil rights activists, and through deceit and force resisted demands for the restoration of democracy. It should not be forgotten that military interventions themselves have often been associated with ethnic rivalry. As we have seen, access to military leadership and the composition of military governments tend to be uneven, mostly to the advantage of the group in power. Because of this, the military has lost the messianic image it tries to present. Practically, it has come to be loathed by ordinary Nigerians as the symbol of oppression and corruption.

Given the distaste for military rule, the question is whether civilians can effectively pursue the democratic approach to nation-state building in Nigeria. As I have already argued, the democratic approach requires political leaders to obtain a mandate from the people, operate under inclusive institutions, and pursue a leadership style that does not discriminate against any ethnic or sectional groups. So far, Nigerians have employed a variety of consociational arrangements to promote a democratic and integrated nation-state. As we have seen from the Nigerian experience, however, consociationalism has the tendency of being transformed into a simple distribution mechanism that undermines the very goals of democracy and nation-state building. Practically, Nigerians have reduced the Federal Character principle (i.e., the main pillar of Nigeria's consociationalism) to a mere quota system. In many other cases, they have used it as a "legitimate" basis for discriminating against other Nigerians who happen to be living away from their ancestral homes. Nigerians have been denied admission into educational institutions and employment in the public services in the states and LGAs where they reside simply because they do not belong to one of the indigenous ethnic groups of the area. By transforming the Federal Character principle into a quota system and extending it to the distribution of basic social services, Nigerians have overstretched the principle. Instead of promoting proper representation, equity, and fairness, the Federal Character principle has now become a source of animosity. Notwithstanding the problems associated with the application of the Federal Character principle, a consociational arrangement is essential for the establishment of a democratic multiethnic nation-state. However, as I have argued, we have to move beyond a mechanical approach to consociationalism that is centered on quotas and the composition of the government. Consociationalism should aim at capacity building and above all promoting a political culture that fosters values such as tolerance, equity, fairness, liberty, and patriotism that promote an inclusive nation-state. As I have demonstrated, the major issues in the development of a democratic and inclusive nation-state in Nigeria are centered on the problems of political representation for the various ethnic groups, and equity and fairness in the distribution of resources.

In order to promote adequate representation, Nigerians need to establish a much more balanced federal arrangement and devolve more power to the state and local governments. Though the creation of states and LGAs has been used to balance the federation, the fact that it has mostly been arbitrarily undertaken by military regimes makes the whole process problematic and open to gross abuse as it occurred during the Babangida and Abacha eras. Instead of empowering the marginalized ethnic groups, boundary adjustment has led to further centralization and strengthened the position of the major ethnic groups that control the federal government. To promote a more representative federation, Nigerians need to simplify the constitutional provisions for boundary adjustment and make it easier to create states and LGAs under a civilian government, as long as it will involve a plebiscite and the new units will be responsible for their operational costs. Furthermore, a balanced federal arrangement would require the devolution of more powers and responsibilities to the lower levels of the federation. The exclusive legislative list should be limited to matters of national significance that cannot be properly handled at the state level such as defense, air and sea transportation, external affairs, bills of exchange, and exploitation of the major minerals. More items, such as taxation, police, agriculture, education, and marriage should be included in the concurrent legislative list or left as residual powers for the states. Given the tremendous ethnic diversity in Nigeria and the limitations of creating a state for each ethnic group that may wish to have a state of its own, it may be necessary to strengthen the powers and responsibilities of local governments and outline them in a separate legislative list. Such enhanced LGAs can protect the interests of ethnic groups that are minorities within a given state. The decentralization of the legislative powers of the three tiers of government should be complemented with the creation of an independent and decentralized judiciary.

As we have seen, the centralization of the Nigerian federation has intensified the struggle for political power to the disadvantage of the smaller ethnic groups. Decentralization would allow the various ethnic groups to take charge of their affairs in matters that are of local and regional significance and reduce the number of issues over which they would have to compete with one another. Instead of seeing the federal government as a honey pot, state and local governments would become the primary generators of revenue and providers of social services. Furthermore, decentralization can allow the federal government to focus on matters that are of national significance and free it from excessive responsibilities and ethnic demands, which often undermined the stability of civilian regimes. By this means, ethnic grievances can be localized and diffused at different layers of the federation without endangering the stability of the nation-state as a whole. Because the federation now consists of smaller and more numerous units, decentralization is less likely to lead to the emergence of the kind of powerful ethnically dominated regions that contributed to the breakdown of the First Republic. To the contrary, decentralization may lead to complex alliances that transcend ethnic, regional, and religious boundaries.

Given the low level of economic development in Nigeria, an inclusive nation-state would also require a much more fair and equitable system of revenue distribution that improves the well-being of the masses. So far, revenue collection has been centralized to the advantage of the federal government and the major ethnic groups, especially the Hausa-Fulani. This has intensified the ethnic struggle to control the federal government. As for the vertical and horizontal revenue distribution formulas, they are simply percentile allocations of cash revenue to the three tiers of government and among the various states and LGAs. Though the assumption is that state and local governments would use their cash allocations to develop the infrastructure in their areas and provide badly needed services to the masses, in practice the system of revenue collection and allocation simply perpetuates dependency and allows politicians, at various levels of the federation, to abuse the resources and intensify ethnicity. For the most part, cash allocations are wasted in excessive administrative costs, embezzled, and used to manipulate ethnic sentiments for political ends. To ensure an equitable and fair revenue distribution system that takes the principles of *derivation* and *even development* into account and improves the material well-being of the masses, Nigerians need to shift from the centralized cash allocation system to a mechanism that allows the units of the federation to generate revenue and take responsibility for their economic and social development. As I have indicated earlier, state and local governments should be empowered to levy a wide variety of taxes, such as sales taxes, property taxes, and import and excise duties, borrow money, and receive donations. In return, each state or LGA must be responsible for covering its administrative cost and promoting economic and social development in its area. Apart from promoting fiscal responsibility, this will also discourage the manipulative creation of states and LGAs as a way of increasing a group's share of the national revenue. Furthermore, because taxpayers will be the ones bearing the cost of running the governments, they will be more likely to scrutinize their governments and hold the leaders accountable.

The most problematic aspect of revenue distribution in Nigeria is the virtual dependence on minerals, especially the huge oil deposit in the minority areas in the South. Evidently, the current revenue collection and distribution system is to the advantage of the major ethnic groups that have dominated the federal government. Not surprisingly, many Nigerians, especially in the oil-rich areas, are calling for greater control of the revenue derived from the minerals in their territory. In particular, they want the vertical revenue distribution formula to be altered to the advantage of the states and LGAs. In terms of horizontal revenue distribution, they are calling for greater emphasis on the principle of derivation. Though such changes can address the grievances of the marginalized ethnic groups, it seems to me that such a revenue allocation proposal dodges the fundamental questions of fairness, equity, unity, and responsibility in the attempt to build a stable democracy and an inclusive nation-state. To begin with, altering the percentile shares of the tiers of government or the derivation principle will not lead to the creation of more wealth. Simply, it will perpetuate the dependency on minerals. Furthermore, if oil-producing states take as much as 50 percent of the oil revenues, as some people are demanding, most of the country will be deprived of badly needed revenues to promote economic and social development. If taken to the extreme, such revenue allocation proposals may create a new form of exclusion, and even threaten the survival of the nation-state. As we have learned from the civil war, Nigerians in the non-oil producing parts of the country are unlikely to let the oil-producing areas go away with the oil.

Instead of focusing on the distribution of the revenues derived from oil, I suggest that such revenues should be dedicated primarily to the financing of concrete economic and social development projects around the country and dealing with ecological problems. To begin with, the distributive pool account should be eliminated. Instead, all revenues generated from minerals should be deposited into a special fund that can only be used to finance specific development projects, such as in the areas of education, health, transportation, communication, agriculture and industry, deal with ecological problems, maintain the infrastructure of the Federal Capital Territory, provide security, and meet the international obligations of the country. States should be given an annual grant to help cover the cost of maintaining security. To ensure equity and fairness, the minimum and maximum amount a state can receive should be clearly stated; and the margin should not be wide. As for the federal government, it should be given an annual grant to maintain the infrastructure of the Federal Capital Territory, cover defense costs, and meet its international obligations. Each tier of government should be eligible to submit proposals for concrete development projects that it would like to undertake. The criteria for funding projects should be based on the profitability of the venture, social needs of the surrounding communities, and even distribution across the country. However, special consideration should be given to oil-producing areas for the ecological hazards that may hinder their ability to generate alternative revenues. To enable these states and LGAs to generate enough tax revenues to run their governments, it will be necessary to support income-generating enterprises in these areas and provide them with generous grants to deal with ecological hazards. Revenues generated from minerals should not be used for the operational costs of any of the three tiers of the government. Like the state and local governments, the federal government should cover its administrative costs through tax-generated revenues, loans, and whatever donations it may receive.

Unlike the government-controlled Petroleum Special Task Fund (PTF) that was created by Abacha, the revenues generated from minerals should be under the control of an independent and representative body. Such a body should be composed of representatives of the federal, state, and local governments. To protect smaller ethnic groups, it is necessary to ensure that all LGAs and states are equally represented; and for the purpose of representation, the federal government should be treated as a state. The sole task of such a body should be to decide on which projects are to be funded. Decisions should be made through an open ballot system, after experts have evaluated the projects for compliance with the funding criteria and passed their report to the delegates. Furthermore, an independent commission should be created to verify whether the projects have been successfully completed. In addition to its own investigations, the commission should be allowed to hear complaints and follow leads from any Nigerian citizen. Governments that fail to complete their projects should be penalized. Project proposals from such governments can be temporarily placed on hold and government officials prosecuted for misappropriation of public money.

Such a revenue generation and distribution system would promote even development without compromising the principle of derivation. Most importantly, it would minimize ethnic conflicts by shifting the focus from simple revenue distribution to revenue generation and the development of concrete economic and social projects that will benefit the masses. Furthermore, it will be much easier to hold political leaders accountable for the funds that have been given to them.

Apart from designing institutions that enhance capacity building, consociationalism should also aim at inculcating values that promote a democratic and inclusive multiethnic nation-state. In this sense, consociationalism should not only be an institutional arrangement, but should also develop into a political culture that promotes tolerance, equity, fairness, liberty, unity, and patriotism. In Nigeria, attempts to promote such a political culture have been made through the adoption of the Federal Character principle and programs such as Unity Schools, National Youth Service, War Against Indiscipline, and Mass Mobilisation for Self-Reliance, Social Justice, and Economic Recovery. However, these programs have all been undermined by the deceit and grudges associated with the politics of distribution and bad leadership. As we have seen from the authoritarian and exclusionary approaches to nation-state building, Nigerian democracy and national integration have been undermined by institutional designs and forms of leadership that marginalize people from certain ethnic groups and thereby undermine democratic values. In order to consolidate democracy and stabilize the nation-state, Nigerians would need to pursue the democratic approach to nation-state building. The democratic approach will combine a democratic mandate with inclusive institutional designs and good leadership. Good leadership will help to promote a political culture that is based on tolerance, equity, fairness, liberty, and patriotism. This is precisely what the civilian governments in Nigeria have been lacking so far. Since good leadership depends on the caliber of the people in power and fluctuates over time, it is extremely important to design an encompassing consociational arrangement that can be monitored and refined as the country matures into a consolidated democracy and an integrated nation-state. Such institutions should be aimed at capacity-building and entrenching the values of tolerance, equity, fairness, liberty, and patriotism.

Notes

1. Among the most notable cases of countries that tried to customize democracy are Nigeria, South Africa, Ethiopia, and Uganda.

2. The immediate post-independence period was their first experience with democracy. However, it was designed by the colonial powers.

Appendix

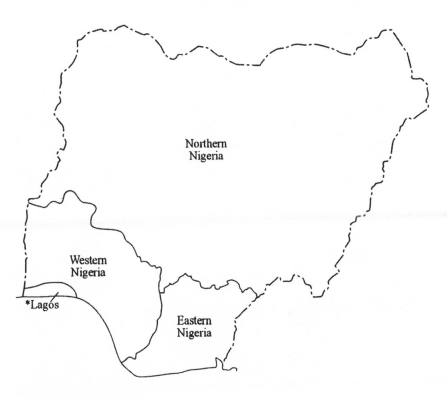

*Federal Capital Territory

Figure A.1: The Three Regions of the Nigerian Federation, 1946 to 1963

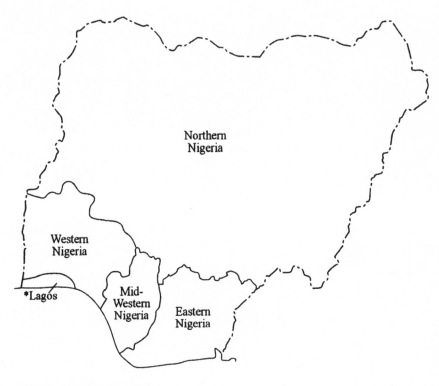

Northern
Nigeria

Western
Nigeria

*Lagos

Mid-
Western
Nigeria

Eastern
Nigeria

*Federal Capital Territory

Figure A.2: The Four Regions of the Nigerian Federation, 1963 to 1967

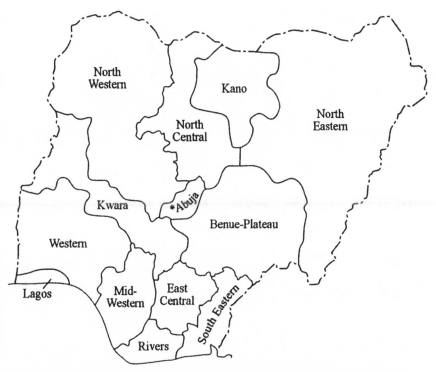

*Federal Capital Territory (The decision to create Abuja and make it the new capital of Nigeria was made in 1976. However, Abuja was not opened until 1991.)

Figure A.3: The Twelve States of the Nigerian Federation, 1967 to 1976

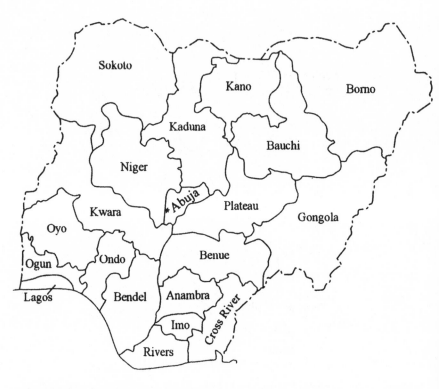

*Federal Capital Territory

Figure A.4: The Nineteen States of the Nigerian Federation, 1976 to 1987

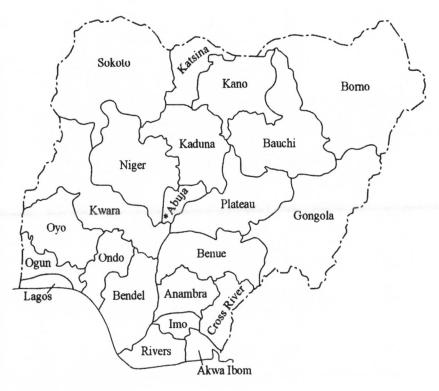

*Federal Capital Territory

Figure A.5: The Twenty-one States of the Nigerian Federation, 1987 to 1991

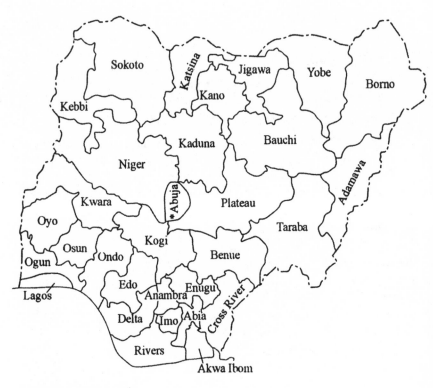

*Federal Capital Territory

Figure A.6: The Thirty States of the Nigerian Federation, 1991 to 1996

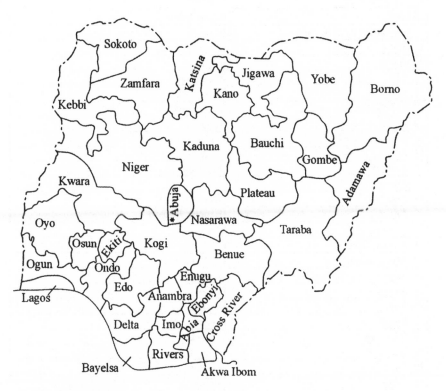

*Federal Capital Territory

Figure A.7: The Thirty-six States of the Nigerian Federation, 1996 to 2004

Sources: Base map from the U.S. Central Intelligence Agency,
Nigeria, 1993. Historical boundaries from Onigu Otite,
Ethnic Pluralism, Ethnicity, and Ethnic Conflicts in Nigeria
(Ibadan, Nigeria: Shaneson C. I. Ltd., 2000).

Table A.1. Ethnic Groups and Their States of Location in Nigeria

Name of Ethnic Group	State of Location
1. Abanyom	Cross River
2. Abua (Odual)	Rivers
3. Achipa (Achipawa Derne)	Kebbi
4. Adim	Cross River
5. Adara (Kadara)	Kaduna
6. Adun	Cross River
7. Aeogworo (KAGORO)	Kaduna
8. Affade	Borno
9. Afizere	Plateau
10. Afo	Nasarawa
11. Aho	Nasarawa
12. Akaju-Ndem (Akajuk)	Cross River
13. Akweya-Yachi	Benue
14. Alago (Arago)	Nasarawa
15. Amo	Plateau
16. Anaguta	Plateau
17. Anang	Akwa Ibom
18. Andoni	Akwa Ibom, Rivers
19. Angas	Bauchi, Plateau
20. Ankwei	Plateau
21. Attakar (Ataka)	Kaduna
22. Atyap (Kataf)	Kaduna
23. Auyoka (Auyokawa)	Jigawa
24. Awori	Lagos
25. Ayu	Kaduna
26. Babur	Borno, Adamawa
27. Bachama	Adamawa
28. Bachave	Cross River
29. Bada	Plateau
30. Bade	Yobe
31. Bahumono	Cross River
32. Bakulung	Taraba
33. Bali	Taraba
34. Bambara (Bambarawa)	Bauchi
35. Bambuka (Bamkuba)	Taraba
36. Banda (Bandawa)	Taraba
37. Bangawa	Kebbi
38. Bankal (Bankalawa)	Bauchi
39. Banso (Panso)	Taraba
40. Bara (Barawa, Badara)	Bauchi
41. Barke	Bauchi

Continued on next page

Table A.1 (continued)

Name of Ethnic Group	State of Location
42. Baruba (Barba)	Niger
43. Bashiri (Bashirawa)	Plateau
44. Bassa	Kogi, Kaduna, Nasarawa, Niger, FCT
45. Batta	Adamawa
46. Baushi	Niger
47. Baya	Adamawa
48. Bekwara	Cross River
49. Bele (Belewa)	Bauchi
50. Betso (Bete)	Taraba
51. Bette	Cross River
52. Bilei	Adamawa
53. Bille	Adamawa
54. Bina (Binawa)	Kaduna
55. Bini	Edo
56. Birom	Plateau
57. Bobua	Adamawa
58. Boki (Nki)	Cross River
59. Bokkos	Plateau
60. Boko (Bussawa, Borgawa)	Niger
61. Bole (Bolewa)	Gombe, Yobe
62. Bollere	Adamawa
63. Boma (Bomawa, Burmano)	Bauchi
64. Bomboro	Bauchi
65. Buduma	Borno, Niger
66. Buji	Plateau
67. Buli	Bauchi
68. Bunu (Kabba)	Kogi, Kwara
69. Bura	Adamawa
70. Burak	Gombe
71. Burma (Bumawa)	Plateau
72. Buru	Yobe, Borno
73. Buta (Butawa)	Gombe
74. Bwall	Plateau
75. Bwanye (Bwatiye)	Adamawa
76. Bwazza	Adamawa
77. Challa	Plateau
78. Cham (Chamawa Fitilai)	Gombe
79. Chamba (Samba)	Adamawa, Taraba
80. Chamo	Gombe
81. Chibok (Chibbak)	Borno
82. Chinine	Borno
83. Chip	Plateau

Continued on next page

Table A.1 (continued)

Name of Ethnic Group	State of Location
84. Chokobo	Plateau
85. Chukkol	Adamawa
86. Daba	Adamawa
87. Dadiya	Gombe
88. Daka	Taraba
89. Dakarkari	Niger
90. Danda (Dandawa)	Kebbi
91. Dangsa	Adamawa
92. Daza (Dere, Derewa)	Bauchi
93. Degema	Rivers
94. Deno (Denawa)	Bauchi
95. Dghwede (Dghuede)	Born
96. Diba	Adamawa
97. Doemak (Dumuk)	Plateau
98. Duguri	Bauchi
99. Duka (Dukawa, Hunnu)	Kebbi
100. Ebana(Ebani)	Rivers
10I. Ebirra (Igbirra)	Kogi, Ondo, Nasarawa
102. Ebu	Edo,
103. Efik	Cross River
104. Egbema	Rivers
105. Egede (Igedde)	Benue
106. Eggon	Nasarawa
107. Egun (Gu)	Lagos
108. Ejagham	Cross River
109. Ekajuk	Cross River
110. Eket	Akwa Ibom
111. Ekoi	Cross River
112. Engenni (Ngene)	Bayelsa
113. Enyima	Cross River
114. Epie	Bayelsa
115. Esan (Ishan)	Edo
116. Etche	Rivers
117. Etolu (Etilo)	Benue
118. Etsako	Edo
119. Etung	Cross River
120. Etuno	Edo
121. Fakkawa (Paeknu)	Kebbi
122. Falli	Adamawa
123. Fantsuam (Kafanchan)	Kaduna
124. Fulbe (Fulani)	Northern States
125. Fyam (Fyem)	Plateau
126. Fyer (Fer)	Plateau

Continued on next page

Table A.1 (continued)

Name of Ethnic Group	State of Location
127. Ga,anda	Adamawa
128. Gade	Niger, Nasarawa
129. Galambi	Bauchi
130. Gamargu-Mulgwa	Borno
131. Ganagana	Kogi
132. GanaWuri	Plateau
133. Gavoko (Govoko)	Borno
134. Gbari (Gbengi)	Kogi
135. Gbedde	Kogi
136. Gelawa	Kebbi
137. Gengle	Adamawa
138. Geji	Bauchi
139. Gera (Gere, Gerawa)	Bauchi
140. Gerka (Gerkawa)	Plateau
141. Geruma (Gerumawa)	Bauchi
142. Gingwak	Bauchi
143. Gira	Adamawa
144. Gizigz (Gizga)	Adamawa
145. Gobirawa	Sokoto
146. Goemai	Plateau
147. Gombi	Adamawa
148. Gomun (Gumun)	Taraba
149. Gongola (Gongla)	Adamawa
150. Gubi (Gubawa)	Bauchi
151. Gude	Adamawa
152. Gudu	Adamawa
153. Gungawa (Reshe)	Kebbi
154. Gure	Kaduna
155. Gurmana	Niger
156. Gurumtum	Bauchi
157. Gusu (GusaWa)	Plateau
158. Gwa (Gurawa)	Bauchi
159. Gwamba	Adarnawa
160. Gwandara	Kaduna, Nasarawa, FCT
161. Gwari (Gbari)	Kaduna, Niger, FCT, Nasarawa
162. Gwom	Taraba
163. Gwoza (Waha)	Borno
164. Gyem	Bauchi
165. Hausa	Northern States
166. Higi (Higgi)	Borno, Adamawa
167. Holma	Adamawa
168. Hona (Hwana)	Adamawa
169. Ibeno	Akwa Ibom

Continued on next page

Table A.1 (continued)

Name of Ethnic Group	State of Location
170. Ibibio	Akwa Ibom
171. Ichen	Taraba
172. Idoma	Benue, Adamawa
173 Igala	Kogi
174. Igbo (Ibo)	Delta, Cross River, and Eastern States
175. Ijumu	Kogi, Kwara
176. Ikom	Cross River
177. Ikwere	Rivers
178. Irigwe	Plateau
179. Isoko	Delta, Bayelsa
180. Isekiri (Itsekiri)	Delta
181. Iyala (Iyalla)	Cross River
182. Izon (Ijo, Ijaw)	Delta, Ondo, Rivers,Bayelsa, Edo
183. Jaba	Kaduna
184. Jahuna (Jahunawa)	Taraba
185. Jaku	Bauchi
186. Jara (Jaar, Jarawa, Jarawa-Dutse)	Borno, Plateau, Bauchi
187. Jere (Jare, Jera, Jerawa)	Bauchi, Plateau
188. Jero	Taraba
189. Jibu	Taraba
190. Jidda-Abu	Nasarawa
191. Jimbin (Jimbinawa)	Bauchi
192. Jirai	Adamawa
193. Jonjo (Jenjo)	Taraba
194. Jukun	Benue, Taraba, Plateau, Gombe
195. Kaba (Kabawa)	Taraba
196. Kadara	Niger
197. Kaje (Kache)	Kaduna
198. Kajuru (Kajurawa)	Kaduna
199. Kaka	Taraba
200. Kamaku (Kamukawa)	Kaduna
201. Kambari (Kambariwa)	Niger, Kebbi
202. Kambu	Taraba
203. Kamo	Gombe
204. Kamukawa (Katsinawa, Laka)	Kebbi
205. Kanakuru (Dera)	Borno, Adamawa
206. Kanembu	Borno
207. Kanikon	Kaduna
208. Kantana	Nasarawa
209. Kanufi	Kaduna
210. Kanuri	Borno, Taraba, Jigawa,Yobe, Nasarawa
211. Karekare (Karaikarari)	Bauchi, Yobe

Continued on next page

Table A.1 (continued)

Name of Ethnic Group	State of Location
212. Karimjo	Taraba
213. Kariya	Bauchi
214. Kelawa	Kebbi
215. Kenem (Koenoem)	Plateau
216. Kenga (Kyenga, Kyengawa)	Kebbi
217. Kenton	Taraba
218. Kiballo (Kiwollo)	Kaduna
219. Kilba	Adamawa
220. Kirfi (Kirfawa)	Bauchi
221. Koma	Adamawa
222. Kona	Adamawa
223. Koro (Kwaro)	Kaduna, Niger
224. Kubi (Kubawa)	Bauchi
225. Kudachano (Kudawa)	Bauchi
226. Kugama	Adamawa
227. Kulere (Kalere)	Plateau
228. Kunini	Taraba
229. Kurama	Kaduna, Plateau
230. Kurdul	Adamawa
231. Kushi	Bauchi
232. Kuteb	Taraba
233. Kutin	Adamawa
234. Kwalla	Plateau
235. Kwami (Kwom)	Gombe
236. Kwanchi	Taraba
237. Kwanka (Kwankawa)	Bauchi, Plateau
238. Kwato	Nasarawa
239. Laaru (Larawa)	Niger
240. Lakka	Adamawa
241. Lala	Adamawa
242. Lama	Adamawa
243. Lamja	Adamawa
244. Lau	Taraba
245. Libbo	Adamawa
246. Limoro (Limaro)	Bauchi, Plateau
247. Longunda (Lunguda)	Gombe, Adamawa
248. Lopa (Lupa, Lopawa)	Niger, Kebbi
249. Mabo	Plateau
250. Mada	Kaduna, Nasarawa
251. Maguzawa	Zamfara
252. Mama	Nasarawa
253. Mambilla	Taraba
254. Manchok	Kaduna

Continued on next page

Table A.1 (continued)

Name of Ethnic Group	State of Location
255. Mandara (Wandala)	Borno
256. Manga (Mangawa)	Yobe
257. Margi (Marghi)	Borno, Adamawa
258. Matakam	Adamawa
259. Mbembe	Cross River, Ebonyi
260. Mbol	Adamawa
261. Mbube	Cross River
262. Mbula	Adamawa
263. Mbum	Adamawa
264. Mernyang (Meryan)	Plateau
265. Miango	Plateau
266. Miligili (Migili)	Nasarawa
267. Miya (Miyawa)	Bauchi
268. Mobber	Borno
269. Montol	Plateau
270. Moruwa (Moro`a, Morwa)	Kaduna
271. Muchalla	Adamawa
272. Mumuye	Adamawa, Taraba
273. Mundang	Adamawa
274. Munga	Taraba
275. Mupun (Mupung)	Plateau
276. Mushere	Nasarawa, Plateau
277. Mwahavul (Mwaghavul)	Plateau
278. Ndoro	Adamawa, Taraba
279. Ngamo	Bauchi, Yobe
280. Ngizim	Yobe
281. Ngweshe (NgosheNdhang)	Borno, Adamawa
282. Nindare	Nasarawa
283. Ningi (Ningawa)	Bauchi
284. Ninzam (Ninzo	Kaduna, Nasarawa
285. Njayi (Nzanyi)	Adamawa
286. Nkim	Cross River
287. Nkum	Cross River
288. Nokere (Nakerey)	Nasarawa
289. Nufawa	Kebbi
290. Nunku	Kaduna, Nasarawa
291. Nupe	Niger, Kogi
292. Nyandang	Taraba, Adamawa
293. Ododop	Cross River
294. Ogoni	Rivers
295. Ogori	Kogi
296. Okobo (Okkobor)	Akwa Ibom
297. Okpamheri	Edo

Continued on next page

Table A.1 (continued)

Name of Ethnic Group	State of Location
298. Olulumo	Cross River
299. Oron	Akwa Ibom
300. Owan	Edo
301. Owe	Kogi
302. Oworo	Kogi
303. Pa`a (Pa`awa, Afawa)	Bauchi
304. Pai	Plateau
305. Panyam	Taraba
306. Pero	Gombe
307. Pire (Pere)	Adamawa
308. Pkanzom	Taraba
309. Polchi Habe	Bauchi
310. Poli	Adamawa
311. Pongo (Pongu)	Niger
312. Potopo	Adamawa
313. Pyapun (Piapung)	Plateau
314. Qua	Cross River
315. Rebina (Rebinawa)	Bauchi
316. Rindire (Rendre)	Nasarawa
317. Rishuwa	Kaduna
319. Ron	Plateau
310. Rubu	Niger
320. Rukuba	Plateau
321. Rumada	Kaduna
322. Rumaya	Kaduna
323. Sakbe	Adamawa
324. Sakkwatawa	Sokoto
325. Sanga	Bauchi
326. Sarkawa	Kebbi
337. Sate	Adamawa
328. Saya (Sayawa Za`ar)	Bauchi
329. Segidi (Sigidawa)	Bauchi
330. Shagawu (Shagau)	Plateau
331. Shanga (Shangawa)	Kebbi
332. Shan-Shan	Plateau
333. Shira (Shirawa)	Bauchi
334. Shomo	Taraba
335. Shuwa	Borno, Adamawa, Yobe
336. Sikdi	Plateau
337. Siri (Sirawa)	Bauchi
348. Srubu (Surubu)	Kaduna
339. Sukur	Adamawa
340. Sura	Plateau

Continued on next page

Table A.1 (continued)

Name of Ethnic Group	State of Location
341. Tangale	Gombe
342. Tarok	Plateau, Adamawa
343. Teme	Adamawa
344. Tera (Terawa)	Borno, Gombe
345. Teshena (Teshenawa)	Bauchi
346. Tigon	Taraba
347. Tikar	Adamawa
348. Tiv	Benue, Taraba, Nasarawa
349. Tula	Gombe
350. Tur	Adamawa
351. Ufia	Benue
352. Ukelle	Cross River
353. Ukwani (Kwale)	Delta
354. Uncinda	Kaduna, Niger, Kebbi
355. Uneme (Ineme)	Edo
356. Urhobo	Delta
357. Utonkong	Benue
358. Uyanga	Cross River
359. Vemgo	Adamawa
360. Verre	Adamawa
361. Vomni	Adamawa
362. Wagga	Adamawa
363. Waja	Adamawa, Gombe
364. Waka	Adamawa
365. Warja (Warjawa)	Jigawa
366. Warji	Bauchi
367. Wula	Adamawa
368. Wula-Matakam	Borno
369. Wurbo	Adamawa
370. Wurkun	Taraba
371. Yache	Cross River
372. Yahe	Cross River
373. Yagba	Kogi
374. Yakurr (Yako)	Cross River
375. Yalla	Benue
376. Yandang	Adamawa, Taraba
377. Yergan (Yergurn)	Plateau
378. Yoruba	Kwara and Western States
379. Yotti	Adamawa
380. Yumu	Niger
381. Yungur	Adamawa
382. Yuom	Plateau

Continued on next page

Table A.1 (continued)

Name of Ethnic Group	State of Location
383. Zabarma (Zarma, Zabarmawa)	Niger, Kebbi
384. Zamfarawa	Zamfara
385. Zaranda	Bauchi
386. Zayam (Zeem)	Bauchi
387. Zul (Zulawa)	Bauchi

Source: Onigu Otite, *Ethnic Pluralism Ethnicity and Ethnic Conflict in Nigeria* (Ibadan, Nigeria: Shaneson C.I. Limited, 2000).

Table A.2. Population of Nigeria: Regional Distribution, 1911 to 1991 Censuses

Population (million)

Region	1911	1921	1931	1952/53	1962	1963	1973	1973	1991
Eastern	4.50	5.11	4.55	7.22	12.33	12.39	18.00	13.75	18.92
Lagos	0.07	0.10	0.13	0.27	0.45	0.68	1.50	2.47	5.69
Western	2.15	2.17	2.95	4.60	8.10	10.28	11.00	8.92	11.91
Mid-Western	1.21	0.78	0.99	1.49	2.40	2.53	3.00	3.24	4.73
Total Southern	7.93	8.62	8.62	13.58	23.28	25.88	33.50	28.38	41.25
Northern	8.12	10.56	11.44	16.84	22.01	29.78	32.00	51.38	47.26
Total Nigeria	16.05	18.72	20.06	30.42	45.29	55.66	65.50	79.76	88.51
Proportion of Southern Population	49.40%	42.64%	42.64%	44.64%	51.49%	46.50%	51.15%	35.58%	46.60%
Proportion of Northern Population	50.60%	56.41%	57.03%	55.36%	48.60%	53.50%	48.85%	64.42%	53.40%

Source: Adewale Maja-Pearce, *From Khaki to Agbada: A Handbook for the February 1999 Elections in Nigeria*
(Lagos, Nigeria: Civil Liberties Organization, 1999).

Table A.3. Population of Nigeria: 1991 Census

State	No. of Households	Males	Females	Both Sexes
Abia	422,032	933,039	980,878	1,913,917
Abuja	86,254	205,299	166,375	371,674
Adamawa	406,683	1,050,791	1,051,262	2,102,053
Akwa Ibom	473,371	1,167,681	1,241,633	2,409,314
Anambra	586,912	1,374,671	1,421,804	2,796,475
Bauchi	510,166	1,443,792	1,418,095	2,861,887
Bayelsa	205,867	584,117	537,576	1,121,693
Benue	498,554	1,368,965	1,384,112	2,753,077
Borno	562,659	1,296,111	1,239,892	2,536,003
Cross River	392,568	956,285	955,312	1,911,597
Delta	573,042	1,271,932	1,318,559	2,590,491
Ebonyi	278,034	670,451	783,431	1,453,882
Edo	441,798	1,085,156	1,086,849	2,172,005
Ekiti	321,864	759,986	775,804	1,535,790
Enugu	449,018	998,157	1,126,911	2,125,068
Gombe	264,388	748,631	740,488	1,489,119
Imo	541,396	1,166,448	1,319,187	2,485,635
Jigawa	570,492	1,455,780	1,419,745	2,875,525
Kaduna	721,784	2,041,141	1,894,477	3,935,618
Kano	1,120,811	2,958,736	2,851,734	5,810,470
Katsina	722,000	1,860,659	1,892,474	3,753,133
Kebbi	380,996	1,035,723	1,032,767	2,068,490
Kogi	395,389	1,039,484	1,108,272	2,147,756
Kwara	326,804	773,182	775,230	1,548,412
Lagos	1,293,379	3,010,604	2,714,512	5,725,116
Nasarawa	204,267	602,535	605,343	1,207,878
Niger	454,143	1,252,466	1,169,115	2,421,581
Ogun	578,835	1,147,746	1,185,980	2,333,726
Ondo	499,367	1,121,898	1,127,650	2,249,548
Osun	485,637	1,043,126	1,115,017	2,158,143
Oyo	769,525	1,711,428	1,741,292	3,452,720
Plateau	374,164	1,054,676	1,049,860	2,104,536
Rivers	609,455	1,655,441	1,532,423	3,187,864
Sokoto	491,162	1,191,617	1,205,382	2,396,999
Taraba	273,951	759,872	752,291	1,512,163
Yobe	288,393	714,729	684,958	1,399,687
Zamfara	404,334	1,017,255	1,055,920	2,073,175
Total	**17,979,494**	**44,529,610**	**44,462,610**	**88,992,220**

Source: Adewale Maja-Pearce, *From Khaki to Agbada: A Handbook for the February 1999 Elections in Nigeria* (Lagos, Nigeria: Civil Liberties Organization, 1999).

Table A.4. 1979 House of Representatives Elections

States	No. of seats	GNPP	UPN	NPN	PRP	NPP
Anambra	29	..	..	3	..	26
Bauchi	20	1	..	18	..	1
Bendel	20	..	12	6	..	2
Benue	19	..	..	18	..	1
Borno	24	22	..	2	..	..
Cross River	28	4	2	22	..	..
Gongola	21	8	7	5	..	1
Imo	30	..	..	2	..	28
Kaduna	33	1	1	19	10	2
Kano	46	..	..	7	39	..
Kwara	14	1	5	8	..	..
Lagos	12	..	12	..	..	..
Niger	10	..	..	10	..	..
Ogun	12	..	12	..	..	..
Ondo	22	..	22	..	..	..
Oyo	42	..	38	4	..	..
Plateau	16	..	..	3	..	13
Rivers	14	..	..	10	..	4
Sokoto	37	6	..	31	..	..
Total	**449**	**43**	**111**	**168**	**49**	**78**
Percent	**100**	**9.6**	**24.7**	**37.4**	**10.9**	**17.4**

Source: Richard Joseph, *Democracy and Prebendal Politics in Nigeria: The Rise and Fall of the Second Republic* (New York: Cambridge University Press, 1987). Reprinted with the permission of the Cambridge University Press.

Table A.5. 1979 Gubernatorial Elections

State	Party	Governor
Anambra	NPP	Mr. Jim Nwobodo
Bauchi	NPN	Alhaji Tatari Ali
Bendel	UPN	Prof. Ambrose Alli
Benue	NPN	Mr. Aper Aku
Borno	GNPP	Alhaji Mohammed Goni
Cross River	NPN	Dr. Clement Isong
Gongola	GNPP	Alhaji A. Barde
Imo	NPP	Mr. Samuel Mbakwe
Kaduna	PRP	Alhaji Balarabe Musa
Kano	PRP	Alhaji Abubakar Rimi
Kwara	NPN	Alhaji Adamu Atta
Lagos	UPN	Alhaji Lateef Jakande
Niger	NPN	Alhaji Awwal Ibrahim
Ogun	UPN	Chief Bisi Onabanjo
Ondo	UPN	Mr. Michael Ajasin
Oyo	UPN	Mr. Bola Ige
Plateau	NPP	Mr. Solomon Lar
Rivers	NPN	Chief Melford Okilo
Sokoto	NPN	Alhaji Muhammadu Kanjiwa

Source: Richard Joseph, *Democracy and Prebendal Politics in Nigeria: The Rise and Fall of the Second Republic* (New York: Cambridge University Press, 1987). Reprinted with the permission of the Cambridge University Press.

Table A.6. 1979 Presidential Election

States	GNPP Waziri	%	UPN Awolowo	%	NPN Shagari	%	PRP Aminu	%	NPP Azikiwe	%
Anambra	20,228	1.67	9,063	0.75	163,164	13.50	14,500	1.20	999,636	82.88
Bauchi	154,218	15.44	29,960	3.00	623,989	62.48	143,202	14.34	47,314	4.74
Bendel	8,242	1.20	365,381	53.20	242,320	36.20	4,939	0.70	57,629	8.60
Benue	42,996	7.98	13,634	2.59	411,638	76.39	2,777	1.35	62,097	11.79
Borno	384,278	54.04	23,885	3.35	246,778	34.71	46,385	6.52	9,642	1.35
Cross River	100,105	15.14	77,775	11.76	425,815	64.40	6,737	1.01	50,671	7.66
Gongola	217,914	34.09	138,561	21.67	227,057	35.52	27,750	4.34	27,856	4.35
Imo	34,616	3.00	7,335	0.64	101,516	8.80	10,252	0.89	1,002,083	86.67
Kaduna	190,936	13.81	92,382	6.68	596,302	43.15	436,771	31.61	65,319	4.72
Kano	18,468	1.54	14,968	1.20	242,643	20.38	907,136	75.89	11,041	0.92
Kwara	20,251	5.71	140,006	39.48	190,142	53.62	2,376	0.67	1,830	0.52
Lagos	3,943	0.48	681,762	82.30	59,515	7.18	3,824	0.47	79,320	9.57
Niger	63,273	16.60	14,155	3.69	287,072	74.88	14,555	3.77	4,292	1.11
Ogun	3,974	0.53	689,655	92.61	46,358	6.23	2,338	0.31	2,343	0.32
Ondo	3,561	0.30	1,294,666	93.50	87,361	4.10	2,509	0.20	11,752	0.80
Oyo	8,029	0.57	1,197,983	85.78	177,999	12.75	4,804	0.34	7,732	0.55
Plateau	37,400	6.82	29,029	5.29	190,458	34.72	21,852	3.98	269,666	49.70
Rivers	15,025	2.18	71,114	10.32	499,846	72.65	3,212	0.40	98,754	14.34
Sokoto	359,021	26.60	34,112	3.20	898,994	66.61	44,977	3.33	12,499	0.92
Total	1,686,489		4,916,651		5,688,857		1,732,113		2,822,523	

Source: Joint Action Committee of Nigeria (JACON), *Way Forward for Nigeria: Revolution Not Transition*, publication no. 4 (Lagos, Nigeria: Joint Action Committee of Nigeria, 1999).

Table A.7. 1983 Presidential Election

State	Total Votes Cast	GNPP		UPN		NPN		NPP		PRP		NPA	
		Votes Received	%	Votes Received	%	Votes Received	%	Votes Received	%	Votes Received	%	Votes Received	%
Abuja	135,351	1,103	-	1,102	-	127,372	-	4,156	-	641	-	977	-
Anambra	1,158,283	36,165	3.12	23,859	2.06	385,297	33.26	669,348	57.79	16,103	1.39	27,511	2.38
Bauchi	1,782,122	37,203	2.09	98,974	5.55	1,507,144	84.57	65,258	3.66	54,564	3.06	18,979	1.07
Bendel	1,099,851	11,723	1.06	566,035	51.46	452,776	41.17	53,306	4.85	7,358	0.67	8,653	0.79
Benue	652,795	19,897	3.05	79,690	12.21	384,045	58.83	152,209	23.31	6,381	0.98	10,573	1.62
Borno	718,043	179,265	24.96	120,138	16.73	348,974	48.60	26,972	3.76	26,996	3.76	15,698	2.19
Cross River	1,285,710	16,582	1.29	506,922	39.43	696,592	54.18	46,418	3.61	8,229	0.64	10,967	0.85
Gongola	723,763	28,407	3.93	182,495	25.21	316,643	43.74	170,535	23.55	12,698	1.77	12,985	1.79
Imo	1,588,975	52,364	3.29	22,648	1.43	398,463	25.07	1,064,436	66.99	18,370	1.16	32,604	2.06
Kaduna	2,137,398	80,862	3.80	225,878	10.57	1,266,894	59.28	225,919	10.58	300,476	14.02	34,369	1.75
Kano	1,193,050	35,252	2.95	48,494	4.06	383,998	32.19	274,102	22.98	436,997	36.63	14,207	1.19
Kwara	608,422	7,670	1.20	275,134	45.22	299,654	49.25	16,215	2.66	3,693	0.61	6,056	1.02
Lagos	1,640,381	11,748	0.72	1,367,807	83.42	126,165	7.65	119,455	7.28	6,570	0.40	8,636	0.53
Niger	430,731	12,984	3.01	15,772	3.66	272,086	63.17	112,971	26.23	8,736	3.06	8,182	1.90
Ogun	1,261,061	6,874	0.55	1,198,033	95.00	43,820	3.47	5,022	0.40	4,449	0.35	2,862	0.23
Ondo	1,828,343	11,629	0.63	1,412,539	77.26	366,217	20.03	20,340	1.11	7,052	0.39	10,566	0.58
Oyo	2,351,000	15,732	0.67	1,396,226	59.39	885,125	37.65	34,852	1.48	9,174	0.39	9,891	0.42
Plateau	652,302	18,612	2.85	38,210	5.86	292,606	44.86	280,803	43.05	11,561	1.77	10,490	1.61
Rivers	1,357,715	12,981	0.96	251,825	18.55	921,664	67.88	151,558	11.16	4,626	0.34	15,061	1.11
Sokoto	2,837,785	46,752	1.65	75,428	2.66	2,605,935	91.83	63,238	2.23	24,280	0.85	22,152	0.72
Total	25,443,087	643,805	-	7,907,209	-	12,081,471	-	3,557,113	-	968,974	-	284,509	-

Source: Joint Action Committee of Nigeria (JACON), *Way Forward for Nigeria: Revolution Not Transition*, publication no. 4

(Lagos, Nigeria: Joint Action Committee of Nigeria, 1999).

Table A.8. 12 June 1993 Presidential Election: Pattern and Order of Voting on State Basis, SDP (Abiola and Kingibe)

State	Number of Registered Voters	% Voter Turnout	Number of SDP Votes	% of SDP Votes	% of State in Total (national)	Ranking
Lagos*	2,397,421	43.10	883,965	85.54	10.60	1
Ondo	1,767,896	59.20	883,024	84.42	10.59	2
Oyo*	1,579,280	40.60	536,011	83.52	6.43	3
Ogun*	941,889	51.50	425,725	87.78	5.10	4
Plateau*	1,513,186	44.70	417,565	61.68	5.01	5
Kaduna*	1,614,258	46.20	389,713	52.20	4.67	6
Rivers	1,908,878	52.30	370,578	36.63	4.44	7
Osun	1,056,690	41.40	365,266	83.52	4.38	8
Bauchi	2,048,627	42.20	339,339	39.27	4.07	9
Delta	1,155,182	40.90	327,277	69.30	3.92	10
Kwara	669,629	52.60	272,270	77.24	3.26	11
Emugu	1,291,750	42.40	263,101	48.09	3.15	12
Benue	1,297,072	33.40	246,830	56.94	2.96	13
Kogi*	978,019	49.90	222,760	45.60	2.67	14
Akwa Ibom*	1,032,955	40.10	214,787	51.86	2.57	15
Anambra*	1,248,226	29.70	212,024	57.11	2.54	16
Edo*	912,680	33.90	205,407	66.48	2.46	17
Cross River	876,599	39.10	189,303	55.23	2.27	18
Katsina	1,661,132	26.60	171,162	38.70	2.05	19
Kano*	2,583,057	12.60	169,619	52.28	2.03	20
Imo	1,141,630	31.10	159,350	44.86	1.91	21
Bomo*	1,222,533	23.10	153,496	54.40	1.84	22
Adamawa	954,680	32.30	140,875	45.72	1.69	23
Jigawa	1,230,215	18.60	138,552	60.67	1.66	24
Niger*	1,002,173	35.70	136,350	38.10	1.63	25
Yobe	663,297	26.50	11,887	63.59	1.34	26
Abia*	991,569	25.90	105,273	41.04	1.26	27
Taraba	n.a.	n.a.	101,887	61.42	1.22	28
Sokoto	1,636,199	28.70	97,726	20.79	1.17	29
Kebbi	824,254	26.10	70,219	32.66	0.84	30
Abuja*	152,686	25.10	19,968	52.16	0.24	31
Total	38,353,578		8,341,309	58.36		

Note: (*) states where election results were released by the NEC

Reprinted from Transition Without End: Nigerian Politics and Civil Society Under Babangida, edited by Larry Diamond, Anthony Kirk-Greene, and Oyeleye Oyediran (Boulder, Colo.: Lynne Rienner Publishers, 1997).

Copyright © 1997 by Lynne Rienner Publishers, Inc. Reprinted with permission of publisher.

Table A.9. 12 June 1993 Presidential Election: Pattern and Order of Voting on State Basis, NRC (Tofa and Ugoh)

State	Number of Registered Voters	% voter Turnout	Number of NRC Votes	% of NRC Votes	% of State in Total (national)	Ranking
Rivers	1,908,878	52.30	640,973	63.37	10.77	1
Bauchi	2,048,627	42.20	524,836	60.73	8.82	2
Sokoto	1,636,119	28.70	372,250	79.21	6.25	3
Kaduna	1,614,258	46.20	356,860	47.80	6.00	4
Enugu	1,291,750	42.40	284,050	51.91	4.77	5
Katsina	1,661,132	26.60	271,077	61.30	4.59	6
Kogi	978,019	49.90	265,732	54.40	4.48	7
Plateau	1,513,186	44.70	259,394	38.32	4.36	8
Niger	1,002,173	35.70	221,437	61.90	3.72	9
Akwa Ibom	1,032,955	40.10	199,342	48.14	3.35	10
Imo	1,141,630	31.10	195,836	55.14	3.29	11
Benue	1,297,072	33.40	186,302	43.06	3.13	12
Adamawa	954,680	32.30	167,239	54.28	2.81	13
Ondo	1,767,896	59.20	162,994	15.58	2.74	14
Anambra	1,248,226	29.70	159,258	42.89	2.68	15
Kano	2,583,057	12.60	154,809	47.72	2.60	16
Cross River	876,599	39.10	153,452	44.77	2.58	17
Abia	991,569	25.90	151,227	58.96	2.54	18
Lagos	2,397,421	43.10	149,432	14.46	2.51	19
Delta	1,155,182	40.90	145,001	30.70	2.44	20
Kebbi	824,254	26.10	144,808	67.34	2.43	21
Borno	1,222,533	23.10	128,684	45.60	2.16	22
Oyo	1,579,280	40.60	105,788	16.48	1.78	23
Edo	912,680	33.90	103,572	33.52	1.74	24
Jigawa	1,230,215	18.60	89,836	39.33	1.51	25
Kwara	669,625	52.60	80,209	22.78	1.35	26
Osun	1,056,690	41.40	72,068	16.48	1.21	27
Yobe	663,297	26.50	64,061	38.41	1.08	28
Taraba	n.a.	n.a.	64,001	38.58	1.08	29
Ogun	941,889	51.50	59,246	12.22	1.00	30
Abuja	152,686	25.10	18,313	47.84	0.31	31
Total	**38,353,578**		**5,952,087**	**41.64**		

Reprinted from Transition Without End: Nigerian Politics and Civil Society Under Babangida, edited by Larry Diamond, Anthony Kirk-Greene, and Oyeleye Oyediran (Boulder, Colo.: Lynne Rienner Publishers, 1997).

Copyright © 1997 by Lynne Rienner Publishers, Inc. Reprinted with permission of publisher.

Table A.10. 1999 Presidential Election

State	Total Votes Cast	APP Chief Falae	% Votes Scored	PDP Olusegun Obasanjo	% Votes Scored
Abuja	99,022	39,788	40.18	59,234	59.82
Abia	535,918	175,095	32.67	360,823	67.33
Adamawa	845,107	177,868	21.05	667,239	78.95
Akwa Ibom	383,278	152,534	17.27	730,744	82.73
Anambra	833,178	199,461	23.94	633,717	76.06
Bauchi	1,176,541	342,233	29.09	834,308	70.91
Bayelsa	610,032	152,220	24.45	457,812	75.05
Benue	1,252,957	269,045	21.47	983,912	78.53
Borno	915,975	334,593	36.53	581,382	63.47
Cross River	876,156	283,468	32.35	592,688	67.65
Delta	816,574	240,344	29.43	576,230	70.57
Ebonyi	345,921	94,934	27.44	250,987	72.56
Edo	679,784	163,203	24.01	516,581	75.99
Ekiti	713,690	522,072	73.15	191,618	26.85
Enugu	835,586	195,168	23.36	640,418	76.64
Gombe	844,539	311,381	36.87	533,158	63.13
Imo	736,106	314,339	42.70	421,767	57.30
Jigawa	548,596	237,025	43.21	3,711,571	56.79
Kaduna	1,676,029	381,350	22.75	1,292,679	77.25
Kano	904,713	222,458	24.59	682,255	75.41
Katsina	1,193,397	229,181	19.20	964,216	80.80
Kebbi	512,229	172,336	33.64	339,893	66.36
Kogi	984,710	476,807	48.42	507,903	51.58
Kwara	659,598	189,088	28.67	470,510	71.33
Lagos	1,751,981	1,542,969	88.07	209,012	11.93
Nasarawa	597,008	173,277	29.02	423,731	70.98
Niger	871,130	140,465	16.12	730,665	83.88
Ogun	475,904	332,340	69.83	143,564	30.17
Ondo	801,797	668,474	83.37	133,323	16.63
Osun	794,639	607,628	76.47	187,001	23.53
Oyo	931,178	693,510	75.29	227,668	24.71
Plateau	672,442	173,370	25.78	499,072	74.22
Rivers	1,565,603	213,328	13.63	1,352,275	86.37
Sokoto	354,427	198,829	56.10	155,598	43.90
Taraba	871,039	81,290	9.33	789,749	90.67
Yobe	311,578	165,061	52.98	146,517	47.02
Zamfara	380,078	243,755	64.13	136,329	35.87
Total	**29,848,441**	**11,110,287**	**37.22**	**18,738,154**	**62.78**

Total number of registered voters: 53,161,687

Source: Joint Action Committee of Nigeria (JACON), *Way Forward for Nigeria: Revolution Not Transition*, publication no. 4 (Lagos, Nigeria: Joint Action Committee of Nigeria, 1999).

Table A.11. State and Local Government Area (LGA) Creation and Structural Imbalances in the Federation, 1914 to 1996: Northern Nigeria

1914	1946	1963		1967	
Protectorates	**Regions**	**Regions**	**Provinces**	**States**	**No. of Divisions**
Northern	Northern	Northern	Sokoto	Kano	2
			Katsina	North Western	7
			Kano	North Central	4
			Kaduna City	Benue-Plateau	9
			Zadauna	Kwara	7
			Zaria	North East	12
			Niger		
			Benue		
			Plateau		
			Kabba		
			Ilorin		
			Borno		
			Adamawa		
			Bauchi		
Total (North)	1	1	14	6	41

* Excluding Abuja

| **Total (South)** | 2 | 3 | 21 | 6 | 45 |

Continued on next page

Table A.11 (continued)

Region	1976		1987-1990		1991		1996	
	States	No. of LGAs	States	No. of LGAs	States	No. of LGAs	States	No. of LGAs
	Kano	20	Kano	46	Kano	34	Sokoto	23
	Kaduna	14	Kaduna	13	Jigawa	21	Zamfara	14
	Sokoto	19	Kastina	20	Kaduna	19	Kebbi	21
	Benue	13	Sokoto	37	Kastina	26	Katsina	34
	Kwara	12	Benue	19	Kebbi	16	Kaduna	23
	Niger	9	Kwara	14	Sokoto	29	Kano	44
	Plateau	14	Niger	10	Benue	18	Jigawa	21
	Borno	18	Plateau	16	Kwara	12	Niger	25
	Gongola	17	Borno	24	Kogi	16	Abuja	6
	Bauchi	16	Gongola	21	Niger	19	Benue	23
			Bauchi	20	Plateau	23	Plateau	17
					Abuja	4	Nasarawa	14
					Borno	21	Kwara	16
					Yobe	13	Kogi	21
					Adamawa	16	Taraba	16
					Taraba	12	Yobe	17
					Bauchi	23	Adarnawa	21
							Borno	27
							Bauchi	20
							Gombe	11
Total (North)	10	152	11	240	*16	322	*19	414
* Excluding Abuja								
Total (South)	9	148	10	208	14	273	17	355

Source: Joint Action Committee of Nigeria (JACON), *Way Forward for Nigeria: Revolution Not Transition,* publication no. 4 (Lagos, Nigeria: Joint Action Committee of Nigeria, 1999).

Table A.12. State and Local Government Area (LGA) Creation and Structural Imbalances in the Federation, 1914 to 1996: Southern Nigeria

1914	1946	1963		1967	
Protectorate	Regions	Regions	Provinces	States	No. of Divisions
Southern	Western	Western	Colony	Lagos	4
			Abeokuta	Western	13
			Ibodan		
			Ijebu		
			Ondo		
			Oyo I		
			Oyo II		
Sub-total		1	7	2	17
		Mid-Western	Port-Harcourt	South Eastern	11
			Calabar	Rivers	5
			Benin	Mid-Western	10
			Ogoja		
			Delta		
			Anang		
			Uyo		
			Degema		
			Yenagoa		
Sub-total	1	1	9	3	16
	Eastern	Eastern	Enugu	Central-East	12
			Abakaliki		
			Umuahia		
			Onitsha		
			Owerri		
Sub-total	1	1	5	1	12
Total (South)	2	3	21	6	45
Total (North)	1	1	14	6	41

Continued on next page

Table A.12 (continued)

Sub-Regions	1976		1987-1990		1991		1996	
	States	No. of LGAs	States	No. of LGAs	States	No. of LGAs	States	No. of LGAs
Western	Lagos	8	Lagos	12	Lagos	20	Lagos	20
	Oyo	24	Oyo	42	Oyo	25	Ogun	20
	Ogun	10	Ogun	12	Osun	24	Oyo	33
	Ondo	17	Ondo	22	Ogun	15	Osun	30
					Ondo	26	Ondo	18
							Ekiti	16
Sub-total	4	59	4	88	5	105	6	137
Mid-Western	Cross-River	17	Cross-River	8	Delta	19	Delta	25
	Rivers	9	Akwa-Ibom	19	Cross-River	14	Akwa-Ibom	31
	Bendel	19	Bendel	20	Edo	14	Edo	18
			Rivers	14	Akwa-Ibom	24	Cross-River	18
					Rivers	24	Bayelsa	8
							Rivers	23
Sub-total	3	45	4	61	5	95	6	123
Eastern	Imo	21	Imo	30	Imo	21	Anambra	21
	Anambra	23	Anambra	29	Abia	17	Imo	27
					Enugu	19	Ebonyi	13
					Anambra	16	Abia	17
							Enugu	17
Sub-total	2	44	2	59	4	73	5	95
Southern Total	9	148	10	208	14	273	17	355
Northern Total	10	152	11	240	*16	322	*19	414

* Excluding Abuja

Source: Joint Action Committee of Nigeria (JACON), *Way Forward for Nigeria: Revolution Not Transition*, publication no. 4 (Lagos, Nigeria: Joint Action Committee of Nigeria, 1999).

Table A.13. Revenue Allocation to States and Local Government Areas (LGAs), 1999

Zones	States	Population (1999 Census)	% of Total Popula.	1999 Budgetary Allocation to States (Naira)	Budgetary Allocation to States as % of Total	No. of LGAs	1999 Budgetary Allocation to LGAs (Naira)	Budgetary Allocation to LGAs as % of Total
North West	Kano	5,810,470	6.53	2,527,588,681.22	3.61	44	2,793,919,607.24	5.32
	Zamfara	2,051,590	2.30	1,529,612,733.20	2.18	14	1,019,627,756.65	1.95
	Jigawa	2,875,625	3.23	1,820,627,470.22	2.60	21	1,634,818,095.35	3.11
	Sokoto	2,418,586	2.72	1,718,236,770.21	2.45	23	1,466,946,821.96	2.80
	Kebbi	2,068,490	2.32	1,652,778,833.22	2.35	21	1,323,291,385.27	2.52
	Kaduna	3,935,618	4.42	2,234,832,603.22	3.19	23	1,898,588,521.96	3.62
	Katsina	3,753,133	4.22	2,170,343,633.22	3.08	34	2,155,550,623.77	4.12
Total		**22,913,412**	**25.74**	**13,654,040,724.50**	**19.46**	**180**	**12,292,742,812.10**	**23.44**
North Central	Kwara	1,548,412	1.74	1,620,307,103.22	2.31	16	1,177,979,693.54	2.25
	Kogi	2,147,756	2.40	1,678,441,029.22	2.39	21	1,329,112,485.27	2.54
	Benue	2,753,007	3.10	1,998,345,216.22	2.85	23	1,695,503,221.96	3.24
	Plateau	2,104,536	2.36	1,628,536,743.22	2.32	17	1,191,709,611.89	2.27
	Niger	2,421,581	2.72	2,000,067,451.22	2.86	25	1,767,349,058.66	3.38
	Nasarawa	1,207,876	1.36	1,411,783,415.22	2.00	14	880,508,538.50	1.68
	Abuja	371,674	0.42	2,624,000,000.00	3.75	6	464,732,510.08	0.88
Total		**12,554,842**	**14.10**	**12,961,480,958.10**	**18.48**	**122**	**8,506,895,119.50**	**16.23**
North East	Taraba	1,512,163	1.70	1,666,215,733.22	2.37	16	1,211,361,393.54	2.31
	Yobe	1,399,687	1.60	1,598,282,759.22	2.27	17	1,171,708,211.88	2.23
	Adamawa	2,102,053	2.30	1,751,603,270.22	2.51	21	1,412,774,985.27	2.69
	Borno	2,536,003	2.85	2,051,389,754.22	2.93	27	1,800,841,295.35	3.43
	Bauchi	2,861,887	3.22	1,826,526,605.22	2.61	20	1,473,673,066.93	2.80
	Gombe	1,489,120	1.67	1,371,912,858.22	1.95	11	818,851,601.81	1.56
Total		**11,900,913**	**13.40**	**10,265,930,980.30**	**14.64**	**122**	**7,889,210,554.78**	**15.05**

Continued on next page

Table A.13 (continued)

Zones	States	Population (1999 Census)	% of Total Popula.	1999 Budgetary Allocation to States (Naira)	Budgetary Allocation to States as % of Total	No. of LGAs	1999 Budgetary Allocation to LGAs (Naira)	Budgetary Allocation to LGAs as % of Total
South West	Lagos	5,725,116	6.43	2,517,888,522.22	3.59	20	2,046,001,766.93	3.91
	Ogun	2,333,726	2.62	1,807,885,849.22	2.58	20	1,359,124,366.93	2.59
	Oyo	3,452,720	3.88	2,058,085,144.22	2.93	33	2,060,667,305.43	3.93
	Osun	2,158,143	2.43	1,674,034,044.21	2.39	30	1,691,592,750.39	3.22
	Ondo	2,249,548	2.55	1,917,913,022.22	2.73	18	1,215,477,530.23	2.33
	Ekiti	1,535,790	1.70	1,394,308,290.22	1.99	16	983,236,893.54	1.87
Total		17,455,043	19.60	11,370,114,872.30	16.21	137	9,356,100,613.45	17.85
South-South	Delta	2,590,491	2.91	3,135,349,572.22	4.47	25	1,623,637,758.66	3.09
	Edo	2,172,005	2.44	1,733,600,811.22	2.47	18	1,329,916,630.23	2.54
	Rivers	3,187,864	3.58	2,644,331,904.21	3.77	23	1,568,192,221.96	2.99
	Cross River	1,911,297	2.15	1,700,358,799.22	2.43	18	1,320,978,930.23	2.52
	Bayelsa	1,121,693	1.20	2,172,881,305.22	3.10	8	669,745,546.77	1.28
	Akwa Ibom	2,409,613	2.71	2,743,773,052.22	3.91	31	1,794,784,668.13	3.41
Total		13,392,963	14.13	14,130,295,444.20	20.15	123	8,307,255,755.98	15.85
South East	Abia	1,913,917	2.15	1,515,885,322.22	2.16	17	1,083,551,211.13	2.06
	Anambra	2,796,475	3.14	1,707,860,155.22	2.44	21	1,487,905,765.22	2.84
	Ebonyi	1,453,876	1.64	1,338,580,248.22	1.90	13	856,493,538.54	1.64
	Enugu	2,125,074	2.38	1,487,586,246.22	2.12	17	1,112,653,311.85	2.12
	Imo	2,485,635	2.79	1,710,218,041.22	2.44	27	1,547,190,695.35	2.96
Total		10,774,977	12.10	7,760,130,013.10	11.06	95	6,087,794,522.09	11.61
Grand Total		88,992,150	100.00	70,141,000,000.00	100.00	1548	52,439,999,377.60	100.00

Source: Joint Action Committee of Nigeria (JACON), *Way Forward for Nigeria: Revolution Not Transition*, publication no. 4 (Lagos, Nigeria: Joint Action Committee of Nigeria, 1999).

Bibliography

Achebe, Chinua. *The Trouble with Nigeria*. Enugu, Nigeria: Fourth Dimension Publishing, 1983.

Ake, Claude. *Democracy and Development in Africa*. Washington: The Brookings Institution, 1996.

————. *The Feasibility of Democracy in Africa*. Dakar, Senegal: CODESRIA, 2000.

Akinola, Anthony. *Rotational Presidency*. Ibadan, Nigeria: Spectrum Books Ltd., 1996.

Akinterinwa, Bola. "The 1993 Presidential Election Imbroglio." Pp. 257-79 in *Transition Without End: Nigerian Politics and Civil Society under Babangida*, edited by Larry Diamond et al. Boulder, Colo.: Lynne Rienner Publishers, 1997.

Alli, M. Chris. *The Federal Republic of Nigerian Army: The Siege of a Nation*. Lagos: Malthouse Press Limited, 2000.

Anderson, Benedict. *Imagined Communities: Reflections on the Origin and Spread of Nationalism*. New York: Verso, 1991.

Awolowo, Obafemi. *The Travails of Democracy and the Rule of Law*. Ibadan, Nigeria: Evans Brothers Limited, 1987.

Bach, Daniel. "Indigeneity, Ethnicity, and Federalism." Pp. 333-49 in *Transition Without End: Nigerian Politics and Civil Society under Babangida*, edited by Larry Diamond et. al. Boulder, Colo.: Lynne Rienner Publishers, 1997.

Bah, Abu. "Approaches to Nation Building in Post-Colonial Nigeria." *Journal of Political and Military Sociology* 32, no. 1 (Summer 2004): 45-60.

————."Changing World Order and the Future of Democracy in Sub-Saharan Africa." *Proteus: A Journal of Ideas* 21, no. 1 (Spring 2004): 3-12.

BBC News. "Six Killed in New Ethnic Clashes in Nigeria," December 31, 1997, http://news.bbc.co.uk/2/hi/africa/43794.stm (June 2000).

————. "Ceremony Sparks Violence in Nigeria." May 26, 1999, http://news.bbc.co.uk/2/hi/africa/353547.stm (July, 15 2000).

————. "Hundreds Flee Nigerian Ethnic Clashes." July 19, 1999, http://news.bbc.co.uk/2/hi/africa/398383.stm (July 20, 1999).

————. "Nigerian Ethnic Fighting Flares." September 28, 1999, http://news.bbc.co.uk/2/hi/africa/460004.stm (February 9, 2000).

————. "More Bloodshed in Delta." November 15, 1999, http://news.bbc.co.uk/2/hi/africa/521424.stm (March 2, 2000).

————. "Nigeria Riots 'Killed 100.'" November 28, 1999, http://news.bbc.co.uk/2/hi/africa/540684.stm (January 10, 2000).

————. "Fighting in Two Nigerian Cities." January 6, 2000, http://news.bbc.co.uk/2/hi/africa/593147.stm (January 8, 2000).

————. "Nigerian Riots Kill Hundreds." March 1, 2000, http://news.bbc.co.uk/2/hi/africa/662246.stm (March 9, 2000).

------. "30 Dead in New Nigeria Clashes." March 6, 2000, http://news.bbc.co.uk/2/hi/africa/667075.stm (March 8, 2000).

------. "Violence Erupts in Northern Nigeria." March 7, 2000, http://news.bbc.co.uk/2/hi/africa/669239.stm (March 15, 2000).

------. "Twenty Die in Lagos Accident." March 8, 2000, http://news.bbc.co.uk/2/hi/africa/670746.stm (March 15, 2000).

------. "Violence Re-Ignites in South-West Nigeria." March 16, 2000, http://news.bbc.co.uk/2/hi/africa/679760.stm (March 16, 2000).

------. "'Nigeria Clashes Kill Ninety' Says Report." May 21, 2000, http://news.bbc.co.uk/2/hi/africa/757986.stm (May 27, 2000).

------. "Ethnic Unrest Erupts in Northern Nigeria." October 20, 2000, http://news.bbc.co.uk/2/hi/africa/979428.stm (October 22, 2000).

------. "New Violence in Niger Delta." May 27, 2001, http://news.bbc.co.uk/2/hi/africa/1354055.stm (June 1, 2001).

------. "Thousands Flee Nigeria Clashes." June 23, 2001, http://news.bbc.co.uk/2/hi/africa/1404521.stm (June 27, 2001).

------. "Villagers 'Massacred' in Nigeria." June 28, 2001, http://news.bbc.co.uk/2/hi/africa/1412289.stm (July 3, 2001).

------. "Scores Die in Nigeria Clashes." September 10, 2001, http://news.bbc.co.uk/2/hi/africa/1535092.stm (September 18, 2001).

------. "Land Clash in Central Nigeria." November 26, 2001, http://news.bbc.co.uk/2/hi/africa/1676925.stm (November 27, 2001).

------. "Nigeria Land Clashes Claim More Lives." January 8, 2002, http://news.bbc.co.uk/2/hi/africa/1748652.stm (January 16, 2002).

------. "Lagos Tense After Riots." February 5, 2002, http://news.bbc.co.uk/2/hi/africa/1802175.stm (February 6, 2002).

------. "Minister Defends Nigeria's Sharia Law." November 4, 2002, http://news.bbc.co.uk/2/hi/programmes/hardtalk/2387627.stm (January 5, 2003).

------. "Nigerian Party Backs Obasanjo." January 6, 2003, http://news.bbc.co.uk/2/hi/africa/2625877.stm (January 8, 2003).

------. "Nigeria Recovers 'Stolen' Money." November 27, 2003, http://news.bbc.co.uk/2/hi/business/3244092.stm (December 2, 2003).

Bratton, Michael, and Nicholas Van de Walle. *Democratic Experiments in Africa: Regime Transitions in Comparative Perspectives*. New York: Cambridge University Press, 1997.

Campbell, Aidan. *Western Primitivism: African Ethnicity; A Study in Cultural Relations*. London: Cassell, 1997.

Citizens' Forum for Constitutional Reform. "Position of the CFCR on the Review of the 1999 Constitution of the Federal Republic of Nigeria." Lagos, Nigeria: CFCR, 2001.

Coleman, James. *Nationalism and Development in Africa: Selected Essays*. Edited by Richard Sklar. Berkeley: University of California, 1994.

------. *Nigeria: Background to Nationalism*. Berkeley: University of California Press, 1958.

Colonial Office. "Nigeria: Report of the Commission Appointed to Enquire into the Fears of the Minorities and the Means of Allaying Them." London: Her Majesty's Stationery Office for the Nigerian Government, 1958.

Dahl, Robert. *Polyarchy: Participation and Opposition*. New Haven: Yale University Press, 1971.

Davidson, Basil. *The Black Man's Burden: Africa and the Curse of the Nation-State.* New York: Times Books, 1992.

Diamond, Larry. *Class, Ethnicity and Democracy in Nigeria: The Failure of the First Republic.* Syracuse, N.Y.: Syracuse University Press, 1988.

————. "Nigeria: Pluralism, Statism, and the Struggle for Democracy." Pp. 33-91 in *Democracy in Developing Countries: Africa*, edited by Diamond et al. Boulder, Colorado: Lynne Rienner Publishers, 1988.

Diamond, Larry, et. al., eds. *Transition Without End: Nigerian Politics and Civil Society under Babangida.* Boulder, Colo.: Lynne Rienner Publishers, 1997.

Federal Republic of Nigeria (FRN). *Constitution of Eastern Nigeria, 1963.*

————. *Constitution of Northern Nigeria, 1963.*

————. *Constitution of the Federation, 1963.*

————. *Constitution of Western Nigeria, 1963.*

————. "Report of the Fiscal Review Commission." Lagos, Nigeria: Federal Ministry of Information Printing Division, 1965.

————. "Constitution (Distributive Pool Account) Decree 1970" (Decree No. 13). Supplement to Official Gazette No. 12, vol. 57, March 12, 1970-Part A .

————. "Off-Shore Oil Revenue Decree 1971" (Decree No. 9). Supplement to Official Gazette Extraordinary. No. 15, vol. 58, March 31, 1971—Part A.

————. "National Youth Service Corps Decree 1973" (Decree No. 24). Supplement to Official Gazette Extraordinary. No. 28, vol. 60, May 22, 1973—Part A.

————. "Report of the Committee on the Location of the Federal Capital of Nigeria." Lagos, December 1975.

————. "Federal Military Government's View on the Report of the Boundary Adjustment Commission." Lagos: Federal Ministry of Information Printing Division, 1976.

————. "Federal Military Government Views on the Report of the Panel on Creation of States." Lagos: Federal Ministry of Information Printing Division, 1976.

————. "Government Views on the Report of the Panel on the Location of the Federal Capital." Lagos: Federal Ministry of Information, 1976.

————. "Government View on the Report of the Technical Committee on Revenue Allocation." Lagos: Federal Ministry of Information, 1978.

————. *Constitution of the Federal Republic of Nigeria, 1979.*

————. "Report of the Presidential Commission on Revenue Allocation," Vol. 1. Main Report. The Federal Government Press, APAPA, 1980.

————. "Civil Disturbances (Special Tribunal) Decree 1987" (Decree No. 2). Supplement to Official Gazette Extraordinary. No. 15, vol. 74, March 20, 1987—Part A.

————. "Directorate of Social Mobilisation Decree 1987" (Decree No. 31).

————. "States (Creation and Transitional Provisions) Decree 1987" (Decree No. 24).

————. *Constitution of the Federal Republic of Nigeria, 1989.*

————. "Treason and Treasonable Offences Decree 1993" (Decree No. 29). Supplement to Official Gazette Extraordinary. No. 10, Vol. 80. May 5, 1993. Part A.

————. *The Constitution of the Federal Republic of Nigeria, 1995.* "Report of the Constitutional Conference Containing the Draft Constitution," Volume 1, 1995. Abuja, Nigeria: Constitutional Conference, Office of the Chairman.

————. "Federal Character Commission (Establishment, etc.) Decree 1996" (Decree No. 34). Supplement to Official Gazette Extraordinary. No. 70, Vol. 83. December 27, 1996—Part A.

————. *Constitution of the Federal Republic of Nigeria, 1999.*

————. "Report of the Presidential Committee on the Review of the 1999 Constitution," Volume 1. Lagos, Nigeria, February 2001.

Federation of Nigeria (FR). "Report by the Nigeria Constitutional Conference" (held in London, May and June 1957). Lagos: Federal Government Printer.

————. "Report by the Resumed Nigeria Constitutional Conference" (held in London, September and October 1958). Lagos: Federal Government Printer.

————. *Constitution of Eastern Nigeria, 1960.*

————. *Constitution of Northern Nigeria, 1960.*

————. *Constitution of the Federation, 1960.*

————. *Constitution of Western Nigeria, 1960.*

Gambari, Ibrahim. "British Colonial Administration." Pp. 159-75 in *Nigerian History and Culture*, edited by Richard Olaniyan. Harlow, Essex, England: Longman, 1985.

Gellar, Sheldon. "State-Building and Nation-Building in West Africa." Pp. 384-426 in *Building States and Nations*, volume 2, edited by Shmuel Eisenstadt and Stein Rokkan. Beverly Hills: Sage Publications, 1973.

Gellner, Ernest. *Nations and Nationalism*. Ithaca: Cornell University Press, 1983.

Herder, Johann G. von. *J. G. Herder on Social and Political Culture*. Edited by F. M. Barnard. London: Cambridge University Press, 1969.

————. *Reflections on the Philosophy of the History of Man*. Chicago: University of Chicago Press, 1968.

Hobsbawm, Eric. *On History*. London: Weidenfeld & Nicolson, 1997.

Horowitz, Donald. *A Democratic South Africa? Constitutional Engineering in a Divided Society*. Berkeley: University of California Press, 1991.

————. *Ethnic Groups in Conflict*. Berkeley: University of California Press, 1985.

Ibrahim, Jibrin. "The Transformation of Ethno-Regional Identities in Nigeria." Pp.41-61 in *Identity Transformation and Identity Politics under Structural Adjustment in Nigeria*, edited by Attahiru Jega. Uppsala, Sweden: Nordiska Afrikainstitutet, 2000.

Imoagene, Oshomha. *Know Your Country Series: Handbooks of Nigeria's Major Cultural Areas; the Hausa and Fulani of Northern Nigeria*, vol. 1. Ibadan, Nigeria: New-Era Publishers 1990.

International IDEA. *Democracy in Nigeria: Continuing Dialogues for Nation-Building*, Capacity Building Series 10. Stockholm, Sweden: International Institute for Democracy and Electoral Assistance, 2000.

Isaacs, Dan. "Profile: Olusegun Obasanjo." *BBC News*. April 23, 2003, http://news.bbc.co.uk/2/hi/africa/2645805.stm (April 25, 2003).

Isichei, Elizabeth. *A History of Nigeria*. New York: Longman, 1983.

Isumonah, V. Adefemi, and Jaye Gaskia. *Ethnic Groups and Conflicts in Nigeria: The Southsouth Zone of Nigeria*, vol. 3. Ibadan, Nigeria: Programme on Ethnic and Federal Studies, University of Ibadan, 2001.

Iweriebor, Ehiedu. "Nigerian Nation Building since Independence." *Nigerian Journal of Policy and Strategy* 5, no. 1 and 2, (June/December 1990): 1-38.

Jibo, Mvendiga et. al. *Ethnic Groups and Conflicts in Nigeria: The Northcentral Zone of Nigeria*. Ibadan, Nigeria: The Lord's Creations for [the] Programme on Ethnic and Federal Studies, Department of Political Science, University of Ibadan, 2001.

Joint Action Committee of Nigeria (JACON). *Way Forward for Nigeria: Revolution Not Transition*, publication no. 4. Lagos, Nigeria: Joint Action Committee of Nigeria, 1999.

Joseph, Richard. *Democracy and Prebendal Politics in Nigeria: The Rise and Fall of the Second Republic*. New York: Cambridge University Press, 1987.

Keay, E. A., and H. Thomas. *West African Government for Nigerian Students*. London: Hutchinson Educational, 1968.

Kirk-Greene, Anthony H. M. *Crisis and Conflict in Nigeria: A Documentary Sourcebook 1966-1970; January 1966-July 1967*, Volume 1. London: Oxford University Press, 1971.

———. *Crisis and Conflict in Nigeria: A Documentary Sourcebook 1966-1970; July 1967-January 1970*, Volume 2. London: Oxford University Press, 1971.

Lijphart, Arend. *Democracy in Plural Societies: A Comparative Exploration*. New Haven: Yale University Press, 1977.

Linz, Juan. *The Breakdown of Democratic Regimes: Crisis, Breakdown and Reequilibration*. Baltimore: The Johns Hopkins University Press, 1978.

Linz, Juan, and Alfred Stepan. *Problems of Democratic Transition and Consolidation: Southern Europe, South America, and Post-Communist Europe*. Baltimore: The Johns Hopkins University Press, 1996.

Lipset, Seymour Martin. *Political Man: The Social Bases of Politics*. New York: Doubleday & Company, 1960.

Mackintosh, John. *Nigerian Government and Politics: Prelude to the Revolution*. Evanston, Ill.: Northwestern University Press, 1966.

Maier, Karl. *This House Has Fallen: Nigeria in Crisis*. New York: Penguin Books, 2000.

Mainwaring, Scott et al., eds. *Issues in Democratic Consolidation*. Notre Dame: University of Notre Dame Press, 1992.

Maja-Pearce, Adewale. *From Khaki to Agbada: A Handbook for the February 1999 Elections in Nigeria*. Lagos, Nigeria: Civil Liberties Organization, 1999.

Mamdani, Mahmood. *Citizen and Subject: Contemporary Africa and the Legacy of Late Colonialism*. Princeton, N.J.: Princeton University Press, 1996.

Mbeke-Ekanem, Tom. *Beyond the Execution: Understanding the Ethnic and Military Politics in Nigeria*. Lincoln, NE: Writer's Showcase, 2000.

Mottoh-Migan, Vivian Roli. *Constitution Making in Post-Independence Nigeria: A Critique*. Ibadan, Nigeria: Spectrum Books Limited, 1994.

Nigeria. "Report of the Fiscal Commissioner on Financial Effects of Proposed New Constitutional Arrangement." Nigeria: Government Printer, 1953.

Nnoli, Okwudiba. *Ethnic Politics in Nigeria*. Enugu, Nigeria: Fourth Dimension Publishers, 1980.

Nwabueze, Benjamin. *A Constitutional History of Nigeria*. New York: Longman, 1982.

O'Donnell, Guillermo, and Philippe Schmitter. *Transitions from Authoritarian Rule: Tentative Conclusions about Uncertain Democracies*. Baltimore: The Johns Hopkins University Press, 1986.

Offe, Claus. *Varieties of Transition: The East European and East German Experience*. Cambridge, Mass.: MIT Press, 1997.

Ojukwu, C. Odumegwu. *Biafra; Selected Speeches and Random Thoughts of C. Odumegwu Ojukwu, with Diaries of Events*. New York: Harper & Row, 1969.

Organisation Mondiale Contre la Torture (OMCT) and Centre for Law Enforcement Education (CLEEN). *Hope Betrayed? A Report on Impunity and State-Sponsored Violence in Nigeria*. Geneva, Switzerland: Organisation Mondiale Contre la Torture, 2002.

Osaghae, Eghosa. *Structural Adjustment and Ethnicity in Nigeria*. Uppsala, Sweden: Nordiska Afrikainstitutet, 1995.

Otite, Onigu. *Ethnic Pluralism, Ethnicity, and Ethnic Conflicts in Nigeria*. Ibadan, Nigeria: Shaneson C. I. Ltd., 2000.

Oyovbaire, Sam Egite. *Federalism in Nigeria: A Study in the Development of the Nigerian State*. New York: St. Martin's Press, 1984.

Oyovbaire, Sam, and Tunji Olagunju, eds. *Crisis of Democratization: Selected Speeches of IBB*, vol. 3. Lagos, Nigeria: Malthouse Press Limited, 1996.

Paden, John. "Nigerian Unity and the Tensions of Democracy: Geo-Cultural Zones and North-South Legacies." Pp. 243-64 in *Dilemmas of Democracy in Nigeria*, edited by Paul Beckett and Crawford Young. Rochester, NY: University of Rochester Press, 1997.

Poggi, Gianfranco. *The State: Its Nature, Development, and Prospects*. Stanford: Stanford University Press, 1990.

Przeworski, Adam. *Democracy and the Market: Political and Economic Reforms in Eastern Europe and Latin America*. New York: Cambridge University Press, 1991.

Riley, Stephen. *The Democratic Transition in Africa: An End to One Party State?* London: Research Institute for the Study of Conflict and Terrorism, 1991.

Saro-Wiwa, Ken. *Genocide in Nigeria: The Ogoni Tragedy*. Port Harcourt, Nigeria: Saros International Publishers, 1992.

Sartori, Giovanni. *Comparative Constitutional Engineering: An Inquiry into Structures, Incentives, and Outcomes*. New York: New York University Press, 1997.

Schumpeter, Joseph. *Capitalism, Socialism, and Democracy*. New York: Harper Colophon Books, 1942.

Sklar, Richard. *Nigerian Political Parties; Power in an Emergent African Nation*. Princeton, N.J.: Princeton University Press, 1963.

Skocpol, Theda. "Bringing the State Back In: Strategies of Analysis in Current Research." Pp. 3-37 in *Bringing the State Back In*, edited by Peter Evans et al. New York: Cambridge University Press, 1985.

Smith, Anthony. *Nationalism and Modernism: A Critical Survey of Recent Theories of Nations and Nationalism*. London: Routledge, 1998.

———. *The Nation in History: Historiographical Debates about Ethnicity and Nationalism*. Hanover, N.H.: University Press of New England, 2000.

Strayer, Joseph. *On the Medieval Origins of the Modern State*. Princeton, N.J.: Princeton University Press, 1970.

Suberu, Rotimi. *Federalism and Ethnic Conflict in Nigeria*. Washington, D.C.: United States Institute of Peace Press, 2001.

———. *Public Policy and National Unity in Nigeria*. Ibadan, Nigeria: Development Policy Center, 1999.

Tamuno, Tekena. "The Independence Movement." Pp. 176-88 in *Nigerian History and Culture*, edited by Richard Olaniyan. Harlow, Essex, England: Longman, 1985.

Thiong'o, Ngugi wa. *Weep Not Child*. London: Heinemann Educational, 1964.

Tilly, Charles, *Coercion, Capital, and European States, A.D. 990-1990*. Cambridge, Mass.: B. Blackwell, 1990.

———. "Reflections on the History of European State-Making." Pp. 3-83 in *The Formation of National States in Western Europe*, edited by Charles Tilly. Princeton, N.J.: Princeton University Press, 1975.

Usman, Yusuf Bala, and Alkasum Abba. *The Misrepresentation of Nigeria*. Zaria: Center for Democratic Development Research and Training, 2000.

Weber, Max (translated, edited, and with an introd., by H. H. Gerth and C. Wright Mills). *From Max Weber: Essays in Sociology*. New York: Oxford University Press, 1946.

Welsh David. "Ethnicity in sub-Saharan Africa." *International Affairs* 72, no. 3 (July 1996): 477-91.

Wiseman, John. *The New Struggle for Democracy in Africa*. Aldershot, England: Ashgate, 1996.

Znaniecki, Florian. *Modern Nationalities: A Sociological Study*. Westport, Conn.: Greenwood Press, 1973.

Index

The letter "t" following a page number denotes a table and the letter "f" denotes a figure.

About the Author

Abu Bakarr Bah is Assistant Professor of Sociology at Northern Illinois University. His research interests include democratization, nation-building, race and ethnicity, and migration. Some of his most recent works have been published by the Programme on Ethnic and Federal Studies at the University of Ibadan in Nigeria; *Journal of Political and Military Sociology*; *Democracy & Development: Journal of West African Affairs*; *Proteus: A Journal of Ideas*; and *Annuaire de L'Universite de Sofia "St. Kliment Ohridski."* He holds a Ph.D. and an M.A. in sociology from the New School for Social Research in New York and a Diploma of Higher Education in sociology from the University of Sofia in Bulgaria.

Made in the USA
Monee, IL
22 August 2021

76264686R00125